"Comrades from all veteran organizations should read this true, personal account of a Vietnam warrior."
>   —Michael J. Kogutek, Past National Commander,
>   The American Legion

"Donahue's work will light you up with the smells, sounds, and imagery of Vietnam. Donahue was there . . . and he didn't run no P.X."
>   —Chad Colley, Past National Commander,
>   Disabled American Veterans

"Fantastic! All freedom-loving people of this world should read this book, for it is through brave soldiers such as these that we can enjoy freedom and liberty today."
>   —Aloysius Bartel, National Service Officer (Retired),
>   AMVETS

"This book was impossible to put down. Not only can you visualize the action and landscape, you can smell them as well. I highly recommend it."
>   —Roy E. Barley, President,
>   75th Ranger Regiment Association, Inc.

"Riveting and emotional, *Mobile Guerrilla Force* describes the cameraderie between Green Berets and their Cambodian troops in a flurry of combat action."
>   —Capt. Rob Krott, USAR,
>   Foreign Correspondent, Behind the Lines

"No Special Warfare library would be complete without *Mobile Guerrilla Force*."
>   —Franklin Mark Osanka, Ph.D.,
>   Author of *Modern Guerrilla Warfare*

MOBILE GUERRILLA FORCE

WITH THE SPECIAL FORCES IN WAR ZONE D

JAMES C. DONAHUE

St. Martin's Paperbacks

Published by arrangement with Naval Institute Press

MOBILE GUERRILLA FORCE

Library of Congress Catalog Card Number: 95-37395

ISBN: 0-312-96164-2

Printed in the United States of America

Naval Institute Press hardcover edition published in 1996
St. Martin's Paperbacks edition/April 1997

St. Martin's Paperbacks are published by St. Martin's Press, 175 Fifth Avenue, New York, NY 10010.

10 9 8 7 6 5 4 3 2 1

*To those Americans and Cambodians
who fought with the Mobile Guerrilla Force
5th Special Forces Group (Airborne)*

ACKNOWLEDGMENTS

This book would not have been possible without the encouragement and assistance of my wife, Sandi, and friends John Truax, Harve Saal, and Jamie Van Eaton. Mrs. Gail Hosking Gilbert, daughter of Master Sgt. Charles Hosking, and the entire Ovsak family were also most cooperative. I would also like to acknowledge the contributions of the following:

Stephen Banko	Sergeant, D Company, 2nd Battalion, 7th Cavalry, 1st Cavalry Division
Roy Barley	Sergeant, E Company, 50th Infantry (Abn), LRP, 9th Infantry Division
Monty Davis	Major, 101st Airborne Division
Aloysius Doyle	Sergeant First Class, Mobile Guerrilla Force, 5th Special Forces Group (Abn)

Dale England   Staff Sergeant, Mobile Guerrilla
                    Force, 5th Special Forces Group
                    (Abn)

John Fiorella   Staff Sergeant, Support Command,
                    1st Infantry Division

James Gritz   Captain, Mobile Guerrilla Force,
                    5th Special Forces Group (Abn)

Michael Holland   Sergeant First Class, Detachment
                    A-343, Duc-Phong, 5th Special
                    Forces Group (Abn)

James Howard   Master Sergeant, Mobile Guerrilla
                    Force, 5th Special Forces Group
                    (Abn)

Hank Humphreys   Specialist Fifth Class, 519th Mili-
                    tary Intelligence Battalion, Gia-
                    Dinh

Richard Jarvis   Staff Sergeant, Mobile Guerrilla
                    Force, 5th Special Forces Group
                    (Abn)

Francis Kelly   Colonel, Commanding Officer, 5th
                    Special Forces Group (Abn)

Donald Koch   Specialist Fourth Class, Detach-
                    ment A-732, Kham-Duc, 7th Spe-
                    cial Forces Group (Abn)

Peter Linkowski   Sergeant, F Company, 2nd Battal-
                    ion, 3rd Marines, 3rd Marine Divi-
                    sion

Kimh Ly	Platoon Sergeant, Mobile Guerrilla Force, 5th Special Forces Group (Abn)
Son Ly	Squad Leader, Mobile Guerrilla Force, 5th Special Forces Group (Abn)
Dennis Montgomery	Staff Sergeant, Mobile Guerrilla Force, 5th Special Forces Group (Abn)
Rex Newell	Specialist Fifth Class, Advisory Team 1, G-2 Section, Da Nang
Jake O'Connor	Airman, USS *Ranger*
Warren Pochinski	Sergeant First Class, Detachment A-343, Duc-Phong, 5th Special Forces Group (Abn)
Alan Pritchard	Sergeant, O Company, 75th Rangers, 82nd Airborne Division
Kien Rinh	Senior Cambodian Medic, Mobile Guerrilla Force, 5th Special Forces Group (Abn)
Hal Slusher	Sergeant, Mobile Guerrilla Force, 5th Special Forces Group (Abn)
Ernest Snider	Sergeant First Class, Mobile Guerrilla Force, 5th Special Forces Group (Abn)

Thai Hien Son   Machine Gunner, Mobile Guerrilla Force, 5th Special Forces Group (Abn)

Shelby Stanton   First Lieutenant, 46th Special Forces Company (Abn), Lopburi, Thailand

Lyndon Steele   Sergeant, Detachment A-341, Bu-Dop, 5th Special Forces Group (Abn)

Ramades Torruella   Sergeant, Detachment A-232, Ban-Don, 1st Special Forces Group (Abn)

Patrick Wagner   Sergeant First Class, Mobile Guerrilla Force, 5th Special Forces Group (Abn)

Scott Whitting   Staff Sergeant, Detachment A-503, Mike Force, 5th Special Forces Group (Abn)

Stephen Yedinak   Captain, Mobile Guerrilla Force, 5th Special Forces Group (Abn)

FOREWORD

U.S. Army Special Forces involvement in the war in Vietnam began in 1957, when a team from the 1st Special Forces Group (Airborne) on Okinawa began training members of the Army of the Republic of Vietnam at the Commando Training Center in Nha-Trang. The trainees would later become the nucleus of the Vietnamese Special Forces.

From 1957 to 1961, Special Forces was primarily involved in training South Vietnam's regular military forces. In late 1961, however, our counterinsurgency effort was broadened when Special Forces teams were assigned the mission of providing training and advisory assistance to South Vietnam's minority groups. These groups included Montagnard tribesmen, Cambodians, Chinese Nungs, and ethnic Vietnamese from the Cao-Dai and Hoa-Hao religious sects.

The development of these paramilitary forces among the minority groups became known as the Civilian Irregular Defense Group (CIDG) program. In 1964 the 5th Special Forces Group (Airborne) deployed to Vietnam; by February 1965 forty-eight CIDG camps had been established by Special Forces A-Teams. The CIDG camps and their light infantry defenders were commanded by the Vietnamese Special Forces. When I assumed command of the 5th Special Forces Group (Airborne) in June 1966, more than 50 percent of our CIDG camps were surrounded by enemy-controlled areas.

With the formation of Mobile Guerrilla Force Detachment A-303 in October 1967, our ability to conduct unconventional operations in enemy-controlled areas and secret zones was significantly increased. Unlike the CIDG, the Mobile Guerrilla Force was organized, trained, equipped, and commanded by U.S. Army Special Forces personnel. In his "Report on the War in Vietnam," Gen. William C. Westmoreland, commander, U.S. Military Assistance Command, Vietnam, stated, "These special operations were highly successful in penetrating isolated enemy bases, disrupting the enemy's lines of communication, attacking his hidden logistical support bases, and gathering intelligence."

In *Mobile Guerrilla Force*, Jim Donahue has captured the essence of the Special Forces soldier in combat. The details of the raids, ambushes, booby traps, air strikes, and parachute resupply drops are authentic. Donahue was there—you feel it, you know it. This is the way it was.

Col. Francis "Blackjack" Kelly, USA (Ret.)
*Commanding Officer, 5th Special Forces Group
(Airborne), June 1966-June 1967*

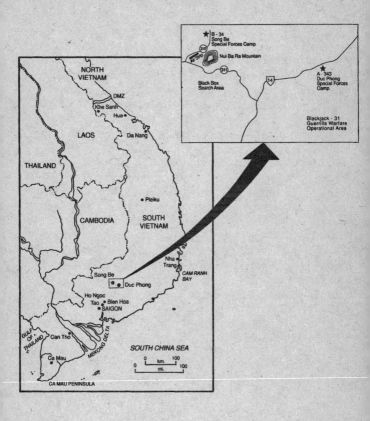

MOBILE GUERRILLA FORCE

INTRODUCTION

In October 1966, Capt. James Gritz was the executive officer and chief instructor at the Recondo School in Nha-Trang, South Vietnam. The school trained volunteers for long-range reconnaissance missions and other special operations in North and South Vietnam, Laos, and Cambodia. Gritz had been at the Recondo School for just a couple of weeks when he received a message to report to Col. Francis "Blackjack" Kelly, commanding officer, 5th Special Forces Group (Airborne). When Gritz arrived, the colonel pointed to a map of War Zone D—a Vietcong (VC) secret zone about which allied intelligence knew little or nothing—and in his booming voice asked Gritz if he thought it possible to take a company-size unit into that secret zone, conduct guerrilla operations for an undetermined length of time, and do it without artillery support or chance of reinforcements. The unit's sole support would consist of a single Forward Air Control (FAC) aircraft and parachute drops of food, supplies, and ammunition.

Gritz told Kelly that, based on his experience, it would be impossible for a company-size unit to conduct operations in War Zone D for more than a few days at best. As soon as they were inserted, they would be found, fixed, fought, and finished by much larger VC and North Vietnamese Army (NVA) forces. But before leaving, Gritz added that if the colonel was seriously considering such a mission, he was volunteering to be its "on-the-ground" commander.

Ten days later Gritz received another message to report to Kelly. When he arrived, Blackjack told him that he had made the decision to introduce American-led guerrillas into the Vietnam conflict. He wanted Gritz to organize, train, and command a Mobile Guerrilla Force (MGF) company that would begin guerrilla operations in War Zone D as soon as possible. When Gritz asked about personnel, weapons, and equipment, Kelly bellowed that there was a difference between questions and problems and that he wasn't interested in listening to Gritz's problems.

A few days later, Gritz caught a flight down to Bien-Hoa, where he met Capt. Steven Yedinak. Prior to coming to Bien-Hoa, Yedinak had served at Suoi-Da, a Special Forces camp located northwest of Saigon in Tay-Ninh Province. That first day in Bien-Hoa, Yedinak sent a coded message to the Special Forces detachments in the III Corps Tactical Zone asking for volunteers for a "one time" guerrilla operation. Gritz and Yedinak also met with Lt. Col. Thomas Huddleston, the C-Team commander, and Sgt. Maj. Richard "Mickey" Finn. Huddleston gave them a couple of desks in his operations office and told them that when their American and indigenous personnel started arriving, they could house them in the adjacent Mike Force (a multipurpose reaction force) compound.

At the time, I was eighty miles north of Saigon at the Duc-Phong Special Forces camp serving as the camp's medical specialist and an advisor to one of its Montagnard light infantry companies. The idea of an American-commanded guerrilla unit was both a challenging and an exciting concept. It was a clear departure from the conventional military thinking that had dominated the American military effort in Vietnam, and in my mind it represented what Special Forces was all about. Although my year in Vietnam was quickly coming to an end, I sent a radio message informing our B-Team in Song-Be that I would extend my tour in Vietnam for another six months in return for assignment to the MGF. Two weeks later, I found myself a member of Mobile Guerrilla Force Detachment A-303 in Bien-Hoa.

To recruit our indigenous force, Yedinak made contact with an underground Cambodian organization known as the Khmer-Serei, or Free Cambodians. Using a Buddhist pagoda on Cong-Ly Street in Saigon as their headquarters, they recruited 263 men. We completed recruiting Cambodian personnel on 10 November 1966 and trucked the company to the flat, sandy terrain of the Ho-Ngoc-Tao Special Forces camp.

Ho-Ngoc-Tao was located on the Saigon-to-Bien-Hoa highway, a few kilometers north of the capital. From 13 November to 15 December 1966 we put the Cambodians (Bodes, as we came to call them) through four weeks of intensive training. Because of their varied military backgrounds they were trained, or retrained, in such basic infantry subjects as marksmanship, tactics, communications, map and compass reading, hand-to-hand combat, and first aid. Additional unconventional training included the use of silent and special weapons, mines, and booby traps; night operations; light and noise discipline; and setting up and securing Drop Zones.

At Ho-Ngoc-Tao, the MGF was organized into a headquarters section, three main-force platoons, and a reconnaissance platoon. Each platoon had fifty-five Cambodians. The headquarters section consisted of Gritz, Sgt. 1st Class Patrick Wagner, our senior radio operator, Sgt. 1st Class William "Buck" Kindoll, our intelligence specialist, and thirteen Cambodians. The reconnaissance platoon was led by 1st Lt. Charlie Chilton and his deputy platoon commanders, Staff Sgt. Joe Cawley and Staff Sgt. Lowell Glossup.

The first main-force platoon was commanded by Master Sgt. Jim Howard, the MGF's senior enlisted man. His deputy platoon commanders were Staff Sgt. Dennis "Monty"

Montgomery and Sgt. Dick Jarvis. The second main-force platoon was commanded by Staff Sgt. Dale England, whose deputy was Yedinak, who also served as the deputy MGF commander. As far as we knew, England was the only staff sergeant in the Army to have a captain in his platoon. Gritz had assigned Yedinak to the second platoon so he would be in position to take command of the company if the head-quarters section were wiped out.

Sgt. 1st Class George Ovsak and I were the two Americans assigned to the third main-force platoon. George served as the platoon commander and a light weapons specialist. I was his deputy platoon commander and one of two medical specialists assigned to the MGF.

After completing our training phase at Ho-Ngoc-Tao, we were trucked to the Air Force base in Bien-Hoa, where we boarded C-123 aircraft and were flown to my former camp at Duc-Phong. The star-shaped camp was located on the northern edge of War Zone D, and its surrounding hills and triple-canopied jungle offered the ideal terrain in which to field-test the tactics developed at Ho-Ngoc-Tao. On our eleventh day at Duc-Phong we planned to quietly fade into the jungle to begin a guerrilla operation that had been code-named Blackjack-31.

When we landed at Duc-Phong we carried American and Khmer-Serei battle flags. Much to our astonishment, the flags struck terror into the hearts of the Vietnamese Special Forces (Luc-Luong-Dac-Biet, or LLDB) detachment, who panicked; a shoot-out between the Bodes and the camp's Montagnard defenders almost resulted. After a few tense moments, Gritz convinced First Lieutenant Thoi, the LLDB camp commander, that we were not part of a coup d'état and that he had nothing to fear from the MGF.

The following morning we received a radio message that Colonel Kelly and members of his staff would be flying in from Saigon. When the colonel arrived, he met privately with Gritz and informed him that Gen. William C. Westmoreland had requested Special Forces assistance in recovering a top-secret Electronic Countermeasure (ECM) System 13A device—a black box—from a downed U-2 spy plane. After the pilot safely ejected, the "Dragon Lady"—CIA designation for the U-2—crashed in the jungle south of the provincial capital of Song-Be. Kelly had evaluated his assets and decided to give the mission to the MGF. Blackjack-31 would be put on hold until the black box was recovered.

An Air Force briefing team arrived the next morning to provide us with the details. The plane was from the Strategic Air Command's 100th Strategic Reconnaissance Wing in Bien-Hoa. While returning from a signal intelligence mission over North Vietnam it encountered a structural problem and broke up at an altitude of twenty-six thousand feet. The Air Force had completed an extensive air and photoreconnaissance search of the area but hadn't turned up any evidence of the missing U-2.

We were also told that the black box was the single most important classified piece of electronic equipment on board the aircraft and that a compromise of this particular technical device would have a grave effect on the national security of the United States. We later learned that the black box's state-of-the-art technology fooled enemy radar into thinking that the U-2 was somewhere it wasn't. Unlike those ECM systems that filled enemy radar screens with clutter, the System 13A device gave no indication to the enemy that the information displayed on his radar screen was false. Although the black box was equipped with a self-destruct device that consisted of nonexplosive incendiary panels which were mounted against its circuit boards, Air Force technicians in Bien-Hoa hadn't yet received instructional manuals on how to connect it.

A technician involved in the briefing also informed us that, based on the U-2's speed and altitude, the Air Force had calculated its landing somewhere within a 440-square-mile cone-shaped area of VC-controlled jungle. He called the mission next to impossible and compared it to finding a very small needle in a very large haystack.

Two days later we were airlifted by C-123 the twenty-six miles from Duc-Phong to Song-Be. The remote airstrip was located north of the base of Nui-Ba-Ra—an extinct volcano whose great green mass rose thousands of feet above the rolling hills of Phuoc-Long Province. After landing, we were picked up by trucks from the Special Forces B-Team and transported to the drop-off point, a short distance southwest of the base of Nui-Ba-Ra. From there we moved south in a column and quietly entered the dark jungle of the search area.

To maximize our chances of recovering the black box, Gritz developed a detailed plan for covering every square kilometer of the search area. Each day the company broke down into platoon-size units, each of which was assigned specific one-thousand-meter grid squares to search. Once a platoon reached its search area, it spread out on line—ten meters between each man—and moved forward on an azimuth.

As we were moving through bamboo and scrub brush on the third day of methodically scouring the steaming jungle south of the mountain, we suddenly came upon a twisted pile of seared metal, wire, and aircraft parts. It was the missing U-2. The Dragon Lady had hit the ground with such impact that it dug a crater measuring thirty meters across and flattened all of the surrounding bamboo. The pungent odor of burnt rubber and jet fuel still filled the air around the crash site, and the only large part still intact was its Pratt & Whitney J75 jet engine. After examining the wreck and thoroughly searching the surrounding area, we found no trace of the black box. We surmised that it must have separated from the aircraft when it broke up at twenty-six thousand feet.

That evening, we set up a mission support site (MSS) on

a nearby hill and the following morning broke down into platoons to continue to search for the black box. Later that morning, Yedinak radioed that his platoon had recovered the device. Three hours thereafter, Capt. Charlie Pocock— an FAC pilot flying an O-1E observation aircraft out of Song-Be—radioed Gritz that a chopper would make the pickup. Gritz told Pocock that the chopper would have to lower a 120-foot nylon rappeling rope into a bomb crater, the only clearing in the area. Thirty minutes later, we monitored another radio transmission; the black box was on board the chopper, intact and uncompromised.

The third platoon made it back to the support site later that afternoon. While positioning the Bodes along our section of the perimeter, George and I ran into Fang, Gritz's Cambodian interpreter. He had been given the nickname because his incisors extended well over his lower lip. In broken English he told us that with the black box safe in American hands, "Captain Gri" now wanted to find, engage, and destroy enemy units that were thought to be operating in the area. He went on to tell us that our first objective would be to raid a VC base complex located a day's march to the east.

While we were still talking to Fang, Gritz radioed that we had captured a prisoner, and he wanted me to treat his wounds. I followed Fang to the center of the perimeter and found Kindoll questioning the prisoner through one of our Cambodian interpreters. The prisoner was sitting on a rotting tree trunk with his hands bound. He appeared to be about sixteen years old, was slight, and was wearing blood-soaked black pajamas and Ho-Chi-Minh sandals. When I placed my medical bag on the ground next to him, I noticed he was trembling. After I cleaned and dressed deep lacerations on his forehead and cheek and gave him shots of penicillin and streptomycin, his hands stopped shaking.

While eating a can of C-ration peaches he told us that

his name was Tranh. Kindoll detected a weakness in him
and handed the prisoner an Air Force "White Dot" signal
mirror. With blood seeping out from under his dressings
and his face reddened and bruised, his wounds looked more
serious than they actually were. Tranh appeared shocked
when he saw his reflection in the mirror, and Kindoll convinced him that he would die if he didn't get to a hospital.
Kindoll also told him that if he agreed to tell us about
enemy units operating in the area, we would med-evac him
to Saigon.

Much to everyone's surprise, Tranh told us that he had
been trained as a sapper, was wounded during the May
1965 attack on Song-Be, and was currently assigned to a
local security platoon. He also let us know that a VC base
camp was located a short distance from our MSS and that
he would show us how to attack it without running into
any of their guards or booby traps. Tranh's reliability was
a gamble, but Gritz decided to act on his information. We
would postpone our march to the east and move swiftly to
attack the base camp.

Less than an hour later we were slipping and sliding
down a muddy gorge when suddenly the smell of wood
smoke and Vietnamese cooking filled the still air. With
Tranh leading on point, we entered an area of felled trees,
punji stakes (sharpened bamboo sticks), and piles of thorn-
covered vines. At the base of the hill we deployed on line
and entered a place where all of the lower levels of foliage
had been cut and cleared. Only the great trees remained,
and they supported a canopy of leaves. The space beneath
the canopy was thick with smoke; everything appeared in
shades of gray. As we moved quietly through the camp's
unguarded latrine area, the silence was broken by the sound
of laughter and Vietnamese voices.

Seconds later, the space beneath the canopy erupted
with the roar of automatic fire and exploding M-79
rounds. While red tracers cut through the smoke at waist

level, we rushed forward at a slow run and leapt over an unmanned trench. Further into the camp we passed a few bamboo-and-thatch structures and two blackened ten-gallon metal pots boiling away over separate fires. Next to them, thick gray smoke billowed from an earthen oven. On the far side of the camp's kitchen we splashed across a shallow stream and caught momentary glimpses of the enemy before they disappeared into the smoke. Twenty meters past the stream we hit a wall of thorn-covered vines.

During a quick search of the camp we discovered that the Vietcong had transformed the bed of the stream into a road. Its hard surface was hidden just a couple of inches below the surface, and unless you walked in the stream, you would never suspect that it was there. Kindoll theorized that it was part of a well-camouflaged east-west transportation system. With every structure in the camp ablaze, we rigged a few booby traps before heading back to our support site.

The following morning we received our first aerial resupply drop. The C-123 was flown by Air Commandos employing the Computed Air Release Point (CARP) system to calculate the point at which the bundles would be dropped. While in Bien-Hoa we had been told that it was an excellent system for resupplying special operations because it enabled aircraft to make accurate drops at night and during bad weather. Apparently, however, the computer didn't calculate the forward throw of the bundles and mistakenly released them when the aircraft was directly over the Drop Zone. Soon after the red, yellow, and green parachutes opened, their attached bundles landed in high trees at the end of the Drop Zone. It took us close to an hour to recover the bundles and another thirty minutes to distribute the food, ammunition, and supplies.

By mid-afternoon on Christmas Eve we were moving

east to position ourselves for a Christmas Day attack on the VC base complex. We were making good time when England's second platoon made point contact with an undetermined number of Vietcong. Although no enemy dead were found at the point of contact, a trail of fresh blood indicated that at least one had been hit. A Bode from the second platoon had his kneecap shot off during the exchange and, after receiving medical treatment, had to be carried in a hammock.

Following the contact we moved five hundred meters to the east before stopping to make our scheduled radio contact with the C-Team in Bien-Hoa. After transmitting our situation report, we received a message from Colonel Kelly informing us that President Lyndon Johnson had been told of the successful recovery of the black box. He also informed us that a Christmas truce had been signed with the Vietcong and that we were to cease all offensive operations until after the holiday. Although we were skeptical of the truce, we obeyed the order and moved to a small clearing to med-evac Tranh and the wounded Bode. Gritz also wanted to send Yedinak out on the chopper so that he could make the necessary arrangements to have our next resupply dropped by A-1E fighter aircraft rather than C-123s.

The helicopter didn't have any trouble landing, but because of a combination of weight and high-air temperature, the pilot couldn't get enough vertical lift to hover straight up until he cleared the trees. After two unsuccessful attempts, we removed Tranh from the chopper; this proved to be just enough lightening of the load to enable the pilot to clear the trees.

With our plans for Tranh scrubbed, we moved to a nearby hill and set up a circular perimeter. While sitting on a fallen tree, George and I reviewed our security plans with Sanh, our Cambodian platoon sergeant. Sanh was a former Viet-Minh who always wore a black beret and spoke English with a French accent. By the time we finished talking, the once bright colors of the jungle were reduced to an inky black. I crawled into my hammock and looked up at a star-filled sky. It was Christmas Eve, and the jungle was alive with the sounds of the night.

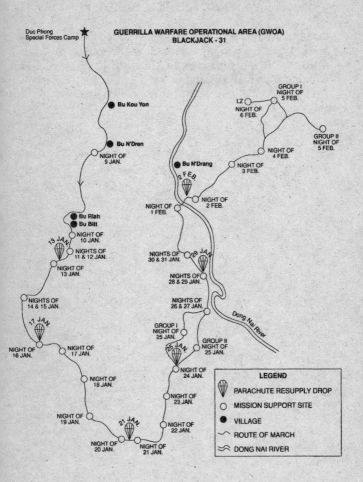

GUERRILLA WARFARE OPERATIONAL AREA (GWOA)
BLACKJACK - 31

Duc Phong
Special Forces Camp

● Bu Kou Yon

● Bu N'Dren
○ NIGHT OF
9 JAN.

● Bu N'Drang
2 FEB.

● Bu Riah
● Bu Bitt
○ NIGHT OF
10 JAN.

13 JAN.

○ NIGHTS OF
11 & 12 JAN.

○ NIGHT OF
13 JAN.

○ NIGHTS OF
14 & 15 JAN.

17 JAN.

○ NIGHT OF
16 JAN.

○ NIGHT OF
17 JAN.

○ NIGHT OF
18 JAN.

○ NIGHT OF
19 JAN.

21 JAN.

○ NIGHT OF
20 JAN.

○ NIGHT OF
21 JAN.

○ NIGHT OF
22 JAN.

○ NIGHT OF
23 JAN.

○ NIGHT OF
24 JAN.

GROUP I
NIGHT OF
25 JAN.

25 JAN.

GROUP II
NIGHT OF
25 JAN.

○ NIGHTS OF
26 & 27 JAN.

Dong Nai River

○ NIGHTS OF
28 & 29 JAN.

29 JAN.

○ NIGHTS OF
30 & 31 JAN.

○ NIGHT OF
1 FEB.

○ NIGHT OF
2 FEB.

○ NIGHT OF
3 FEB.

○ NIGHT OF
4 FEB.

LZ
NIGHT OF
6 FEB.

GROUP I
NIGHT OF
5 FEB.

GROUP II
NIGHT OF
5 FEB.

LEGEND

🪂 PARACHUTE RESUPPLY DROP
○ MISSION SUPPORT SITE
● VILLAGE
⌒ ROUTE OF MARCH
≈ DONG NAI RIVER

CHAPTER ONE

0002, 25 DECEMBER 1966

I WAS SOUND ASLEEP in my hammock when I awoke to the distant rumble of thunder. Heavy rain was working its way through the canopy of trees overhead, and it drummed on the poncho that was stretched tight above me. After rubbing my eyes and yawning, I checked my watch and realized it was Christmas Day. Raising my head to look over the side of the hammock, I found the cool night air heavy with moisture and the smell of rotting vegetation. The low-hanging storm clouds that blanketed Phuoc-Long Province blocked out the light of the moon and the stars, leaving the jungle pitch black. I soon noticed that with every flash of lightning the jungle lit up as though someone were using flashbulbs. For a second I caught a momentary glimpse of George's hammock and poncho a few feet to my left.

"Pssst! George." I reached out into the rain and gave a tug on his hammock. There was a "swish" of quick movement, and lightning framed him in a sitting position.

"What's wrong?" he hissed.

"Merry Christmas," I whispered.

"You scared the piss outta me," he said as he lay back down. "I was in the middle of a dream." He rolled on his side, reached under his hammock, and removed something from his rucksack. "Here you go, Jimmy." He extended his arm and fumbled for my hand. "Merry Christmas."

"What is it?" I examined what felt like a can of liquid.

"Pepsi. I've had it in my ruck since Ho-Ngoc-Tao."

"Got any ice?" I joked.

"I'll get some from the cooler," he laughed.

"Hey, I've got something for you." I reached under my hammock and removed a plastic bag from my rucksack. A few days before leaving Ho-Ngoc-Tao, I received a fruit-cake from home and still had two pieces left. I placed the bag on my chest and, after opening it, passed a piece to George. "Merry Christmas," I said softly again.

"Thanks, Jimmy." He reached to shake my hand. "May you live a hundred more."

I popped the lid on the can and took my first sip. "Boy, there's nothing like a Pepsi when you've been in the bush for a few days," I said before biting into the fruitcake.

"You said it. I can think of a lot of places I'd rather be on Christmas, but here in War Zone D it don't get any better."

"You're right. We could be out in the mud somewhere. At least we're warm and dry."

"This your first Christmas in the field?" George asked.

"Yeah, I've been on duty before, but this is my first one in the bush. Last Christmas I was home on leave from A Company of the 7th."

"Lotta snow in Buffalo."

"Yeah, we get a good hundred inches a year," I said.

When I thought about it, I realized that this was actually my second Christmas on duty. As George and I enjoyed our feast I told him about my first—Christmas 1961. At that time I was assigned to the Marine barracks in Sanford, Florida, and was on guard duty at the main gate—Post #1—on the midnight-to-four watch. I still had to laugh whenever I thought about it. A couple of minutes after midnight, a Navy cook—a chief petty officer—drove up to the gate in his 1948 Chevy and wished me a Merry Christmas. The chief was drunk and handed me a freshly cooked, king-size turkey leg. Just as I was about to take my first bite, the first sergeant—probably the strictest first sergeant in the Marine Corps—arrived to inspect my post. I quickly hid the turkey leg in one of the desk drawers, licked my fingers clean, and snapped to attention as he approached.

My heart was beating a mile a minute as he barked a couple of quick questions. Every Marine in the company was scared to death of him, and as he looked through the logbook I prayed he wouldn't smell the turkey. While ordering me to recite a couple of my general orders, he went through all of the drawers except one—the one with the turkey leg. After completing his inspection he climbed back into his gray pickup and headed for Post #2. I couldn't believe my luck, and as soon as he got out of voice range, I let out a loud "Yahoo!"

After telling George the story, we finished what was left of our Pepsi and fruitcake and continued to whisper.

"The first sergeant must've been a terror," George added.

"Yeah," I laughed, "but he paid a price for messing with the troops."

"How's that?"

"Whenever we cleaned his office, we pissed in his coffee cup." George broke into uncontrollable laughter and choked as he tried to suppress it.

"Shhhh." I reached out into the rain to pull on his hammock. "Every Cong in the area's gonna hear you."

After a couple of minutes he settled down. "That's a classic," he laughed. "You know, I wouldn't mind being here on Christmas if I didn't have a family."

"You've got three kids, don't you?"

"No, I've got *four* great kids. My son, George Junior, and daughters Jackie, Terri, and Dena—Dena's the youngest."

"She's the one who's been sick?"

"Yeah, it's been rough with me gone. She's been in and out of the hospital," he answered sadly in the darkness.

"Aren't you getting short?"

"Yeah, I'll be goin' home after the next mission," he said. "What about you?"

"I extended to come to the Mobile Guerrilla Force, so I'll be here until September."

"You been here almost a year?"

"Just about," I said. "We got here right after New Year's. When we landed in Nha-Trang, Colonel McKean assigned us the mission of building a new camp at Duc-Phong."

"Time flies when you're having fun," George chuckled.

"I can't complain. I probably learned more than I did during the first twenty-three years of my life."

"Yeah, wars are like that. You learn a lot about people and better appreciate what's really important in life," George agreed. "Hey, it's getting late. We'd better catch some Zzzzs. It'll be morning before you know it."

"You're right." I reached down to the foot of my hammock and pulled a piece of camouflaged parachute nylon up to my neck. "Merry Christmas."

"Merry Christmas, Jimmy."

Although the rain had stopped, drops were still drumming a beat on my poncho. From what I could see, the storm was moving east, but distant flashes continued to light up the jungle beneath the trees. I felt good after having talked to George and, wrapped in the warmth of my parachute nylon, quickly drifted off into deep sleep.

Whoomph. There was a loud explosion just outside the western edge of our perimeter. "Sounded like a grenade," George murmured as I sat up, reached under my hammock, and quickly slipped into my wet boots.

"Think it was one of our booby traps?" I asked while hastily lacing my boots.

"Don't know." I could hear George adjusting the squelch on our radio as I pulled the quick-release knots on my hammock and poncho. The midnight air was cold and wet, and my hands shook as I stuffed them into my rucksack. Another flash of lightning lit the space beneath the canopy, and I saw George standing with the radio handset pressed against his ear.

"Hear any . . ."

Thoomp. I was interrupted by an explosion somewhere farther west than the first. My heart shifted into second gear as I buttoned my fatigue jacket and put on my bush hat.

"Mortars!" George called under his breath.

"Shit." I quickly slipped into my ammunition harness and picked up my M-16. Thoomp. Another one on the way.

"Get on the other side of the tree," George said. I grabbed one of the straps on my rucksack and quickly dragged it to the other side of a large cypress. Thoomp. Number three. We both hit the ground behind the tree. I was on the left and George on the right. I could hear voices over the radio, but because the handset was pressed to George's ear I couldn't understand a word. Thoomp, thoomp. Two more in the air.

"So much for the truce," I wisecracked.

"Bastards used the sound of the grenade to sight the mortar," he added.

Thoomp, thoomp . . . "Seven on the way," I said. With the top of my head pressed against the tree, I pulled my rucksack up against the side of my head. Whoomph. A mortar round exploded off to our left, and my heart rate shifted into third gear. "Here we go," I said to myself. George and I were squeezed side by side, and I could feel his body heat through my wet fatigues.

Whoomph. A second round exploded even closer to our position. I wondered if they had a ground assault ready to follow up the mortar barrage.

Whoomph. The ground shook and shrapnel cut through the leaves and thumped into the tree trunks. "Stay low." George put his arm over my back.

"I'd have to unbutton my jacket to get any lower," I

said with a nervous laugh. Whoomph, whoomph. Two bright flashes exploded to our left front, the earth shuddered beneath my chest, and my ears rang with a high-pitched whistle.

Our faces weren't more than a couple of inches apart, and I could hear George counting the seconds between the blasts as debris rained down on us. "Four, one thousand, five, one thousand . . ."

Suddenly, I detected a faint whistle streaming in from high above the canopy. "Aw shit." I covered my head with my arm and waited for the blast. Whoomph. Another flash, and a deafening metallic crack sounded just a few meters on the far side of the cypress. The hot blast rolled my rucksack over my head until it came to a rest on top of my legs.

Thump. Something smacked into the soft mud to the right of George's head. "What the hell was that?" I raised my head to look over the top of George. For a second I thought it might have been a piece of the tree.

"My God. It's gotta be the seventh round," George muttered softly. I pushed the rucksack off my legs and sprang to my feet. George was on his hands and knees, and in the next flash of lightning I saw him touching what looked like the fins of a mortar round. "It *is* the seventh round," he gasped in disbelief.

I grabbed his shoulder. "Don't mess with it."

"I may be seven-fifths crazy, but I ain't dumb." He reached out and grabbed my pant leg. "You stand over it. Make sure no one steps on it." He pulled my hand down and guided it to the cold steel fin. Running my fingers carefully over the round's cast-iron body and steel fins, I concluded that it was a 60-mm high-explosive cartridge—probably Chinese Communist.

"This round's got a point-detonating fuse," I said. "If it didn't blow on impact, it probably won't."

"You sure?"

"Yeah." Stumbling in the dark I felt my way back to my rucksack.

"Swamp Fox, this is Fox Three, over." George's voice was barely audible as he spoke into the radio handset.

"Fox Three, this is Swamp Fox," Captain Gritz responded. "Wait one."

"Fox One, are you there?" Gritz asked.

"Roger, Swamp Fox," Howard responded.

"Swamp Fox, this is Fox Two." England checked into the net.

"Fox Four, are you there?" Gritz asked.

"That's a Roger, Swamp Fox. Fox Four standing by," Chilton responded.

"This is Swamp Fox," the captain said. "Break out on your assigned azimuths. We'll RV [rendezvous] after first light. Swamp Fox, out."

We heard a hiss of static. "That's it, Jim. Let's get the third herd ready to roll." George stuffed his hammock and poncho into his rucksack.

"Hey, George," I whispered as I picked up my rucksack and swung it around to my back. "Tell me you don't believe in Santa Claus."

CHAPTER TWO

0025, 25 DECEMBER 1966

"*BAC-SI!*" A VOICE WHISPERED in the darkness. To most of the Cambodians I was Bac-si—Vietnamese for doctor.

"Over here." I bounced a couple of times to adjust the weight of my rucksack on my back.

"Is Sanh, Bac-si." He grabbed my arm with a sense of urgency. "I have Dung. He is wounded." Dung was a thin seventeen year old who had come to the MGF from the Buddhist pagoda in Saigon. Prior to his becoming a soldier he had studied to be a monk.

"Okay." I slipped out of my rucksack and lowered it to the ground. I asked Dung where he was wounded. My Cambodian wasn't all that great, but the Bodes usually understood what I was trying to say. Dung told me that it was his arm.

"I gave him morphine," Sanh said.

"Let's sit him down against my ruck." I grabbed Dung by the rear straps of his ammunition harness, and we slowly lowered him to the ground. I knelt at his left side, and, after locating his shoulder, felt my way down his arm. Just above his elbow I found a cloth tourniquet.

"He lose much blood," Sanh said with concern.

Working my way down from Dung's elbow I felt the

sleeve of his fatigue jacket suddenly turn cold and wet with blood. The sleeve had been torn by the mortar blast. Reaching in through one of the holes, my fingers came in contact with something hard, wet, and slippery. It was the two bones of his lower arm. I estimated that seven to eight inches of tissue had been blown away. Karoumph, karoumph. Two artillery rounds exploded far to the north.

"What you think, Bac-si?" Sanh murmured anxiously in the darkness.

"Let me check his pulse." Leaning over Dung, I found his right wrist: his pulse was racing and weak—somewhere around 165 beats a minute. He was in shock.

"Sanh, tell him we're gonna start an IV," I said.

Sanh said a few words in Cambodian and Dung immediately began chanting in whispers.

"Jimmy!" It was George.

"Over here."

His hand touched my shoulder. "Ready to move?" he asked as I rose to my feet.

"Dung's hit. If we move now, he'll die."

"Damn," he paused. "It's your call, Jim."

"Gotta get some serum albumin into him," I said.

"How much time?"

"A couple of hours."

"You got it." George placed a hand on my shoulder. "I'll pull in the platoon and form a perimeter. Let me know when you're ready to move."

"Okay." I was relieved with George's decision. It would contribute to the trusting relationship that was developing between the Americans and the Cambodians. One of the lessons of Vietnam was that trust was an essential part of leadership. With trust all things were possible.

"Bac-si," Sanh grabbed my arm, "one more wounded." Behind him someone was gasping for air with short, quick breaths.

"Who is it?"

"Hoa," Sanh told me. Groping in the darkness I found

Hoa being helped along by two other Bodes.

"Where's he hit?" I asked.

"His chest," Sanh replied.

"Let's sit him down next to Dung."

Sanh said a few words, and then we lowered Hoa to a sitting position, with his back braced against a couple of stalks of bamboo.

"I give him morphine?"

"No, not for a chest wound. It could kill him. He cough up any blood?" I asked.

"No cough," Sanh said.

"Bac-si," a hand touched my arm. "Is Luc, Bac-si. I bring M-5 kit."

"Good man," I said as Luc handed me the medical kit. Luc was our curly-haired, cheerful sixteen-year-old platoon medic. Although he didn't know much about medicine, he was very dependable. Kneeling in the mud between Dung and Hoa, I placed the kit on the ground and felt for Hoa's shoulder. He grabbed my hand. I told him to place my hand on his wound. He guided it toward his chest.

"Ouch." Something stuck the palm of my hand—it stung like a needle. Feeling further, I discovered a pencil-shaped, three-inch piece of metal with jagged edges sticking out of the left side of his chest. Unbuttoning his fatigue jacket, I reached under it to feel for any signs of bleeding. His chest was cold and clammy and his body was shaking. I felt around the piece of shrapnel. There was some slippery oozing, but as far as I could determine, he wasn't bleeding seriously, nor was air escaping from the wound.

Whump-whump-whump. Automatic rifle fire burst to the south of our perimeter. It sounded like an AK-47. I fumbled through the M-5 kit until I found the stethoscope. With Luc helping Hoa lean forward, I lifted the back of his fatigue jacket and listened to his lungs. The right side sounded clear, but when I attempted to listen to the left side, I couldn't hear anything—something was obstructing the sound of his breathing. He wasn't coughing so I had to conclude that the space between his chest wall and lungs was filling up with blood.

My thoughts were interrupted by the soft muted sounds of someone talking to George in low tones. It was England; his slow West Virginian accent was one of a kind. He had come to the MGF from Hiep-Hoa—a Special Forces camp located west of Saigon in Hau-Nghia Province. He was generally a quiet, easygoing person. Because he didn't say a lot it took me a while to get to know him, but when I did, I found him to be an uncommonly deep-thinking person.

"Ji-im." Only England pronounced Jim with two syllables.

"Yeah." I rose to my feet and bumped into him.

"Look," he grabbed my arm, "I'm gonna stay here with you and George. My platoon will take the eastern half of the perimeter—zero to one-eighty."

"We'll take one-eighty to three-sixty," George said.

"Keep 'em close enough to touch the next guy without moving," I said to Sanh.

"If they gotta piss, they do it in place," England said. "And we don't open fire unless we're attacked."

"*Oui, Trung-si* [Sergeant]," Sanh whispered.

"Okay, Jimmy," George said, "I'll take Sanh and Ly with me. We'll RV here when everyone's in place."

I followed the sound of breathing back to Dung. He was still sitting with his back against my rucksack so I placed my hand on the back of his neck, pulled the rucksack off to the side, and slowly lowered his trembling body to the ground. With him lying flat I removed a poncho from my rucksack and positioned the ruck under his feet so that his legs would be elevated. I then used the wet rubber poncho to cover him from head to toe. Luc was near Dung's head, and after telling him to move to Dung's other side, I slipped under the poncho and pulled in the medical kit.

In the confined space, my nostrils filled with the smell of blood, sweat, and rubber. Reaching into my breast pocket I removed my pen flashlight. As soon as Luc was under the poncho I turned on the light. Dung's face was a stark indicator of his condition. His eyes were glassy and beads of sweat slowly dripped down his ashen face. The flesh on the inside of his forearm had been blown from the bone; three inches down from his elbow I spotted a large white blood vessel sticking out a quarter of an inch. Even though he had a tourniquet on his arm, he was still losing blood through the torn vessel.

After handing Luc the light I removed a hemostat clamp from the medical kit, clamped it to the end of the bleeding vessel, and tied off the end using a piece of black surgical thread.

"Okay, my friend, let's get some serum albumin into him." I reached into the medical kit and removed a bottle of the blood-plasma expander. I handed Luc the bottle, and he reached out from under the poncho and taped it to a stalk of bamboo. With everything ready, I found what looked like a good vein on the inside of Dung's wrist. It was getting hot beneath the poncho, and I could feel beads of sweat dripping from the end of my nose.

"Get the light closer," I told Luc as a mosquito buzzed in my ear. With my face just a few inches from Dung's hand, I worked the needle into his vein. "Got it." I removed the clamp from the IV tubing. The sight of the life-giving liquid flowing into his vein provided a great sense of relief. While Luc held the light, I packed the wound with sterile gauze, then wrapped his entire lower arm with an Ace bandage—it would hold everything in place and keep it clean.

"Let's check his blood pressure," I said to Luc.

Whoomph. What sounded like a hand grenade exploded to the east of our perimeter. I removed the blood-pressure cuff from the medical kit and after applying it to Dung's arm found that his systolic blood pressure reading was only ninety-two. I was worried that if it went much lower he wouldn't make it. I hoped to get it up to at least 100 before we had to move.

"Turn off the light," I told Luc. "Let's get the poncho over Hoa." The light clicked off and we were again in total darkness.

Slipping out from under the poncho, I felt the damp, cold night air and breathed in the smells of decayed vegetation and mold. I pulled the poncho from Dung and—down on my knees—moved the short distance to where Hoa was sitting against the bamboo. I carefully slipped the poncho over his head while Luc worked his way around to his other side. After adjusting the poncho, I crawled under it and could hear Hoa's now-familiar raspy breathing a few inches from my face. By the time I pulled in the medical kit, Luc was also under the poncho. When he clicked on the light, it illuminated Hoa's pain-stricken face. His eyes too were glassy, and his olive skin had a bluish tint to it. Looking at his chest, I spotted the piece of metal protruding from the left side of his camouflaged fatigue jacket.

Like Dung, Hoa was just a teenager. He had a great tenor's voice, and I had joked that his ancestors must have come from Ireland. When we were at Ho-Ngoc-Tao, I taught him a couple of verses from Barry Sadler's "The Ballad of the Green Berets," and he got to the point where he could sing them well.

With Luc holding the light, I unbuttoned Hoa's jacket. Then, using scissors, I cut the jacket so it fell away from the piece of shrapnel. There was no major bleeding; only a small amount of blood oozed from around the piece of metal. I then took his blood pressure: his systolic reading was merely ninety-seven. Like Dung, Hoa was in real danger.

"Let's get an IV going," I said to Luc as I removed a slimy leech from my face, squished it between my fingers, and dropped it to the ground. While Luc got the serum albumin ready I found what looked like a good vein on Hoa's right hand. Much to my relief the IV needle slipped right in. After filling a syringe with a hundred milligrams of Demerol, I slowly injected the painkiller into the IV tube that ran into his arm. Hoa would soon be on cloud nine.

"Gotta wait for the Demerol to work," I told Luc. For fifteen minutes we sat in the darkness listening to the occasional trumpeting of a nearby elephant. "Okay, Luc." There was a click, and the small space beneath the poncho filled with light. "Tell him that as soon as I pull out the shrapnel, he's gotta take in a deep breath," I said as I wrapped a piece of gauze around the sharp piece of metal. With one hand pressed against his chest, I gripped the gauze-wrapped piece of shrapnel with my other hand and carefully began to pull. It was stuck! A barb was probably hung up on a rib.

Getting a better grip, I steadily increased the pressure and started twisting. With Hoa groaning from deep in his chest, the barb suddenly released its hold and slid out from between his ribs. Hoa took in a deep breath, and I placed some petrolatum gauze over the hole; ideally, it would form an airtight seal. While I examined the bloody piece of metal, Luc covered the gauze with a few strips of surgical tape.

"Tell him we're gonna use a syringe to get the blood out of his chest. Once it's out he'll feel a lot better," I said. While Luc explained the procedure, I attached a needle to a syringe. Luc slipped behind Hoa and, after raising the back of his fatigue jacket, he placed a hand on each of his shoulders and pressed him forward. I moved behind Hoa and, using my fingertips, found a location between his seventh and eighth ribs. It would be our entry point for drawing the blood. After swabbing the area with betadine, I slowly worked the needle between his ribs; the syringe began to fill with blood.

Whump. A shot was fired to the east of our perimeter.

When the syringe was full I squirted the blood onto the jungle floor. I repeated the procedure six times. When the seventh syringe was about half full, I began to get air. With the blood removed from his pleural space, Hoa appeared to be breathing easier. I covered the needle marks with a band-aid and wrapped his chest with an Ace bandage.

With Hoa in relatively good shape, we returned to Dung and found his bottle of serum albumin almost empty. "Disconnect it and plug in a bottle of normal saline," I told Luc. As soon as Luc had the normal saline flowing, I again checked Dung's blood pressure and found that it had risen to ninety-nine. Both patients were now in relatively good shape.

I crawled out from under the poncho. It was 0217, and the cool night air was filled with the buzzing of mosquitoes and the chirping of crickets.

CHAPTER THREE

"DONAHUE," A FAMILIAR VOICE whispered.

"Over here." I rose to my feet and, reaching into the darkness, I touched a face.

"It is Rinh," he said. "I have three wounded."

Rinh was our chief Cambodian medic. He was also a good friend who spoke excellent English. Behind him I could hear more than one person breathing.

"What d'ya got?"

"Binh has a large piece of shrapnel in his leg."

"Can he walk?" I asked.

"Yes, I gave him morphine and meprobamate."

"How about the other two?"

"Kien had part of his ear blown off."

"Any head damage?" I asked.

"Just his scalp. I put a dressing on it and gave him Demerol."

"Good. What about the last one?"

"Danh has shrapnel in his hip."

"Can he walk?"

"Yes. I gave him morphine and meprobamate."

"What about antibiotics?"

"Not yet, Donahue."

"Can they walk without help?" George asked from behind me.

"Yes, I gave their rucksacks to their squad leaders."

"Dung and Hoa are wounded and in shock," I told Rinh. "I've got IVs going. We're not gonna move until we get 'em stabilized."

I pulled Rinh a few feet in my direction and put his hand on Dung's foot.

"This is Dung," I said. "Hoa's to his left."

"I understand," he said quietly.

"Put your three on the ground to the left of Hoa," I told him.

"I will take Dung and Hoa's blood pressure every fifteen minutes," Rinh said.

"Okay, my friend." I sat near Dung's feet and reached to make sure my M-16 was still leaning against my rucksack. A few feet to my right I heard muffled voices over our PRC-25 radio (a battery-powered frequency modulated—FM—radio that had a range of eight kilometers, or nearly five miles). Reaching in the direction of the radio I touched an arm.

"It's me, Jimmy," George whispered. "We've got two LPs [listening posts] out."

"Good."

To my left I heard Sanh chattering under his breath to the squad leaders over his HT-1 radio (a walkie-talkie-type radio with a range of one kilometer).

"Hey, look at that," George said. "A Christmas star."

I looked up and a drop of water hit my face. Through a small hole in the overhead foliage I saw a single star brushed by fast-moving clouds. "Cloud cover's breaking up."

"In one hour, all cloud go east," Sanh said.

"You a weatherman?" George chuckled.

"I'll take him back to Buffalo and get him a job on TV," I joked.

"Good idea, Bac-si." Sanh patted my knee. "After

Khmer-Serei kill Sihanouk, I come America.''

Karoumph, karoumph. Two more artillery rounds exploded to the north.

"He's too ugly to be on TV," George mused.

"When I was young man I very handsome," Sanh tried to convince us. "I have too many girlfriend."

"Why don't you like Sihanouk?" I asked. "I thought he was a neutral.''

"Sihanouk bullshit everyone," Sanh said with anger. "When Japanese leave, America and France have much power so he tell them he against Communist. They think he stop Communist in Cambodia, so they give him much money and help him become president. When Communist strong in Vietnam he tell them he support Communist."

"Why doesn't the Khmer-Serei work out a truce with him?" I asked.

"Yeah," George said, "a coalition government?"

"Ah, Trung-si. Problem go back long time. Before Japanese come here, Khmer-Serei was right wing of resistance, and Sihanouk was left wing. When Japanese army come Cambodia, our leader Son-Ngoc-Tran support Japanese. Now Sihanouk say Khmer-Serei is fascist and work for CIA."

"He supported the Japanese?" George was surprised.

"You must understand, Trung-si. Khmer-Serei then see French imperialist as number one enemy. Son-Ngoc-Tran think he use Japanese to get French out of Cambodia."

"A dangerous game," George said.

"What's the Khmer-Serei want?" I asked.

"Democratic government in Cambodia," Sanh said.

"How you gonna get Sihanouk outta there?" asked George.

"We train our soldier in Vietnam and then we send some to Cambodia," answered Sanh. "They join army and tell Sihanouk we love you too much. Since army in Cambodia not good, our soldier become officer. One day we have coup in Cambodia."

"How in the hell did all you Cambodians end up in Vietnam?" George asked.

"Ah, Trung-si. Long time ago, the land south of Saigon part of Cambodia. Now this land is South Vietnam; maybe half a million Cambodian live there. In Vietnam we are oppressed minority."

"George," a voice hissed from the darkness.

"Over here," he said.

"England?"

"Yeah." He sat on the ground a few feet from us. "I'll tell you what," he said in his familiar West Virginian drawl. "I ain't ever seen a night this dark."

"Donahue," Rinh touched my shoulder, "their blood pressure is over 105."

I looked at my watch; it was 0347. "Go ahead and disconnect the bottles. Leave the needles in their veins and tape the tubes to their arms."

"I understand."

If one of them developed a problem during the move, it would be a simple procedure to untape the tubing and plug in another bottle of normal saline.

"They about ready?" George asked.

"A few minutes," I replied.

"Okay," said George, "we move at 0415."

"Look, you've got the wounded. I'll lead out with my platoon," England volunteered.

"Okay," George agreed. "You take point and we'll fall in to your rear."

"I'll stay on three-sixty until first light," England told us.

"Shouldn't take long to reach the RV," said George.

"Sanh," I called, "pass the word that if anyone gets separated they should stay on 360 degrees until they hit the road. We'll have a truck from the B-Team pick 'em up."

"*Oui,* Bac-si."

England and his radio operator headed back to their platoon.

"Jimmy, meet me up at the head of the column at 0400," George said.

"Right."

George, Sanh, and Ly left, and I could see that Rinh had the wounded on their feet. Looking up through holes in the canopy, I saw that the clouds had moved to the east and that the sky was white with stars. In scattered spots the light from those stars penetrated all the way to the jungle's floor. In those few areas everything was visible in tones of gray; everywhere else remained black as tar.

Reaching down, I grabbed my rucksack and swung it around to my back. With my sixty pounds in place, I picked up my M-16 and mentally pictured how we were going to keep everyone together during our trek. Movement through the jungle during the day required that you maintain visual contact with the person to your front. Failure to do so could result in your becoming separated and possibly lost. Since visual contact generally couldn't be maintained at night, it had to be replaced by physical contact.

Rinh had the wounded lined up and ready to move. Hoa was first, followed by Luc and Rinh. Behind Rinh I found Dung with a tight grip on Rinh's rucksack. To his rear Binh, Kien, and Danh were ready to head north. When I reached Hoa, I had him grab a strap on the back of my rucksack. Like a slow-moving train we began working our way north in three-inch steps. By the time we reached George, the first of England's men were already feeling their way north.

CHAPTER FOUR

THERE WAS MOVEMENT IN our shadowy world beneath the canopy. As the ghostlike figures of England's men continued to pass in front of George, the third platoon waited its turn to move. The rain had stopped, but drops continued to filter through the canopy. Behind George, Ly had the radio handset pressed to his ear. Sanh was third, followed by me and the wounded. The machine-gun section fell in to the rear of the wounded, and behind them were the remainder of the platoon. We were pressed together—hand to rucksack—ready to move.

"Jim," George called in low tones, "you count the paces."

"Okay." I pulled a two-foot section of parachute line from my pants pocket. One end was tied to my belt. Every hundred paces I would tie a knot in it; once the sun came up, I would count the knots and figure how far we had traveled. If we kept track of the distance and direction, we would be able to compute our location. Navigation in War Zone D could be difficult because there were few prominent terrain features on our 1:50,000 maps. (One inch on the map equaled fifty thousand inches on the ground.) One jungle-covered hill came after another, and they all looked pretty much the same. The landscape resembled a pool table packed tight with balls. You knew when you were at the crest or the base of a hill, but you weren't always sure which hill it was.

As we waited in the darkness, I rested my M-16 on my ammunition belt and could feel Hoa gripping the back of my rucksack. "Hold on partner," I urged encouragingly.

"Okay, Bac-si," a weak voice responded. To our right front the gray shadows of the last of England's men were approaching George. They'd take a step or two, stop for a few seconds, and then take another couple of steps. When the last man passed, George grabbed the back of his ruck-sack. I held a strap on the rear of Sanh's rucksack, and a few seconds later he took his first steps. We were finally on our way. We moved downhill through a tangled mass of wet leaves and vines, and the jungle soon became alive with the predawn chirping of birds.

By the time we reached the top of the next hill, dawn was breaking; the grays slowly turned to dull shades of yellow, green, and brown. In the lower levels of the canopy, gnarled brown-and-green vines twisted off in every direc-tion and dangled like limp tentacles from branches over-head. In the higher elevations the leaves disappeared into a thick morning mist. Growing between the towering tree trunks were stands of lime green bamboo and leaves of every size and shape. The air was absolutely still. Just be-yond the crest, Sanh raised his hand over his head and the column stopped. In front of him I heard the muffled tones of George making radio contact.

"Psst." George waved me forward.

"What's up?" I murmured.

"Little over a klick [a thousand meters] to the RV."

"About an hour," I estimated.

"England's gonna move on 320 degrees for five hundred meters and then shoot an azimuth to the RV."

Halfway down the hill we changed direction and began moving north-northwest, an azimuth of 320 degrees. At the bottom of the hill we hit a wall of leaves, thorn-covered vines, and foul-smelling ankle-deep water. Because of the thickness of the undergrowth England's point man had to use a machete to cut a tunnel through the tangle. Feeling our way through the dark tunnel, our boots sank six inches into soft mud; behind me I could hear Hoa gasping for air. When we emerged from the swamp, we returned to daylight and began working our way up yet another hill.

Near the crest the foliage thinned and we found ourselves surrounded by exotic trees. Their thick branches grew parallel to the ground, ten to twenty feet above it. Limp tentacles hung from the branches and grew into new trees wherever they touched the ground. It was, in fact, a single tree that had grown to cover the entire area. It struck me as the ideal setting for a horror movie about a man-eating tree.

Moving over relatively open terrain, George put out flank security—four-man fire teams on either side—and I assume England did the same. If contact was made, it would most likely be at the head of the column, but flank and rear contact were always possible. It was therefore essential to have all-around security whenever we moved. The general rule was that flank-security units would maintain visual contact with the main body at all times. As the jungle thinned, the units moved farther out, and as it thickened, they moved in close. In dense foliage it was sometimes impossible to maintain flank security, but no matter what the terrain, point and tail-gunner (rear) security was always preserved.

As the sun continued to rise, the mist above our heads glowed white, and here and there brilliant shafts of sunlight penetrated to the jungle floor. Treading left and right around fifty-foot mango trees I found myself softly humming Christmas songs as my brain sorted every shred of stimuli for possible danger: the smell of smoke, a muffled cough, a shadow that didn't fit. Twenty minutes later we changed direction and followed a thirty-five-degree azimuth past large banana plants whose clumps of small green bananas hung under large drooping leaves.

Sometime thereafter we broke onto a grass-covered circular field measuring 150 meters across. The area was located on the west side of a hill that had been cleared by Montagnards for slash-and-burn agriculture. Decaying tree stumps dotted the clearing, but nowhere was there any evidence that crops had been planted in recent years. The field's wet grass grew ankle high, and clumps of small yellow flowers grew everywhere.

Looking up the hill I saw a few camouflaged uniforms standing in the mist-shrouded wood line. It looked like our headquarters section. Halfway up that hill England's platoon was moving to the left side of the clearing. I was only a short distance into the clearing when George stopped.

"Jimmy, we're gonna set up security on this end. Gritz wants you to bring the wounded up to headquarters."

"They got a chopper on the way?" I asked.

"As soon as the mist burns off."

"Okay."

George said a few words to each of the wounded, then I led them up the hill. In the wood line to my right I spotted Jim Howard and Dick Jarvis. Howard had been in the army for fifteen years, and prior to volunteering for the MGF he had served as the team sergeant of Special Forces Detachment A-331 at Loc-Ninh. It was one of the hottest camps in III Corps, and while there he developed a hard-earned reputation as one of the best team sergeants in the 5th Special Forces Group. Although he never said anything about it, I knew him to be a deeply religious man. He carried a small Bible, and during quiet moments I often saw him reading from it.

Jarvis had also served at Loc-Ninh before coming to the MGF. During his time in Vietnam he had become an expert on enemy booby traps, and he took great joy in improvising his own. He was one of the best-natured people I knew, always wearing a smile on his face.

Near the top of the hill the mist turned a brilliant white, the temperature shot up, and overhead a few small patches of blue appeared. The morning would soon turn into a steam bath. At the top of the hill I found Captain Gritz standing at the edge of the clearing. His tiger-striped fatigues and soft bush hat were soaked from the rain; his face bore a serious expression as he pressed the radio handset to his ear. While talking, he fingered through a canvas map case that hung at his side. On his right hip a dull black holster concealed a 9-mm Browning automatic pistol. Green tape secured a U.S. Navy survival knife to the left shoulder strap of his ammunition harness, and a green triangular bandage hung loosely around his neck.

Fang stood to Gritz's left and held the captain's 9-mm Swedish K submachine gun under his arm. To the captain's right, Pat Wagner had ignited two pieces of C-4 (high-explosive compound) and was heating a couple of canteen cups of water. A few meters to their rear and just inside the wood line Tranh was sitting on the ground talking to Buck Kindoll through an interpreter.

"Merry Christmas," Gritz smiled as we approached.

"Merry Christmas, sir." I shook his hand.

"Roger, Sidewinder. The west side of the hill, over," Gritz said into the handset and then paused while the FAC said something I couldn't understand.

I turned to Rinh. "Sit 'em down next to Sergeant Kindoll." As each of the wounded passed, the captain gave him a few words of encouragement and shook his hand.

"You made it," Kindoll smiled as he rose to shake my hand.

"Yeah, I'm glad we didn't have to carry anyone." I lowered my rucksack to the ground. "How's the prisoner doing?"

"He's got the ass," Kindoll said with a sardonic smile.

"What's his problem?" I removed a canteen from my harness and took a drink.

"Well," Kindoll grinned, "he figured out that his wounds weren't all that serious."

Gritz had to laugh at Kindoll's comment. "Are you telling me he thinks you fed him a line of bullshit?" Kindoll shrugged.

"Hey, Jimmy," a gravel voice called, "want some tea?" Wagner rose to his feet with a steaming cup in each hand.

"Yeah, nothing like tea in the morning."

"It's hot." He handed me a cup.

"Thanks." I took a couple of sips and smacked my lips before passing the cup to Rinh, who gave some to each of the wounded and then took a sip himself.

"Jimmy," Gritz motioned with his hand.

"Yes, sir." I took a few steps to where he was listening to the radio.

"How are they doing?" he asked.

"Well, sir, Dung's gonna lose the arm. His soldiering days are over."

"He got a family?"

"Yes, sir. A wife and blind kid."

"I'll talk to Colonel Huddleston," the captain said with concern. "Maybe we can get him a job with C-3 security."

"He'd appreciate it," I said. "Sir, we heading north from here?"

"Affirmative. One recon section's halfway to the highway."

"Swamp Fox, this is Sidewinder, over," the FAC interrupted.

"Sidewinder, this is Swamp Fox, over," Gritz responded.

"Swamp Fox, this is Sidewinder. I'm holding west of the mountain. Will remain this location until it clears, over."

"Roger, Sidewinder. We're getting some sky down here. Would estimate another one five minutes, over."

"Swamp Fox, this is Sidewinder. Let me know when you're clear, over."

"Roger, Sidewinder. Swamp Fox, out." Gritz passed the handset to Wagner.

"Jimmy, take a look at Clyde [the VC prisoner]."

"Yes, sir."

"Jim." A hand touched my shoulder. I turned and saw that it was Denny Montgomery, one of three former Marines on the team. Montgomery was not only an outstanding medic, he also had a solid infantry background. He knew weapons and tactics as well as anyone, and so was a real asset to the team.

"Hey, Monty." I shook his hand. "Merry Christmas."

"Merry Christmas, Jim." While Montgomery talked to the captain I grabbed Fang and walked over to talk to Tranh. When Fang and I knelt on the ground in front of the prisoner, I noticed that much of his face had turned black and blue from the blast and that he was trembling. I asked if he was hungry. He shook his head. With a shaky voice he told me the captain had given him food.

"*Ho se giet toi knong,*" he trembled.

"What'd he say?" I asked Fang. Tranh grabbed Fang's arm and started talking a mile a minute.

"Bac-si, he say the ugly one will kill him," Fang told me.

"What!" I assured him that he was going to the hospital in Saigon. By the expression on his face I could tell he wasn't convinced.

"Hey, Pat, get over here."

"What's his problem?" Wagner walked over with a cup of tea.

"Tranh thinks you're gonna kill him," I smiled.

"Gimme a break," Wagner said. "Here, kid, have some tea."

Wagner handed the prisoner the cup. Tranh said something in Vietnamese and pointed to Kien. Kien was a short stocky Bode, somewhere around twenty-five years old, who was always chewing on a half-smoked unlit cigar. With the Ace bandage wrapped tightly around his head and a half-inch growth on his chin, he could easily have passed for a Moroccan.

"Bac-si," Fang shook his head, "not Trung-si Wagner. He say Kien kill him." Tranh pointed his blood-and-dirt caked finger at Kien. Kien was sitting a few meters away with his M-16 lying across his outstretched legs. The muzzle was pointed at Tranh's chest and Kien's face was full of hate. Fang jumped to his feet and, while pounding a finger on Kien's chest, said something in harsh muffled tones.

"Fang, you tell him that it's a life for a life," Gritz said. "If he kills the prisoner, it'll cost him his life."

"He say he like to kill VC," Fang told us, "but he not do today."

"Tell him he's a good soldier," Gritz said before picking up his radio handset. The prisoner looked relieved and, after taking a couple of sips of tea, handed the cup back to Wagner, who passed it to Kien. The Bode refused to drink from the same cup as the Vietcong prisoner.

"We're gonna have to warn the chopper crew to keep an eye on the Bodes," Kindoll said.

"Yeah," Montgomery agreed, "they'll throw Tranh's ass out the door in a heartbeat."

"Roger, Sidewinder," Gritz spoke into his handset as he checked his compass. "You're northwest of the LZ. If you shoot a one-sixty, you'll come in right above us, over."

"Roger, Swamp Fox."

Walking into the clearing I heard the faint hum of the FAC's engine. Mist still drifted among the leaves, but the sky overhead was clear and blue. When the hot rays of the sun came in contact with the wet grass, beads of moisture sparkled like crystals, and here and there trails of steam worked their way skyward.

"Sidewinder, this is Swamp Fox," Gritz said into the handset. "If you look to your left-front you'll see the clearing, over."

"Roger, Swamp Fox."

"Hit him with a mirror," Gritz told Wagner.

I looked up and saw the O-1E against the blue sky. At an altitude of a few thousand feet it looked like a black bird with outstretched wings. Wagner walked a few meters into the sunlight and removed his White Dot signal mirror from his pocket. Raising it to eye level he looked through a small hole in the mirror. When he had the plane sighted through it he began rocking the mirror back and forth. Its reflective surface caught the rays of the sun and flashed a signal to the aircraft.

"I got you, Swamp Fox," the FAC reported. "Estimate dust off your location in zero five minutes, over."

"Roger, Sidewinder. Thank you much. Swamp Fox, out."

The steady hum of the O-1E's prop changed pitch as it dropped down and passed over us at treetop level. After waving, the pilot returned to altitude to await the arrival of the chopper.

"Jimmy, the guy with the head wound—what's his name?" Gritz asked.

"That's Kien, sir."

Gritz grabbed Fang by the arm. "Fang, you tell Kien that I'm holding him personally responsible for the prisoner's safety."

Fang translated the captain's words and Kien jumped to his feet and saluted.

"I do Captain Gri," he smiled. In Asian cultures a smile is often a sign of submission. Gritz returned the salute. To the north I could hear the familiar wap, wap, wap of the approaching Huey. It sounded close, but sound could be deceptive. If it was flying at treetop level, you would pick up the sound of its rotors at about three miles. If it was approaching at five thousand feet, however, you could hear it up to ten miles away. Three thousand feet overhead, the FAC continued to drift in lazy circles.

"Pop a smoke," Gritz told Wagner, who removed a smoke grenade from his ammunition harness, pulled the pin, and tossed it into the clearing. By the time it hit the ground, a trail of thick red smoke poured from the canister and slowly twisted skyward. While Gritz talked to the FAC, Montgomery, Rinh, and I got the wounded on their feet and lined them up along the edge of the clearing.

"Here he comes," Kindoll said. Looking north I saw the green hull of the Huey gliding in just above the mist. Seconds later the nose of the craft rose slightly, and it slowed to fifty miles per hour. With the rotor blades slapping the moist morning air at more than three hundred revolutions per minute, the pilot slowed to five miles per hour and, at the last possible second, lowered his nose and set down twenty meters into the clearing.

We covered our eyes with our arms to protect against the pieces of grass kicked up by the prop wash and followed the captain and Kindoll out to the chopper. As I neared the front of the Huey, I saw Gritz standing on the skid step talking face to face with the pilot. The pilot had his helmet pulled half off so he could hear what Gritz was yelling over the noise of the engine and rotors.

"Get 'em aboard," Gritz motioned with his arm. When we reached the side door we found a medic anxiously awaiting the wounded. Montgomery and I helped Dung and Hoa climb in, and the medic put them into position with their backs against the fire wall. Binh, Kien, and Danh quickly climbed aboard and took up positions with their backs to the pilot stations.

"Where are you taking them?" I hollered to the medic.

"Cong-Hoa Hospital," he yelled. Tranh was standing on the skid and was about to climb aboard. Suddenly, Gritz jumped from the step and, from behind, grabbed Tranh around the neck. Tranh's feet dangled a foot off the ground and his eyes bulged.

"The pilot's an asshole," Kindoll yelled in my ear. "He won't take the prisoner without security."

Gritz pulled his 9-mm Browning automatic from his holster, cocked the hammer, and pressed the muzzle against

Tranh's temple. The prisoner turned white and appeared close to passing out. "Okay," Gritz shouted, his grip preventing Tranh from collapsing on the ground. "This one's for you."

"What?" The pilot was shocked.

"When you lift off, I'm gonna kill him," Gritz roared. "You can come back any time, look down, and know there's one planted here in your name." Tranh had no idea what was going on. With the cold steel muzzle pressed tight against his temple, tears began welling in his eyes. The pilot turned and exchanged a few hurried words with a crew member, then he turned back to Gritz. With each pass of the rotor blades overhead, rays of sunlight passed through one of the cockpit's overhead windows and flickered across the pilot's face.

"It's your decision," Gritz bellowed as the prop wash tugged at his uniform. "Make it."

"Get him on board," grumbled the angry pilot. "You're gonna hear about this."

Gritz released his grip on Tranh and tapped his butt. Wearing a confused expression on his face, he didn't waste any time climbing aboard. He took a seat on the chopper's honeycombed floor with his feet dangling out over the skids. When he turned and saw Kien sitting behind him, he quickly crawled to a more secure position. Once Tranh was on board, the pilot made a quick pre-takeoff check and then slowly pulled back on his collective.

We ran in a low crouch, retracing our path back to the wood line. As the helicopter hovered a few feet off the ground, a stream of hot air poured from its Pratt & Whitney engine. With a final surge of power, it tilted, transitioned to forward flight, and climbed across the clearing, thrashing the tops of the trees with its departing down wash.

"Would you have shot him?" I asked Gritz as we stood in the wood line.

"Jimmy, let me tell you something. Given the choice of life or death, Americans will almost always choose life."

Gritz turned to Wagner. "We move in five. One, three, headquarters, and two."

"Yes, sir." Wagner reached down and picked up his radio handset. I swung my ruck around to my back, and Montgomery and I headed back to our platoons.

"Captain could end up in deep shit," I said as we moved across the clearing.

"Yeah," he smiled, "maybe they'll send him to Vietnam."

CHAPTER FIVE

I STOOD IN A shadowy tangle at the base of a great cypress tree and bounced up and down a couple of times to adjust the weight of my rucksack. Looking up through a hole in the canopy I saw yellow butterflies drifting in and out of a brilliant shaft of sunlight that penetrated to the jungle floor. The few patches of mist that remained clung to the leaves in the upper reaches of the canopy. Minutes later the third platoon followed Howard's first platoon north from the Landing Zone (LZ). The headquarters section fell in to our rear, and behind them England's second platoon. With our green-and-black column stretched out over two hundred meters, we slipped silently through the wet undergrowth.

When we hit the faded blacktop of Highway 311, I stomped my feet to remove the mud from my boots. On both sides of the road green stalks of bamboo grew to within a foot of the pavement. Near the ground the fifty-foot-high stalks seemed bundled together, but at the higher levels the weight of their leaves bowed them over the road to form a tunnel of green. Three hundred meters down the road we found the Popular Force (PF) outpost where the trucks from the B-Team were waiting to pick us up. Theirs was a square-shaped compound surrounded by a red earthen wall, evenly spaced punji stakes, and a few strands of barbed and concertina wire.

Thirty minutes later, we boarded the trucks and headed for Song-Be. The Bodes were quiet until we hit the village of Son-Thuy. Once back into friendly territory, they relaxed and began singing as we sped down the narrow road. After a few Cambodian songs, Jim "The Great Caruso" Howard broke in with a song that was sung to the tune of "My Bonnie Lies Over the Ocean."

> Her mother's a Montagnard sergeant.
> Her father's an LLDB.
> And each night about midnight,
> they turn into hard-core VC.

Nearing the airstrip I spotted an Air America DC-3 sitting on the apron. A half-dozen skinny men dressed in black pajamas were unloading baskets of live chickens and ducks onto a two-and-a-half-ton truck. Waiting in the shade under one of the wings were a missionary and a couple of Vietnamese officials dressed in suits. At the entrance to the airstrip we turned onto the apron and parked. After unloading the troops and equipment, we set up a defensive perimeter in a grassy area between the runway and the road. Once security was in place Captain Gritz informed us that our C-123s had been diverted to another mission, so we would be picked up at 0800 the next morning. The good news was that half of the company could go into Song-Be for three hours. When they returned, the other half would go in.

George insisted that I go first, so I jumped on the back of one of our trucks and headed into town with Pat Wagner, Lowell Glossup, Sanh, and a load of Bodes. Prior to their assignment to the MGF, Wagner and Glossup had served with Detachment A-312 at Xom-Cat, a Special Forces camp located north of Saigon in Long-Khanh Province. Glossup was the team's intelligence sergeant and Wagner its radio operator.

Sanh stared at Nui-Ba-Ra with a faraway look on his face as we sped down the narrow road. The towering extinct volcano rose thousands of feet above the rolling green hills to touch the sky.

"What's on your mind?" I asked.

"Ah, Bac-si," he paused, "many comrades die here."

"When was that?"

"French have penal colony by mountain." He pointed to Nui-Ba-Ra. "It very bad place."

"A penal colony?"

"Yes, Bac-si. Vietnam have many secrets."

Thinking about what Sanh had told me, I looked at the trees at the base of the mountain; hidden beneath their leaves I pictured the prison's crumbling vine-covered walls. How interesting it would be to spend some time nosing around such a place. "There's a Montagnard village at the base of the mountain where I used to hold sick call," I told Sanh.

"Hey, Jimmy," Wagner yelled from the other side of the truck. "There anywhere we can get a cold beer?"

"Yeah, the B-Team's got American beer. If you like Biere La Rue or Ba-mui-ba, there are a few places in town."

"I like Biere La Rue," he said, smacking his lips.

"I told you he's a sick man," Glossup laughed as he put his hands around Wagner's neck and pretended to strangle him. Nearing Song-Be we passed a few farms along the side of the road. For the most part, the houses were small structures with woven bamboo walls and thatch roofs. Next to them grew a few banana, orange, palm, guava, and breadfruit trees. Behind some of the houses women dressed in black pajamas and conical hats could be seen cleaning their pigsties or feeding chickens.

Entering the outskirts of town, we kicked up a cloud of red dust as the truck slowed to avoid hitting one of the many people who walked the streets. Most were soldiers holding hands—a Vietnamese custom. Some wore the maroon berets and camouflaged fatigues of the 31st Ranger Battalion, while others wore the green fatigues and baseball caps of the 49th Infantry of the Army of the Republic of Vietnam (ARVN). A few jeeps and military trucks roved through town, but most of the people relied on bicycles or foot power to get around. A few of the wealthier residents owned Honda motor scooters that belched clouds of black smoke as they sputtered down the street.

As we neared the central market, we saw women balancing across their shoulders long bamboo poles, with a wicker basket attached to each end. They carried everything from fresh fruit, vegetables, and rice to hundred-day eggs and dried fish. For the most part, the buildings in downtown Song-Be were one- or two-story structures built of concrete blocks, stuccoed and roofed with tin. Mainly they were dingy white with streaks of rust and black mold running down their walls. The coffin maker had a dozen wooden coffins stacked out front; his business was always good.

High-pitched singsongy Vietnamese music blared from portable radios, while a hundred different smells assaulted my nostrils. Vendors in their stalls used small charcoal fires to cook a variety of dishes. A Vietnamese Ranger sat on a stool while a man with no nose cut his hair. In another stall a woman sold herbs, roots, and a variety of concoctions that were believed to cure everything from the common cold to tuberculosis. Others sold goods ranging from American toothpaste to tiger skins. Song-Be was alive and well and hadn't changed much since my last visit.

Beyond the market we hit a straight section of road that was used as a landing strip by the FAC and helicopters. At its far end lay the province chief's headquarters: a two-story stucco building whose large pillars held up the front section of its tiled red roof. Our driver parked in front of the building; Wagner and Glossup immediately headed into town with the Bodes. I wanted to stop at the Special Forces compound to see if any of my friends were still stationed there. Their buildings were wedged between the province chief's compound and another one that housed an ARVN unit.

The Special Forces compound was surrounded by aprons of barbed wire; over the gate was a sign that read, *De Oppresso Libre* (Liberate the Oppressed). Standing under it, a smiling Vietnamese soldier—dressed in tiger stripes and an olive drab cowboy hat—snapped to attention and greeted me. Just inside the gate was an open parking area that was surrounded on three sides by buildings. The smell of freshly brewed coffee was in the air, so I followed my nose straight to the mess hall, located on the left side of the compound.

I was greeted as I walked into the building by the smell of broiled steak and the sound of the Beatles' "I Feel Fine" playing on the speaker system. It was good to hear Western music again, and I was amazed at how clean everything looked. White cloths covered the tables, curtains hung over the windows, and handpainted Special Forces emblems and group beret flashes were displayed on freshly painted walls. Three MACV officers sat eating lunch at one of the tables.

Behind the steam table were two young girls with large almond-shaped eyes and long black hair—a symbol of virginity—waiting to dish out the meal. Both wore loose-fitting black silk pants and short-sleeve white shirts with high collars. They immediately recognized me from when I had been there almost a year earlier, and they giggled as I approached. I didn't remember their names.

"*Chao,* Bac-si," one of them smiled. "You come back Song-Be?"

"No," I replied. "I live in Bien-Hoa now."

"Oh," she smiled. "Ha want you come back here." Ha turned red with embarrassment, covered her face with her hands, and started giggling.

"How you want?" a short stocky cook asked while holding a steak on a fork.

"Medium rare." I spooned some french fries and corn onto a tray, fixed a salad, and filled a cup with steaming coffee. While waiting, I took a few sips and listened to Simon and Garfunkel's "The Sounds of Silence."

"Sit," the cook motioned, "I bring." I sat at the nearest table and a few minutes later Ha brought me the steak and a piece of cherry pie. "When a Man Loves a Woman" was playing in the background, and the combination of good food and music had a hypnotic effect on me.

"Ha, would you like to dance?" I joked. She turned red, giggled, and shuffled off to the back room. After thoroughly enjoying the meal, I waved to the girls and walked out into the hot sun.

"Trung-si Donahue," a voice bellowed from the far side of the compound. It was Sergeant Duc, the Vietnamese Special Forces team sergeant at Song-Be. He was wearing freshly starched French camouflaged fatigues, a faded green beret, spit-shined jump boots, and wraparound sunglasses. On his hip a brown leather holster bulged with a Russian Tokarev pistol. Duc was one of the best soldiers I had ever known; he was also a good friend.

"Duc!" I raised my arms over my head. He grabbed me around the waist and lifted me off the ground.

"You get too skinny, Donahue," he said. "We go restaurant." I was stuffed but knew that he would be insulted if I didn't go. He jumped into an old Japanese-made jeep. "Come, we go."

I climbed into the passenger seat and we sped toward town, the jeep shaking and belching a trail of black smoke. Once into the downtown area Duc slammed on the brakes when we spotted Howard walking down the street.

"Where you headed?" I yelled.

"Looking for some seafood," he answered.

I turned to Duc. "This place got fish?"

"They have," he nodded. Howard leapt into the back of the jeep, I introduced him to Duc, and a block down the street we pulled up in front of the restaurant: a two-story cinder block building sporting a large sign over the entrance. It wasn't anything fancy. A half-dozen worn wooden tables, each with four chairs, were evenly spaced on its concrete floor. The smell of incense and jasmine tea filled the air; a Buddhist painting was the only decoration on its unpainted walls.

The cook was sleeping in a hammock strung up between a couple of poles in the rear of the restaurant. Above his hammock, smoke from a slow-burning coil of incense drifted close to the ceiling. Duc woke the cook—an older man dressed in a T-shirt, shorts, and sandals—while Howard and I selected a table near the entrance. Soon after Duc sat down, the cook brought out a steaming ceramic pot of jasmine tea—a sign of welcome—and three handleless cups. "I order for you, Donahue," Duc said proudly. I nodded in agreement and hoped it wouldn't be too much.

"What you want?" Duc asked Howard.

"Aw, any type of seafood," he shrugged. Duc said something to the cook. "He say he have . . ." Duc paused. "I not know word. Maybe you call pincher?" He made a pinching movement with his fingers.

"Lobster," I guessed.

"Not lobster," Duc said.

"Crab?" Howard asked.

"Yes, Trung-si. Crab."

"Super," Howard said. "Haven't had crab in years."

The cook took the order, and as we waited we sipped tea, watched the passersby, and talked about the good old days.

"Do you remember VC tailor?" Duc laughed and slapped my leg.

"How could I forget?" I joined in the laughter. I explained to Howard that I had brought six red, blue, and yellow cargo parachutes to a local tailor and asked him to make the canopy material into VC flags for me. He agreed but cautioned that there would be serious consequences if he were caught. Once the flags were made I planned to take them to Saigon to trade for needed food and supplies. A week later I was attending a joint Vietnamese-American dinner when Duc remarked that he had jailed a VC tailor who had the unmitigated balls to tell him that he was making the flags for the Americans.

As we reminisced, the cook brought out a plate of sticky rice served on a banana leaf. The rice had been mixed with coconut, sesame, and a variety of oriental spices.

"You like *zoi?*" Duc asked.

"My favorite," I smiled.

"Smells great," Howard nodded. A minute later the cook returned with two more banana leaves.

Piled high on one leaf were small pieces of browned chicken that had been basted with spices and cooked over hot coals. On the other were dark pieces of crabmeat that had been similarly prepared. "I fix," Duc offered as he leaned forward and used his chopsticks to cover our plates with a layer of rice. "A little *nuoc-mam.*" He picked up a small brown bottle from the center of the table and sprinkled drops of the fermented fish sauce on our rice. "And now the chicken and crab," Duc smiled. Using his chopsticks again he placed a dozen pieces of chicken on top of my rice and an equal amount of crab on Howard's. "Eat," he gestured before covering his plate with rice. The chicken was tender, moist, and delicious.

"Mmmm, best chicken I ever had," I said.

"Nothin' like this in the States," Howard agreed.

Duc smiled at our satisfaction and placed a chicken head in the middle of my plate.

"Thanks." I tried to figure how I was going to get out of eating it. The Vietnamese considered the head the best part of the chicken, and to refuse it would be an insult. As we enjoyed our meal the cook brought out some deep-fried rice-paper rolls and three glasses of hot rice wine. I had learned that it was best not to ask what was wrapped in the rice paper.

"I piss." Duc stood up and walked through a beaded doorway into a back room. I took advantage of his absence and slipped the chicken head into my pocket.

"I like Duc," Howard commented while chewing on a piece of crab.

"A great soldier. They don't make 'em any better than Duc," I concurred.

Duc returned to the table and I raised my glass of wine. "A toast." Duc and Howard picked up their glasses. "To Duc. The best there ever was."

"To Duc," Howard echoed as our glasses clinked.

"Thank you, my friends." Duc was visibly moved by the toast. As the three of us sipped our wine, a jeep with a .30-caliber machine gun mounted on it sped by the restaurant. Duc's facial muscles tightened just before he jumped to his feet and dropped some piasters on the table. "We go," he told us.

Howard and I grabbed our M-16s and followed Duc out into the hot glare of the street. A block to our left we saw a crowd of people standing in the street. Duc pulled his Tokarev from his holster. "Stay behind me," he cautioned. We moved at a slow run, and I soon saw that the crowd had gathered in front of the pool hall. The jeep with the machine gun was parked to the rear of the crowd; a Vietnamese soldier had the .30 caliber pointed at the building. At the front of the crowd a Vietnamese officer was hollering at whoever was inside the pool hall. Trapped between the officer and the pool hall were Glossup and Wagner.

Quickly slipping through the crowd, we followed Duc to where they were standing. Just inside the dingy, smoke-filled pool hall a Vietnamese soldier was screaming in a shrill voice while using his sleeve to wipe blood from what appeared to be a broken nose. He pointed at Winh—a Bode from the recon platoon. Winh was the only member of the MGF who wore a flak jacket; with it zipped up tight, he stood defiantly with his M-16 in hand. Behind him I spotted Thach and five other Bodes with their M-16s pointing at the Vietnamese soldier. Thach was one of the third platoon's squad leaders and a veteran of Dien-Bien-Phu. He stood about chest high, was lean and sinewy, and his face was leathery and covered with scars. He had a stone-cold expression on his face; hate burned in his eyes.

"Soldier say Cambodian with flak jacket took his money," Duc told us.

"He's full'a shit," Wagner said.

Thach hollered something at the Vietnamese soldier. I think he called his mother a whore. The Vietnamese captain's face flushed red with anger, and he turned and said something to Duc. "The captain wants him arrested," Duc told us.

"No fucking way," Wagner shook his head.

"Hey," Glossup grabbed Howard's arm, "it ain't the Bode who should be arrested," he said in his slow Tennessee drawl. "They bet on a game of eight-ball, and the Bode won fair and square."

"That's right," Wagner told Duc. "He wouldn't pay up. He deserved an ass kicking."

"Trung-si," Glossup said to Duc while pointing at the soldier in the jeep, "y'all might wanna tell that boy that if he don't point that machine gun elsewhere, I'm gonna wrap it around his neck."

"Whoa, time out." Howard held his arms over his head. "Let's everyone back off." Howard convinced the Bodes to lower their weapons; Duc did likewise with the Vietnamese.

"Donahue," Duc grabbed my arm, "take my jeep to the B-Team and bring Major Bien here." After Howard motioned for me to go, I ran back to the jeep and tore off to the compound. When I pulled up in front of the headquarters building I found Kindoll standing in the doorway.

"Buck," I yelled, "you seen Major Bien?"

"Yeah, they got a problem down at the pool hall. He and Gritz are with the province chief."

"Good."

"The province chief's threatening to call out his APCs [armored personnel carriers]," Kindoll told me.

"Big mistake," I said.

"You got that right. Every camp in the province has Cambodian troops."

"He'll get his ass kicked."

"Here they come," Kindoll pointed to the gate. Behind Gritz and Major Bien were a half-dozen Americans and Vietnamese. When they reached us, Gritz stopped to talk while the others entered the building.

"We got thirty minutes to get the Bodes outta Dodge," Gritz told us.

"That mean we've worn out our welcome?" Kindoll smirked.

"An understatement," Gritz said. "The province chief says he's filing a formal complaint with Colonel Kelly."

"How do you wanna handle it, sir?" Kindoll asked.

"They're sending Major Bien down to the pool hall. As soon as he clears the Vietnamese, we'll pick up the Bodes."

"Anything we can do, sir?" I asked.

"Yeah," Gritz looked at his watch, "give it thirty minutes, then take my jeep and make a sweep of the town."

"Yes, sir," we answered in unison.

"Buck," Gritz said, "I need someone to keep an ear to the ground. Stay here for the night and see if you can pick up anything. This province chief could be trouble."

"Yes, sir. I'll catch a ride out to the strip first thing in the morning."

"One other thing," Gritz said before walking into the building. "I've decided to give the Bodes a few days of R and R. Their sperm count's running a little high."

While Kindoll talked to a sergeant from the B-Team, I ran over to the mess hall and picked up a steak, a bag of fries, and a cold beer for George.

By the time we got back to the airstrip, the sun had lost a touch of its intensity and the heat of the day was beginning to subside. Kindoll dropped me off on the tarmac before heading back to town, and I walked the short distance to where I had left my gear to dry. With everything from radios to web gear to poncho liners laid out in the sun, the place looked like a flea market. Many of the Bodes were busy cleaning their weapons; the smell of solvent and oil filled the late afternoon air.

While I was repacking my gear, I noticed George and Sanh working on our machine gun. "George," I yelled. He looked up. "Got something for ya," I said.

"With you in a minute, buddy."

I tied off the top of my ruck, looked up, and saw him walking toward me. "Brought you some grits," I smiled.

"Great, I'm starving." I reached into my pocket and handed him the chicken head. "I'm gonna beat you to a pulp." He grabbed me, and I fell to the ground laughing hysterically.

"It's in the bag," I hollered as we rolled on the ground. George reached over and opened the bag. When he looked inside, a smile appeared on his face.

"Now that's food." He sat on his poncho, tore open the bag, and used it as a tablecloth on his outstretched legs. "Thanks, Jim. I appreciate it."

I left George to enjoy his meal and walked over to where Sanh was watching one of our squad leaders inspect weapons. "How they looking?" I asked Sanh.

"Good, Bac-si. They clean and oil."

"Have 'em check the receivers and the bolt carrier keys for carbon," I said. "It'll cause malfunctions."

"*Oui,* we have that problem at Ho-Ngoc-Tao."

"Jim," George called. I headed back to where George was sitting on his poncho.

"You done stuffing your ugly face?" I asked.

"Yup," he belched. "I'm gonna sleep good tonight."

"Yeah, it's been a long day," I said as I positioned my gear to his left and stretched out on my poncho with my back against my rucksack. "What's the deal on security?" I asked.

"Two LPs from each platoon," he replied. "They'll move into position at last light."

"What about the road?" I asked. "Friendlies don't use it at night."

"Two squad-size ambushes."

"Good." I was concerned because intelligence had reported that elements of the 320th North Vietnamese Division were operating in the area. It had also been reported that a VC battalion had moved into position to the west of Song-Be.

"Hey, Jim," George smiled, "your eyes look like a couple of pee holes in the snow. Why don't you catch some Zzzzs?"

"Sure you don't need me?"

"Yeah, get some sleep."

I rested my head on my rucksack; within a few minutes I was deep in sleep. While I slept the sun sank slowly into Cambodia. Later that night—at 2300—I awoke to a chill. George was sound asleep and a guard was sitting at our feet monitoring the radio. After covering myself with my piece of camouflaged parachute nylon, I lay back and looked up at a star-filled sky. It was a beautiful night.

CHAPTER SIX

THE BODES CHEERED WHEN our C-123 lifted off the runway. I was wedged between George and Sanh in one of the nylon web seats that lined both sides of the cabin. The floor in front of us was crammed with Bodes, rucksacks, and weapons. We weren't in the air for more than a few minutes when the steady hum of the engines lulled me to sleep. I awoke sometime later and saw Bien-Hoa's eleven thousand feet of concrete runway on the horizon.

"Four hundred year ago the land south of here part of Cambodia," Sanh pointed out the window.

"Saigon was part of Cambodia?" George asked.

"*Oui,* Trung-si. Saigon called Prey-Nokor and Bien-Hoa called Kampong-Sraka-Trey."

The wheels whined down and we banked to the right. Looking out the window again, I saw we were a hundred feet over the Dong-Nai River. A few sampans with yellowed sails moved slowly through its muddied waters, and women could be seen washing clothes along its bank. Just past the river's edge we felt a thump when our wheels touched down. The Bodes let out a loud *Tay-yoo* (a battle cry), and the cabin filled with the faint smell of scorched rubber. Halfway down the runway the pilot reversed the pitch of the propellers, and we slowed to a crawl before turning into a taxiway.

When we finally came to a stop, the rear ramp slowly cranked down, and the cabin instantly filled with bright sunlight. We picked up our rucksacks and weapons and walked down the ramp into the torrid mid-morning sun. Parked and waiting to pick us up were Captain Yedinak and a line of two-and-a-half-ton trucks. Their Chinese Nung drivers wore the black-and-white skull and crossbones patch of the III Corps Mike Force.

After loading the vehicles, we drove past the Post Exchange and a field where Americans were playing baseball—a piece of Americana in the middle of Vietnam.

Outside the front gate we hit Bien-Hoa's main street. A policeman dressed in a white uniform stood on a fifty-five-gallon drum that had been cut in half; he was blowing a whistle and waving his arms as he tried to speed our convoy through the intersection. As we made the turn, our passing trucks engulfed him in a cloud of fine red dust and black diesel exhaust fumes.

Once through the intersection we were enmeshed in heavy traffic. The road was jammed with Vespas, Lambrettas, bicycles, jeeps, and a few Vietnamese buses whose roof racks overflowed with suitcases and baskets of live chickens. Some of the Vespas were driven by pretty girls dressed in white *ao-dai*'s and wraparound sunglasses, and when they passed, the Bodes howled. It was good to be home.

Their horns blaring in frustration, vehicles of every size and shape slowly worked their way through town. On both sides of the road we passed cheap souvenir shops, bars, uniform shops, and whorehouses. The sidewalks were crowded with American and Vietnamese troops; the air was stifling with its dust, exhaust fumes, and the smell of untreated human waste.

A short distance past Bien-Hoa's strip we turned into the III Corps compound. It was surrounded by strands of rusted barbed and concertina wire overgrown with tall grass and weeds. Down the road from the newly constructed Vietnamese Officers Club we were waved through the entrance to the Mike Force compound by a one-legged Chinaman armed with a Thompson submachine gun. Our trucks pulled up in front of the Mike Force team house and parked.

Once our accountable items were locked in CONEX containers and the Bodes were paid, Captain Gritz held a company formation. He used the opportunity to praise everyone for a job well done and passed on congratulatory messages from Colonel Kelly and the Strategic Air Command. The formation was then released.

George, Jarvis, and I picked up our rucksacks and walked the short distance to our room in the C-Team compound. After washing our hands and faces, we met the rest of the team at the mess hall. Over lunch, Gritz informed us that we would be returning to Duc-Phong on the morning of the twenty-eighth and that Yedinak had made the necessary arrangements for our next mission to be resupplied by fighter aircraft from the 14th Air Commando Wing in Pleiku. Yedinak explained that the A-1E fighter aircraft would be dropping napalm containers attached to T-7A reserve parachutes. The aluminum containers would be packed with food, ammunition, and supplies and would be dropped every four days.

Gritz pointed out that it was an ideal method for resupplying clandestine operations because the enemy would never suspect that fighters were being used to parachute-drop supplies. Unlike C-123s, the A-1Es wouldn't compromise our location. When we finished talking about the A-1Es, Gritz went over a long list of things that had to be accomplished before the Bodes returned from their R and R.

"Jimmy," the captain said. "We've got a chopper leaving for Duc-Phong at 0800. Get up there and make sure our gear's ready to go."

"Yes, sir," I said. "When we left, everything was under guard in the inner perimeter."

"We're gonna be on a short fuse, and I don't want any last-minute problems," he said.

Following lunch I returned to my room and packed my gym bag with a few things. I had less than twenty-four hours to spend in Bien-Hoa and wanted to see Ngoi before leaving for Duc-Phong. She was a beautiful eighteen-year-old girl I had met when Sgt. 1st Class Warren "Po" Pochinski and I taught English to a group of Vietnamese civilians at Song-Be. She was in Bien-Hoa studying to be a community health worker, and I hoped to take her to dinner and a movie. My bag packed, I walked back to the Mike Force compound to pick up the jeep that I had stolen from the Saigon docks months earlier and left with Master Sgt. Charles "Snake" Hosking when we deployed to Duc-Phong.

Outside the gate of the III Corps compound I pulled up in front of a barbershop. While Vietnamese music played in the background, the barber gave me a whitewall haircut and used a straight razor to shave my face. When he finished, I relaxed in a steam room that smelled of wintergreen. Its hot vapors drew sweat and filth from my pores. Afterwards, I took a cold shower, splashed some lilac water on my face, and slipped into a set of heavily starched jungle fatigues and a pair of spit-shined jungle boots. I felt human again.

Ngoi and her uncle's family lived in a small Masonite house that was surrounded by an eight-foot wall. After parking in front, I walked up to a wrought-iron gate and pulled a string that rang a bell. Looking in the small mirror attached to the gate, I adjusted my beret. Ngoi's uncle believed the mirror would protect the house against evil spirits. If an evil spirit tried to enter, it would see its ugly reflection and be scared away. I rang the bell a few more times, but no one answered.

I was disappointed that I had missed Ngoi but decided

that I had enough time to make it into Saigon. I would pick up a few things at the central market before it got dark and then have dinner by candlelight at the My-Canh floating restaurant. The My-Canh was located at the foot of Tu-Do Street near the Majestic Hotel, and it boasted some of the best seafood in Saigon. Seated at a table near the railing you could enjoy your meal while watching rusty freighters and sampans moving in slow motion through the murky waters of the Saigon River. It was especially beautiful at night.

When I left Ngoi's I took Highway 1A the fifteen miles to Saigon. The four-lane expressway was less crowded than usual, and I sped all the way. Once in the city, I down-shifted where the highway turned into Phan-Than-Gian Street. The bottleneck was bumper to bumper with jeeps, trucks, buses, and blue-and-white Peugeot taxicabs. Both sides of the street were lined with two-story dirty-white Masonite buildings with first-floor shops. At the intersec-tion of Dinh-Tien-Hoang Street traffic inched its way for-ward in a cloud of dust and exhaust fumes. A policeman stood in the street directing traffic around a woman who had been hit by an American flatbed truck. The vehicle was parked on the sidewalk while the woman lay on the pave-ment next to her twisted bicycle. Her head had been flat-tened by the truck, and all that remained was a mess of hair, bone, brain, and teeth.

When I spotted the Avenue de Pasteur sign, I turned left onto a tree-lined boulevard and found myself in another world. On both sides of the street were stately white villas with red-tile roofs. The French colonial homes were sur-rounded by high walls topped with broken pieces of glass set in concrete. Most had iron gates and were guarded by uniformed men standing behind sandbagged barricades. Saigon was a city that offered the best and worst of every-thing. A few blocks from Pasteur's mansions the city's working class lived in mud-and-straw houses with tin roofs or homes constructed from beer cans. This "Paris of the

East" didn't have a sewage system, and human waste could be seen floating in the listless waters of its many canals.

When I saw the twin towers of the Notre Dame cathedral and the manicured grounds of Gia-Long Palace, I knew I was getting close. Following a couple of quick turns I found myself in front of city hall—a large white building with pillars, arched doorways and windows, and a parking lot full of shiny Citroëns and Peugeots. On Nguyen-Hue Street I found a parking spot in front of the USO. After chaining and padlocking the steering wheel, I grabbed my gym bag.

"I watch jeep?" asked a barefoot boy with a dirty face.

"How much?"

"One hundred P."

"Ten P," I countered.

"No way, GI," he shook his head. "You cheap Charlie. You give me fifty P."

"Twenty-five now, and twenty-five when I come back."

"Okay," he nodded and extended his hand. I slipped him the money and he jumped into the passenger seat. I only had a few piasters on me, so I walked to a bookstore on Le-Loi Street that exchanged U.S. greenbacks at a conversion rate that was much higher than the official one.

"May I help you?" asked a bearded Indian with an English accent.

I slipped a one-hundred-dollar bill into a Bible that was always kept on the counter. "I'll take this one," I said, handing him the Bible.

"Yes, sir." He smiled before carrying it into the back room. A minute later he returned and placed the book on the counter. When I was sure no one was looking, I flipped open the cover, slipped the piasters into my pocket, and strolled down Le-Loi in the direction of the central market.

The market was located in a huge white stucco building with a red-tile roof and a high clock tower, its vendors overflowing into the surrounding streets and alleys. In the street outside the market building, I passed farmers selling breadfruit, bananas, and sugarcane. Bakers peddled long loaves of fresh French bread, and mobile kitchens cooked and hawked soup and noodles and a variety of Vietnamese dishes. As I walked through the market, Vietnamese music blared from loudspeakers and drowned out the sound of a thousand voices.

"*Vit-loi?*" a woman with no teeth bid from behind a basket of eggs.

"*Da khong,*" I shook my head. I'd have to be really hungry to eat a half-hatched duck egg. The aroma of meats being prepared over small charcoal fires competed with that of rotting fruit and vegetables. In the absence of refrigeration, the tropical sun made quick work of the produce that didn't sell. Piled to the rear of the vendors were heaps of spoiled food.

"*Pho?*" An old woman standing next to a wheeled soup cart grabbed my sleeve.

I smiled and shook my head no, stepping around customers who squatted in the street eating bowls of her soup and noodles. Just beyond the soup stand I found a section of the market that sold everything from food to clothes to eyeglasses. In a stall operated by a man who had lost much of his face, I picked up a roll of green tape, a bottle of Hoppe's #9 cleaning solvent, and a silicon cloth. In a nearby stall I bought a bag of homemade coconut candy and two Swiss Army knives. In still other stalls you could buy squid, clams, octopus, or shark. If you were in the mood for something different, monkey meat, pig face, dog, snake, hog intestines, and other delicacies were also on display.

I finished shopping at the market and headed back up Le-Loi in the direction of Lam-Son Square. The sun was sinking into Cambodia; the sky had turned a slate gray. I still had some time to kill before dinner and decided to stop at the Bo-Da Ice Cream Parlor, where I ordered a chocolate malt and sat at one of the tables. Sitting hand in hand at the other tables were a half-dozen smiling young Vietnamese couples who occasionally kissed as they shared a bowl of ice cream. Listening to their laughter, I suddenly felt terribly alone.

For close to an hour I sat sipping my malt and thinking about Ngoi as I watched the passersby. Saigon was a great city for people watching, and I had often thought that I wouldn't mind living here after the war. With the influx of refugees, American troops, and dollars, it had lost some of its charm, yet it still held a certain fascination for me.

By the time I finished my milkshake the sky had turned black, but the street outside the Bo-Da remained bright with street lamps, neon signs, and headlights. Walking across Lam-Son Square, I passed a leper dressed in rags sitting next to the fountain. He had a small basket between his legs and was begging for money. As I reached into my pocket, he looked up; in the beam of a passing headlight, I saw a face covered with pea-size magenta nodules—only a dark hole remained where his nose once was. When I reached down to drop a hundred piasters into his basket, he grabbed my hand; only grotesquely deformed stumps of fingers with long black nails remained of his.

"*Cam on ong*," he thanked me.

I told him he was welcome and turned quickly to look for a place to wash my hands. Beyond the fountain was the National Assembly building—an impressive white structure with a two-story arched entrance. On the stairs leading to its entrance stood Buddhist monks dressed in saffron robes, illuminated by a spotlight from a police car. It looked like a demonstration—a good place to avoid—so I headed across the square to the Caravelle Hotel, where the lobby smelled of cigar and pipe smoke and bustled with people carrying briefcases and luggage. On my way to the men's room I passed civilians—reeking of Aqua-Velva and Old Spice—dressed in fashionable suits.

Out once more on the square, I turned left on Tu-Do, figuring to take a slow walk down to the Saigon River and then over to the My-Canh for dinner. Tu-Do was lined with bars, restaurants, cinemas, and shops that sold everything from cheap souvenirs to the most expensive jewelry, perfumes, and clothing. Parked under the street's many chestnut trees were French automobiles and cycalos (three-wheeled bicycle taxis for transporting one or two passengers). The sidewalks were usually crowded with people just after dark, but for some reason they were almost deserted. Something was wrong. From a few doors down the street country western music boomed from a dimly lit smoke-filled bar. Standing at the door, a beautiful woman wearing a tight yellow silk dress that was slit to the waist and black high heels beckoned, "You buy me Saigon tea?" She smiled as Johnny Cash sang in the background.

"Hey, you!" a voice bellowed from behind me. I turned to see two helmeted military policemen running in my direction. They were a block away and closing fast. I looked around to see who they were calling; no other Americans were in sight.

"Shit," I said to myself. I had a French 9-mm MAT-49 submachine gun and a couple of grenades in my gym bag. It was against regulations to bring weapons into Saigon, and if they caught me, I'd probably be arrested. I glanced back at the MPs and then bolted into a restaurant, where I startled two Vietnamese couples who were enjoying a quiet dinner. Running through the kitchen, I scared the hell out of the cook when I ran into him and knocked him flat on his back. I apologized as I helped him to his feet, then I fled out the back door into a darkened alley full of garbage. When my heels landed on something slippery, I fell on my butt.

Back on my feet, I grabbed a CS gas grenade from my gym bag, pulled the pin, and dropped it as I ran. If the MPs were still behind me it would slow them down. When I reached the street, I glanced back and saw a gray cloud following me down the alley.

I spotted my jeep up the street and, after sprinting back to it, found the boy still sitting in the passenger seat listening to a portable radio. Out of breath, I jumped into the driver's seat and removed the padlock and chain from the steering wheel. As soon as I had it started, I did a quick U-turn and peeled away. Wearing a "What the hell's going on?" expression on his face, the boy hung on for his life.

Glancing back over my shoulder I saw the MPs in the glow of a street lamp. It looked as though they were both leaning against a parked car, gagging. I hoped they didn't have a radio. As soon as I made a left on Le-Than-Ton I pulled over in front of city hall and slipped the boy a hundred piasters. He gave me a dirty look and told me I was crazy before jumping out of the jeep.

I then turned on my lights, made a quick right on Pasteur, and headed back to Bien-Hoa. Except for a few military police vehicles and a roadblock near the Dong-Nai Bridge, the highway was almost deserted.

By the time I pulled into the III Corps compound, my stomach was growling, so I stopped at the Vietnamese Officers Club to get something to eat. The place was smoky and packed with American and Vietnamese soldiers: many were lined up three deep at the bar, others sat at tables eating and drinking. Up on an elevated platform a Vietnamese girl wearing a cowboy hat, jeans, and a sequined western shirt was singing "Your Cheating Heart" with a Vietnamese accent. Hank Williams would have been impressed.

George, England, Wagner, and Jarvis were sitting at a long table sharing a pitcher of beer. The floor near the table was slippery with vomit, and I almost fell when my feet flew out from under me. I grabbed a nearby chair and pulled it up between George and a soldier who had passed out at the table. He had an MACV (Military Assistance Command, Vietnam) patch on his left shoulder and was face down in a puddle of beer.

The others had already eaten, so I ordered a couple of cheeseburgers and some fries. I asked the waitress where the men's room was, and she told me that I had to go through the kitchen to get to it. Outside the men's room I passed a leg of beef lying on the floor. A woman with a cigarette hanging from her mouth held the carcass still with her foot while she used a butcher knife to cut off a piece of meat—I was glad I hadn't ordered steak. The men's room was just a round hole in the floor over which you squatted. The area around the hole was piled high with shit, and a urine-soaked roll of toilet paper sat in the corner.

When I returned to the table I asked where the rest of the team was.

"Howard's over at Mike Force," England said. "Glossup was here but he went to Rosie's [a Special Forces hangout]."

"Yedinak and Chilton went down to Ho-Ngoc-Tao," Jarvis told me.

"Yed had to leave," George cracked. "He lit one of his after burners and almost burned the place down."

"Yeah," Wagner laughed. "He lit a glass of brandy and let it burn too long before he tried to drink it."

"Anyone see Captain Gritz?" I asked.

"He went to Cambode alley to see his girlfriend," George said.

"He's in love," England told me.

"No shit," Wagner said. "Someone's gonna have to talk to that boy."

The waitress brought out my cheeseburgers and fries and used a rag to wipe up the beer and cigarette ashes from the table.

Smack. I turned toward the bar just in time to see an Air Force officer falling to the floor. He landed with a thud and lay there with outstretched arms—out cold. He had been punched by a Special Forces master sergeant who returned to drinking at the bar. As the girl up on the stage sang the Beatles' "Twist and Shout," a couple of Vietnamese women grabbed the officer by his fatigue jacket and dragged him into the kitchen. "We were headed down to the Sporting Bar," George said, "but Saigon's off limits."

George's comment took me by surprise. I was lucky the MPs didn't catch me.

By the time we finished talking it was past midnight. Jarvis and I had to get up early so we left the guys and drove back to our room. Sometime later I awoke to the sound of a rooster crowing. It was still dark, but I smelled coffee and bacon. I could have slept for a few more hours, but knew I had to get moving if I was to catch the chopper to Duc-Phong. Jarvis and I were quiet so as not to wake George, and after shaving and showering, we walked into the mess hall where we met Sgt. Maj. Richard "Mickey" Finn.

"Got an Irish pennant there, Dunahoo," he said as he pulled a piece of thread from my starched fatigue jacket.

"Thank you, sergeant major," I smiled.

The mess hall wasn't ready to serve breakfast so we sat at a table drinking coffee. Thirty minutes later the cook asked what we wanted to eat. I ordered bacon and eggs and Jarvis ordered chipped beef on toast. After breakfast we were loading the jeep when Snake Hosking pulled up in another jeep. Hosking was dressed in camouflaged shorts and shower shoes, and he had almost as many tattoos as he had scars. With bloodshot blue eyes he looked as though he had just gotten out of bed.

"Hey, Snake, how ya doing?" I called cheerfully.

"Not good," he said. "You seen Gritz?"

"Not since yesterday," I said.

"There a problem?" Jarvis asked.

"Could be," he said. "The Bodes say he shot up Cambode alley last night."

"Oh, shit." Jarvis shook his head.

"You been to his girlfriend's?" I asked.

"No, I'm heading there now." He shifted into reverse and backed out in a cloud of dust.

Worried about the captain, Jarvis and I jumped into the jeep and headed for the chopper pad. A fiery sun was just peeking over the horizon and we could hear the wap, wap,

wap of an approaching Huey. When we arrived at the pad, the chopper was sitting on the ground with its rotor blades slicing the still morning air. Jarvis pulled up as close as possible and waited while I loaded my gear.

"I'm gonna see if I can find Gritz," Jarvis yelled over the noise of the engine and rotors.

"Okay," I waved, before climbing aboard. "See you at Duc-Phong."

"Never a dull day," he shouted as he pulled away.

CHAPTER SEVEN

1345, 27 DECEMBER 1966

WAP, WAP, WAP. At five thousand feet, a cool rotor wash blew through the open cabin and tugged at my fatigues. I was sitting in a web seat with my back against the fire wall. In the jump seats, to my left and right, door gunners sat relaxed behind their M-60 machine guns. We cruised at ninety knots beneath dense white cloud formations that billowed like towering mountains in the blue sky. A mile below, shadows drifted across the broccoli-topped mountains of War Zone D. In the valleys between the green and purple peaks, light brown streams disappeared into patches of mist. Except for a few deserted Montagnard longhouses with collapsed roofs, there were no signs of human habitation.

Looking down at the enemy secret zone, I found myself wondering how many VC and NVA units might be hidden beneath the canopy. It was a question that would be answered in the days and weeks ahead.

My thoughts were interrupted when the pilot turned his head and pointed down and to his front. I stood up and, leaning forward over the pilot stations, spotted the star-shaped camp and three-thousand-foot-long dirt runway. The camp was built on a gently sloping hill that had been cleared of rubber and bamboo; its red volcanic soil was surrounded by a sea of green.

Beyond the camp, sections of Highway 14's faded black-top stretched across the horizon. A few kilometers northeast of the camp the town of Duc-Phong straddled the highway, populated by seven thousand Vietnamese, Montagnards, and Cambodians. The jungle surrounding the town was inhabited by elephants, tigers, boar, and leopards; before the war, hunters traveled from around the world to hunt its game.

Directly over the camp, the pilot pulled back on his stick, slightly raised the nose of the chopper, and slowed our forward speed. Blades slapped the humid air as we banked and began our descent. To avoid enemy ground fire from the area around the camp, we flew in a tight corkscrew pattern. As we descended in graceful circles, I leaned out the door and saw a thin veil of white cooking smoke drifting from all five points of the star. Outside the inner perimeter a thick plume of black smoke twisted skyward from where someone was using diesel fuel to burn out one of the camp's four-hole latrines.

At an altitude of one hundred feet the pilot leveled off over the runway and followed it the short distance to where a three-quarter-ton truck was waiting for us. When the chopper touched down on the airstrip it kicked up a cloud of red dust. I ran to the truck with my M-16 and rucksack. The driver was a sergeant first class wearing jungle fatigues and a green beret. "I'm Jim Donahue," I yelled as I reached to shake his hand. "I'm with the Mobile Guerrilla Force."

"Al Doyle," he shook my hand. "Senior radio operator."

Wap, wap, wap. The chopper took off amid a dusting of crimson powder. With the dust settling on our uniforms and sticking to our sweaty faces, we drove up the hill toward the main gate. Along both sides of the road were deep drainage ditches and aprons of barbed wire. The point of the star-shaped camp that extended to our right was defended by the Montagnard light infantry company that I once advised. Some of its troops were working with picks and shovels on improvements to their trench line and its sandbagged bunkers. The point to our left was manned by a Vietnamese Special Forces detachment, a few Cambodian troops, and the crews of two 105-mm Howitzers. The olive drab muzzles of the artillery pieces pointed skyward and extended above their bleached sandbag emplacements.

"Trung-Si Donahue!" a voice called from the medical tent on the left side of the road, just outside the main gate. It was my friend Kimh. Having served as Rinh's assistant when I was at Duc-Phong, he spoke English fairly well.

"Hold up," I told Doyle. "Kimh's an old friend." I jumped to the ground and gave him a bear hug in the sweltering heat. "How you doing?" I asked.

"Many sick." He pointed to about twenty people sitting on benches outside the medical tent. "How Rinh?"

"Oh, he's fine," I replied, smiling. "He went down to the delta to see his wife."

As we talked, a hand touched my shoulder. I turned and saw that it was Ka and his son Djeng. Ka was one of the local Steing Montagnard chiefs. He had a muscular, chestnut-colored body, deep-set friendly black eyes, and dirty black hair that hung to his shoulders. Tattooed circles of blue dots decorated his chest, and a black-and-red loincloth was bound around his waist. With pieces of elephant tusk piercing both earlobes and a half-dozen brass bracelets jangling from his wrists, he looked like someone out of the Stone Age. Djeng was a good-looking six year old. He had short black hair, wore no clothes, and was missing his right hand. We had had to amputate it after he was bit by a cobra. The Montagnards are close to their children, and during Djeng's recovery period, Ka visited his son often. Consequently, he and I became good friends.

"Ka," I smiled, "good to see you again." I shook his hand, and when I bent over to say hello to Djeng, he grabbed me around my neck and wrapped his legs around my waist. Ka put his hand on my shoulder and said something I didn't understand. The Yards spoke a very guttural unwritten language, and although I knew some words, I didn't know enough to carry on a conversation.

"He say you come village," Kimh told me.

I looked at my watch.

"You can take the truck," Doyle said from the vehicle.

"Will you come?" I asked Kimh. "I'll need an interpreter."

"I go," he nodded.

"Okay," I said while lowering Djeng to the ground. "Tell the chief I'll meet him here in fifteen minutes."

Doyle and I left and drove through the main gate. Passing additional rows of barbed and concertina wire and a wave of foul-smelling black smoke, we entered the camp's inner perimeter. Inside its circle of wire were five long, narrow buildings laid out in the shape of a pentagon. The edges of their overhanging tin roofs were just a few feet above the ground because their floors were four feet below ground level. Our engineer sergeant had designed them so we would have some protection from enemy rifle fire and the shrapnel of exploding mortar and artillery rounds. The design also allowed the open-sided building to be used as fall-back fighting positions if any or all points of the star-shaped camp fell to the enemy.

Doyle led me to the building where our ammunition and supplies were piled high on wooden pallets. Sitting on a box of C-rations was a Montagnard guard armed with a .45-caliber Thompson submachine gun. After checking each of the pallets, Doyle directed me to the end of the building and a folding cot. Removing a few things from my rucksack, I thanked him for his help, grabbed my M-16, and drove back to the dispensary. When I pulled up, Ka, Djeng, and Kimh jumped into the seat next to me. It was a bumpy drive down the rutted dirt road, and if Djeng's eyes were any indication, it was an experience he would never forget. We sometimes forgot that the Yards still believed that the world was flat and lived an existence similar to that of American Indians a few centuries ago.

The ride also stimulated many memories and emotions in me. I had been so busy in recent months that I hadn't realized how much I missed the Yards. They didn't lie or steal, they lived in harmony with nature, and they took care of their family and friends. Some Vietnamese called them *moi,* or savages, but I found them to be the most civilized people I had ever known.

My thoughts were interrupted when we reached the point where the road ended and the jungle began. We followed the chief and his son up a narrow well-used trail that cut through double-canopied jungle. As we walked I saw signs that we were nearing the village: a piece of string tied to a branch, a charred monkey skull on a flat rock. The string may have been a warning to outsiders; the skull was likely the remains of a ritual sacrifice that had been performed by the village sorcerer. The Yards believe that spirits inhabit every object; consequently, their lives are centered around rituals and sacrifices intended to pacify those spirits.

As Ka led us up the winding track, barking dogs warned of our approach. At the trail's end we came upon the village in an oblong-shaped clearing. Along both sides were three longhouses, and at its center stood a five-story cypress tree with a thick, mottled-gray trunk. The longhouses had thatch roofs and walls of woven bamboo; a thin layer of wood smoke drifted in the hot air above them. Before entering Ka's longhouse, Kimh and I removed our boots and left them at the entrance—a three-foot hole cut in the woven bamboo. The entrance was so small that a person had to bend over in order to enter. If an unwelcome visitor tried to enter forcibly, his head could be fractured by a club or split by an ax.

Inside it was dark, and the air was filled with the smell of wood smoke. To the left, a bamboo sleeping platform stretched the entire length of the building. The chief's extended family lived in the structure, and each of his married children had their own sleeping area, separated by walls of woven bamboo. The dirt floor on the right had been swept clean, and in front of each family's sleeping area was a blackened fire pit. The chief's area was near the center of the longhouse; when we got there, we found his wife grilling meat over an open fire. Because no hole had been cut in the roof for ventilation, the room was filled with thick gray smoke. Even though it burned my eyes, it served to keep the longhouse free of malaria-carrying mosquitoes.

Along with Ka's spears and crossbows, a collection of animal skulls, skins, and bones hung from the walls. Ka's wife was a pleasant woman. She wore nothing but a black skirt; her large breasts sagged to her waist. Her lips were stained red from chewing betel nut—an opiate—and the whites of her black eyes flashed back and forth under a tangle of thick black hair. Spreading a few animal skins on the floor around the fire, she motioned for us to sit. The smoke close to the ground wasn't as thick as it was near the ceiling, and from behind me a basket of cinnamon bark gave off a pleasant aroma.

The chief's wife took Djeng into the next room while Ka lit a cigar that smelled of burning hemp. Using Kimh to translate, he told us how much our medicine had helped his people and that he wanted his oldest son to become a medic. The chief's vision indicated just how much progress had been made with the Steing. Less than a year had passed since they relied solely on the village sorcerer to treat their medical problems. Although they were quick to accept modern medicine—they especially like injections—they resisted most Western values. Thinking about it, I concluded that they were probably better off that way.

"Chief ask, you remember Vietcong come here?" Kimh relayed.

"Yes," I nodded. It was a day etched in my memory. I always came to the village in the morning to hold sick call, and afterwards we often sat in the shade of the great cypress tree drinking tea, eating breadfruit, and talking for hours about everything under the sun. I told Ka about America, he told me about the tribe, their legends, and their hopes and fears. On that particular day Kimh and I were sitting under the tree with Ka when two armed Vietcong stumbled out of the jungle. Our weapons were lying on top of a medical kit a short distance away; before we could get to them, the enemy soldiers had the drop on us. Both were armed with rusty Chinese 7.62-mm K-50M submachine guns and wore torn, dirty black pajamas and Ho-Chi-Minh sandals. The exposed parts of their skin were covered with cuts, and it appeared as though they hadn't eaten in days.

Ka told them to leave, but from what I could understand, they wanted to kill Kimh and take me prisoner. The chief refused, and a heated argument followed. When one of them pushed Ka to the ground, the villagers ran from their longhouses carrying crossbows, spears, knives, and axes. A crowd formed a tight circle around us. After a few tense minutes the two agreed to join us for lunch. Over tea, breadfruit, and roasted monkey, hostilities quickly subsided. The five of us sat talking, and during the conversation they told us that they were lost. I invited them to turn over their weapons and return to the camp with us, but they didn't think much of the invitation. It was the first time I had ever talked to enemy soldiers who weren't prisoners, and I found them to be very committed to their beliefs. In some ways, they were a lot like us.

After lunch they went on their way and Kimh and I drove back to camp and reported the incident to Sgt. 1st Class Mike "Big Mike" Holland, our intelligence sergeant. It was a day I'd never forget, yet it was so typical; Vietnam was like that.

"Tell Ka I brought him something," I told Kimh. Reaching into my pocket I removed one of the Swiss Army knives I had purchased in Saigon and handed it to him. His face beamed with excitement as I explained its many blades and tools. As the chief sat examining the knife, we continued to talk about the war. Ka explained that the tribes had always been oppressed by the Vietnamese. Although they liked the Americans—especially Special Forces—they saw no difference between the Vietcong and the government of South Vietnam and one day hoped to form an independent Montagnard nation.

Ka's wife brought us three bowls of coconut milk and two wooden plates. One was piled high with sections of breadfruit and the other with small pieces of grilled meat. The Yards don't use chopsticks, so we sat eating with our fingers and sipping coconut milk. "This is really good," I told Kimh. "Ask Ka if it's monkey."

They exchanged a few words. "Rat," Kimh smiled and ran his fingers along the ground while making squeaking noises. I shouldn't have asked.

"Outstanding." I forced a smile, and the chief motioned for us to eat some more. Chewing what looked like a leg, I thanked God that the dinner didn't include such Montagnard delicacies as insects and grubs. As Kimh continued to eat, Ka moved a large earthenware vat from the corner and positioned it on the ground in front of us. "Oh, no," I thought, "rice wine." Once the Yards get to drinking, they have a tendency not to stop until they are flat on their backs.

Light from the fire illuminated Ka's face as he pulled a plug of leaves from the neck of the vat. He then inserted a long bamboo straw. Kneeling next to the vat with a grin on his face, he put the straw in his mouth and started sipping. Drinking what must have been a good pint of the wine, he stopped and let out a belch. He then used a gourd to add water to the vat and motioned that it was my turn. I rose to my knees, grabbed the bamboo straw, and started sipping. When the wine hit my lips, it took my breath away. "Whew!" I choked. "That's strong stuff." After a few sips I handed the straw to Kimh.

"Ah," Ka raised his hand and grunted his displeasure.

"He say you drink more." Kimh pointed to a line on the straw.

"Damn," I thought, "no way I'm gonna get outta this." Two lines had been scratched around the bamboo straw. When it was your turn, you had to drink until the level of the wine reached the bottom line. After each person finished, the chief poured in enough water to raise the level back to the top line. After the first round my head began to spin, and I questioned how we were going to make it back to camp. By the end of the third round, I saw that Kimh's condition was quickly deteriorating.

"Ka," I raised my hand, "we must return to camp before dark." He beamed and told us we could stay the night. I tried to convince him that the Americans would think that we had been killed by the Vietcong. He thought about it and agreed that we should depart as soon as possible.

When we stumbled from the longhouse I took a deep breath of fresh air to relieve the burning in my lungs. It was almost dark, the wind was blowing, and shades of red streaked the steel-gray sky. Kimh and I sped back down the bumpy road; halfway back, he passed out. When I pulled in the front gate I parked the truck, and two security guards carried Kimh to his cot.

It was dark when I reached my cot, so I slipped into a pair of shorts and crawled under the mosquito net. I instantly fell asleep. Sometime later, I awoke to the crack of thunder and the drumming of rain on the tin roof. I was soaked with sweat, my head was pounding, and my stomach was churning. It was 0230. Reaching under my pillow I found my flashlight and slipped into a pair of shower shoes. The beam from my light caught the glowing red eyes of two large rats moving close to the wall. I could taste vomit rising in my throat.

I headed for the latrine, and when I walked out the door I was hit by a cascade of cold water falling from the roof. After a couple of steps I stopped to vomit, and when I tried to move again found both shower shoes stuck in the mud.

With heavy rain beating down on me I continued barefoot through the mud. Even with a flashlight, I couldn't see more than a few meters. Halfway to the latrine I developed explosive diarrhea and had to stop two more times. Finally, I took off my shorts and carried them.

When I reached the four-hole latrine I sat on the toilet seat closest to the door and found it covered with mud. "Damn," I shook my head. The Yards still insisted on standing on the toilet seats. I switched on my flashlight and leaned over the next hole. The area around it was crawling with bugs—they looked like cockroaches. With my head over the hole I alternated between vomiting and defecating. The smell of the burnt diesel fuel only added to my nausea.

Then, figuring I didn't have a drop of fluid left in my body, I reached for the toilet paper—there wasn't any. As the water dripped through the leaky roof onto my head I started laughing. It had to be the worst night of my life. I finally composed myself and headed out into the rain. I made my way back to the cot, and before crawling under its mosquito net, I dried myself and wiped the mud from between my toes. Shaking from the wet chill, I covered myself with a poncho liner and in its warmth soon fell once again into a deep sleep.

CHAPTER EIGHT

1530, 28 DECEMBER 1966

UNDER A BLAZING AFTERNOON SUN, purple smoke drifted
across the red clay runway. Two miles to the southwest a
C-123 was on its final approach. Flying a few hundred feet
above the trees, its silver hull appeared to shimmer as it
moved through wave after wave of rising heat. First Lieutenant Thoi, the LLDB camp commander, stood with me
at the side of the runway. He wore camouflaged French
fatigues and a faded green beret, and he was puffing on a
cigarette. Although he was smiling, I sensed that he didn't
approve of the MGF. He may have viewed us as a threat
to LLDB interests because, unlike other Special Forces detachments, we were not commanded by an LLDB officer.

"Sir, what d'ya think of the Mobile Guerrilla Force?" I
asked.

"No problem, Bac-si," he grinned. I knew he wasn't
leveling with me, but I didn't press the issue. It was common for the Vietnamese to tell Americans what they
thought we wanted to hear. In fact, it had reached the point
where the words "no problem" immediately alerted me to
a potential problem.

The aircraft kicked up a cloud of dust and abruptly
slowed to a crawl. When it came to a stop in front of us,

both engines continued to run while its rear cargo ramp whined down. Captain Gritz and Fang were the first to step to the runway. They were followed by Chilton, Cawley, Kindoll, and the Bodes from the headquarters section and recon platoon. They held their bush hats in place as they followed Gritz through the prop blast and blowing dust and moved to the side of the runway.

"Good afternoon, sir." I saluted the captain.

He returned my salute but didn't say anything. He appeared deep in thought.

"Anything wrong, sir?" I asked Chilton. Out of the corner of my eye I watched a smiling Lieutenant Thoi welcome Gritz back to Duc-Phong.

"Half the Bodes didn't make it," Chilton whispered.

"What?" I found it hard to believe. "We still a go?"

"Yeah, if Gritz ain't relieved of his command," Chilton said before joining Gritz and Thoi.

"What's goin' on?" I looked questioningly at Cawley and Kindoll. They pulled me aside.

"Some staff puke's trying to get the captain relieved," Cawley explained.

Kindoll grabbed my arm and moved close to my ear.

"We were all down on Pasteur having a few drinks and telling lies when this lieutenant colonel told us there was a floor show over at Camp Goodman and that we could have his table," he said.

"They had a couple of round-eyed strippers coming in from Australia," Cawley added.

"So we piled into a couple of jeeps and drove over to Goodman," Kindoll continued. "It turned out to be the best table in the place."

"By the time the show started, the guys were getting a little rowdy," Cawley said as he crushed a scorpion with his heel. The C-123 took off behind us.

"First time I ever saw Gritz get drunk," Kindoll said. Gritz, Chilton, and Thoi continued talking as they walked up the road into camp.

"This stripper was doing her thing when Jarvis got up and started dancing with her," Cawley continued, adjusting the weight of his rucksack. "Before you knew it, he had pulled her G string off with his teeth, and they both fell over a table."

"All officers," Kindoll smiled.

"One of them was this staff puke who got the ass and ordered Gritz to get us outta the club," Cawley chimed in.

"Yeah," Kindoll laughed as the Bodes from the recon platoon walked past us. "Gritz told him he'd rather have a sister in a whorehouse than a brother in the Quartermaster Corps."

"The major was pissed," Cawley said.

"Next thing we knew, he put us under house arrest and told Gritz he was reporting the incident to Colonel Kelly," Kindoll sighed.

"Can't take you guys anywhere," I shook my head.

"The shit hit the fan when we left Goodman without permission," Kindoll smiled. "By two in the morning, we were speeding through back alleys with the MPs in hot pursuit."

"Who was this major?" I asked.

"I called him Major Space," Kindoll said. "His only purpose in life was to occupy space."

"When we were loading the 123s, he pulled up in a jeep and told Yedinak he wanted to see Gritz," Cawley said.

"Yeah," grinned Kindoll, "Yed kept him busy while Gritz escaped on the first plane out."

"Think he got to Kelly?"

"Don't know," Kindoll replied as particles of red dust began sticking to his sweaty face.

"What about the Bodes?" I asked.

"Our TO&Es [organization and equipment tables] are out the window," Cawley said. "All we got is 108 Bodes."

"What the hell happened?"

"The Chams [Cambodians who practice Hinduism] said

they couldn't go on an operation over some Hindu holy day,'' Kindoll shrugged.

"We're gonna be a little light for War Zone D,'' I lamented.

"Time will tell,'' prophesied Cawley as he and Kindoll followed the last of the Bodes up the road.

I turned to see a second aircraft come to a stop. George and Sanh were the first to step off the ramp.

"Hey, George,'' I yelled as they moved through the prop blast holding their hats.

"You get the bad news?'' George asked, shaking my hand.

"Yeah; how many we got?''

"Twenty-six.'' George shook his head. Two Bodes chased their blowing hats down the runway.

· As we walked up the hill, George and Sanh gave me a rundown on everything that had taken place. After dinner, Gritz got the Americans and our Cambodian platoon sergeants together to rework our organization and equipment tables. It was a mess because each platoon had different problems: one lost all of its squad medics, another its machine-gun section. Howard lost his platoon medic, so we transferred Luc to the first platoon and told Rinh he'd have to serve as medic for both the headquarters section and the third platoon. We were up past midnight trading personnel among platoons and redesignating assignments within each platoon. The third platoon ended up with twenty-three Bodes.

The following day, Howard coordinated a number of organizational and planning meetings and the development of a revised training schedule. Since there had been major shifts in Cambodian personnel assignments the training was to concentrate on such critical areas as immediate action drills, patrolling, raids, ambushes, link-ups, guerrilla base security, breakouts, and drop zones.

During the days that followed, the training went well, but problems continued with the LLDB. Every move outside the camp had to be approved in advance, and they did everything possible to put obstacles in our way. Tensions peaked on the morning of 7 January, when an LLDB ambush fired on a patrol led by Denny Montgomery. No one was hit, but the incident served, nevertheless, to increase the Bodes' already intense distrust of a couple of the LLDB. We feared the Bodes would use the incident as an excuse to settle old scores. Much to our relief, they didn't retaliate.

So it was that at 0700 on 8 January, the recon platoon—nineteen Cambodians and three Special Forces personnel—slipped out of camp to begin the ground infiltration of War Zone D. Their objective was to set up an MSS eleven kilometers south of Duc-Phong.

At 0600 the following morning a heavy mist blanketed the camp as we held what was to be our last formation at Duc-Phong. Following a head count, we conducted a final weapons and equipment check. Though the Bodes appeared ready, I sensed that something was wrong. When we finished the inspection, we had the Bodes place their rucksacks at their feet and kept them in formation. George and I stood a few paces in front of our platoon and waited for orders. Twenty meters away, Gritz, Yedinak, Howard, and Fang stood knee deep in the slow-moving mist, talking to four Bodes. The sun hadn't yet come over the mountains; their peaks appeared black against a crimson sky.

"Bull shit!" I heard Gritz yell. He was pissed about something.

"Everyone over here." Yedinak raised his arm over his head and rotated it in small circles.

The troops gathered around Gritz and Fang and sat in a circle. "A few minutes ago," admonished Gritz in a stern voice, "I was told that the Cambodian members of this company are refusing to leave Duc-Phong because they believe the LLDB has betrayed us to the enemy."

As Fang translated his words, George looked at me in disbelief.

"All of you are here today because you have demonstrated your faith in me," Gritz said. "If you think back to Ho-Ngoc-Tao, you'll remember the day I called you into the headquarters tent. There was a hand grenade sitting on the table, and when I asked you to pull the pin and release the spoon, you did so without hesitation. You had no way of knowing that the detonator had been removed, yet you obeyed my order without hesitation. You did it because you have the same faith in me that I have in you."

After Fang completed his translation, a few heads nodded their agreement.

"As I stand here today, I give you my word that other than a few Americans, no one knows of our mission. It would be impossible for anyone here at Duc-Phong to betray us to the enemy because no one—including the Americans—has been briefed."

I knew that the Bodes had complete trust in the captain, but I sensed that he hadn't changed their minds.

"To demonstrate my faith in the security of this mission, I will walk point today," he said. "If we have been betrayed, I will be the first to die."

Upon hearing Fang's translation of the captain's speech, a young Bode from the second platoon snapped to attention. In broken English he told Gritz that their Cambodian friends at Duc-Phong had informed them that the LLDB was plotting with the Vietcong to have everyone in the MGF killed. As Fang whispered something to Gritz, Rinh tapped my back.

"Did you know that Lieutenant Thoi was Viet-Minh?" he whispered.

"What!" I found it hard to believe.

"Yes, Donahue. He was Viet-Minh for nine years. After the 1954 truce, he joined the Popular Force and later the LLDB."

"That doesn't mean he's VC," protested George.

"The LLDB and the Vietnamese government fear Cambodian nationalism," Rinh said. "When they look at our new M-16s and their old carbines, they become very unhappy.''

George raised his hand to stop the conversation when the captain began speaking again.

"When we were at Ho-Ngoc-Tao, each of you swore a blood oath to me and to the Mobile Guerrilla Force," Gritz said solemnly. "On the souls of your dead ancestors you swore your allegiance."

The Bodes began to mumble during Fang's translation of those words. Gritz had struck a sensitive chord. His voice grew louder.

"By breaking your blood oath you will not only disgrace yourselves but also your fathers and their fathers. Through eternity you will be remembered as men who broke a sacred blood oath. I believe that this would be a great injustice because I know you to be soldiers; I know you to be men of honor."

A chilling silence followed.

"Tay-yoo!" A Bode from the rear yelled the Cambodian battle cry at the top of his lungs. It sent a sensation up the entire length of my spine.

"Tay-yoo, tay-yoo, tay-yoo," the Bodes chanted as they sprang to their feet with their fists clenched over their heads.

"This mean we're a go?" George beamed.

Sanh grabbed my hand. "For Captain Gri they will die."

"I know," I grinned. For the first time, I realized how special our relationship with the Cambodians had become.

It was 0720, and at a short meeting with the Americans, Gritz instructed England and Yedinak to move their platoon out as soon as possible. To make it appear as though this was just another day of training, each platoon would depart separately and rendezvous later in the day at the MSS. The second platoon slipped out of camp at 0730. An hour later they were followed by Howard, Montgomery, Jarvis, and the first platoon. Gritz, Kindoll, Wagner, and the headquarters section accompanied the first platoon.

The third platoon was the last to leave. We lifted our seventy-pound rucksacks to our backs at 0900 and headed out the front gate. I was on point, followed by George, Sanh, the machine-gun section, and the rest of the platoon. After months of training, we were finally on our way.

The sun had burnt the mist from the mountains to the east of the camp, and its warm rays felt good as they touched my face. It was a beautiful morning.

At the end of the runway we passed a few thatch huts and splashed across a knee-deep stream whose fast-moving waters appeared white and sparkling as they flowed over smooth black rocks. On the far side of the stream we entered the silent domain of evenly spaced rubber trees. Although no one had collected rubber for years, dirty white collection bowls still hung from some of their trunks. I picked up the pace as we moved in and out of the shadows. Fifty meters to my right I spotted the red clay surface of the north-south trail that appeared on our maps. We wouldn't risk walking on it; rather, we would skirt it south into the heart of War Zone D.

Before long we left behind the rubber trees and moved downhill through a sunny area of lime green clumps of bamboo. At the bottom of the hill we waded across a shallow stream whose stagnant water was covered with a crust of green algae. The stench of decaying flesh filled the still air, and we soon passed a partially decomposed tiger carcass that buzzed with blue-green flies. The pale yellow and black-striped hulk weighed a good three hundred pounds and was so bloated that it appeared ready to explode.

A hundred meters past the tiger we waited while Sanh positioned a four-man stay-behind ambush—our tail-gunner section. They would remain in position for thirty minutes and would ambush any enemy trackers who were attempting to follow us. Farther south, we would make extensive use of booby traps to discourage trackers, but this close to Duc-Phong, we didn't want to risk them being triggered by friendly troops.

As we threaded our way through scrub brush and bamboo I thought about the "Enemy Order of Battle" map that Kindoll had used during our pre-mission intelligence briefing. He had identified enemy infiltration routes and lines of communication with black lines on the map and used colored pins to plot enemy units. Three green pins showed the last reported locations of the 145th, 186th, and 8840th Vietcong Battalions; five yellow pins represented VC companies; four red pins placed enemy platoons. Kindoll was convinced that these units posed the most danger to our operation because they were manned by local Vietcong who possessed detailed knowledge of the area.

At the briefing Kindoll also let us know that MACV suspected that main-force regiments of the Vietcong's 7th and 9th Divisions might be operating in Phuoc-Long Province. Gritz added that the Combined Intelligence Center in Saigon believed that elements of the 101st, 141st, and 250th Regiments of the NVA were also operating in the area. Yedinak predicted that enemy trackers would attempt to follow us when we left Duc-Phong. If they were able to track our movement, they would deploy their main-force units against us.

As we continued south, I thought about the enemy and how we would react if contact was made. As guerrillas, we wanted to avoid decisive engagements with main-force enemy units and fight only when we were confident of quick and decisive victory. Our basic tactical philosophy at the squad, platoon, and company levels was to shoot first and move first. If point, flank, or rear contact was made, we would quickly develop fire superiority and immediately assault the enemy. If it turned out to be a small unit, we would overrun it. If it was determined that we had locked horns with a large enemy force, we would break contact. Once contact was broken, we would heavily booby-trap our route of withdrawal.

It was a game that had to be played well—a game you lost only once. George and I would use our whistles to signal commands if we made contact with the enemy. One blast on the whistle was the signal to deploy on line, two meant assault, and three to break contact. A whistle was the most effective way to communicate commands during a firefight; hand and arm signals couldn't be seen in thick vegetation, and the noise of battle often drowned out voice commands.

At 1130 we reached a bright clearing. It was the deserted village of Bu-Kou-Yon. All but one of a dozen thatch-and-bamboo huts had collapsed, and the unattended grass grew knee high.

"Take ten," George passed the word to Sanh.

While Sanh positioned the Bodes in a small defensive perimeter at the edge of the village, George and I lowered our rucksacks at the base of a banana plant. Kneeling in the shade of its large oval leaves, I removed a canteen from my rucksack and took a long drink. Not more than ten meters away, an anteater appeared undisturbed as it dug deep into a large termite mound. A short distance into the village I noticed a Bode looking through one of the collapsed huts. He had a short stocky build, and from the rear he looked a lot like Kien. I knew it couldn't be him because he and the other wounded had been med-evacked to Saigon. My curiosity got the better of me, however.

"Who is that?" I picked up my M-16 and walked out into the sunlight.

The Bode was on his knees looking into a bomb shelter; when he glanced to the side, I spotted a half-smoked, unlit cigar sticking out of his mouth. It *was* Kien!

"What the hell are you doing here?"

"Bac-si." He rose to his feet with a nervous smile on his face.

"What's going on?" George walked to where we were standing.

"I okay," Kien grinned. "Hospital numbah ten. They no like Cambodian."

"Is that so?" I mused.

Rinh walked up and asked him a few questions while I examined his head wound. The top half of his ear had been sliced off by the exploding mortar round, and a dozen sutures had been removed from his scalp.

"He says that he, Binh, and Danh came to Duc-Phong on an Air America plane," Rinh reported.

"Binh and Danh?" George asked.

Kien sheepishly pointed to where two Bodes were sitting with their backs to us.

"Get their butts over here," George told Sanh.

"No sweat, Trung-si."

Kien chewed on his cigar. "We go operation."

Sanh summoned Binh and Danh to where we were standing.

"We okay," Danh said.

"Let me see your wounds." I motioned for them to drop their trousers.

Removing their ammunition harnesses, they unbuttoned their trousers and dropped them to their ankles.

"Jeez." The areas around their stitches were red and oozing pus. "Stitches shoulda been taken out," I told George.

"Should I remove them?" Rinh asked.

"Yeah, clean them up with hydrogen peroxide and take 'em out. Put both men on penicillin and streptomycin."

"I don't know if I should kick your butts or give you medals," George said, shaking his head.

Rinh translated George's remarks and everyone broke into laughter. I could feel myself being overcome by emotion. They were good soldiers, and it was good to have them back.

Binh said something to Rinh. "He said that they amputated Dung's arm," Rinh relayed to us.

"I'm sorry to hear that," George said quietly.

"What about Hoa?" I asked.

"He good," Kien said. "He go C-Team hospital in Bien-Hoa."

"Glad he's okay."

As soon as Rinh finished removing the sutures, we moved out and continued south past giant cypress trees. The ground beneath them was carpeted with red seeds.

Whack-whack-whack. A burst of M-16 fire, far to the south.

George closed the gap between us. "M-16s," he confirmed as we walked together.

"Yeah," I said, "probably recon."

At 1400 we were moving east around clumps of bamboo and scrub brush.

"Psst," George hissed. I stopped, and he advanced to where I was standing. "Fifteen minutes to the RV," he said. "Wagner says they're at 455 954." Using a ballpoint pen, he pointed to the spot on the map.

Whack-whack-whack. Whump-whump-whump. Another exchange of fire resounded through the jungle.

"M-16s and AK-47s," George whispered.

Twenty minutes later, we were moving past fallen moss-covered trees and large ferns. Suddenly, I sensed movement to the right of my head. I turned and found myself face to face with a lime green snake with large yellow eyes. It was stretched out over a few branches. Instinctively, I slashed it across the head with the barrel of my M-16. When it hit the ground, I stomped its bloody head into the mud while the remainder of its body continued to whip back and forth. My heart was pounding in my chest.

"Bamboo viper." George reached forward and cut it in half with a machete. "One bite from that sucker and you'd be going home in a box."

A few minutes farther on I spotted a yellow platoon scarf hanging from a branch over the trail. We had closed the gap with the first platoon. I stopped and strained for a sign of someone.

"WETSU [We Eat This Shit Up]," I called softly.

"WETSU." A well-camouflaged Bode startled me from

behind a fallen tree. I turned and gave George a thumbs-up.

A few meters down the trail I ran into Jarvis.

"About time you got here," he kidded.

George moved forward with his radio handset pressed to his ear. "How's it going?" he asked.

"Recon made two contacts," Jarvis replied. "Two squad-size units moving south on the big trail—about five klicks south of here."

"Anyone hit?" I asked.

"Killed two, wounded two, and captured a few weapons and documents."

"Any friendlies?"

"One Bode got hit in the arm. Gritz is waiting for an update on his condition."

"You know what they were wearing?" George asked.

"Black tops and khaki trousers."

"Could be a good sign," I said. "If they knew we were here, they wouldn't be using the trail."

Frenchie, Jarvis's interpreter, signaled that the column was moving out. I followed Jarvis back to where he had left his rucksack. "You ask Gritz about what happened in Cambode alley?" I asked as he bounced to distribute the weight of his ruck.

"Hell no," he laughed. "The Bodes told us he found some Air Force guy in bed with his girlfriend."

"Oh."

"He emptied his Swedish K into the wall over the guy's head," continued Jarvis. "Fang saw him running down the alley with nothing on."

"Yeah, not something you'd wanna bring up," I nodded as the column started moving again.

I stayed ten paces behind Jarvis and followed him for an hour. At 1730 we were moving past one-hundred-foot-tall trees and clumps of green bamboo when the column suddenly stopped. The jungle was still steaming from the day's bake, but the shadows were lengthening as the sun arched into Cambodia.

"We're there." George pointed to a spot on his map.

"Eleven klicks south of Duc-Phong," I said. "Just inside their artillery fan."

Moving ahead slowly we soon came to the support site. It was an area of towering black-brown trees and thick overhead foliage. Packed between the great trees were large ferns and stalks of green, tan, and brown bamboo. The ground was covered with decaying vegetation that smelled of mold; with each step, I sank ankle deep into its tangled web.

Twenty meters ahead we found Gritz standing at the base of a tree talking into his PRC-25 radio handset. Wagner and two Bodes were using machetes to clear a fifty-foot path for our PRC-74 radio antenna. The headquarters section was at the center of what would be a circular perimeter measuring seventy to eighty meters across.

"Third platoon," Kindoll whispered, "zero to 120 degrees." That meant that our platoon would be responsible for defending one-third of the perimeter—twelve o'clock to four o'clock. I signaled okay with my thumb and followed my compass due north. Forty meters out, I ran into England positioning three of his Bodes. England's second platoon had from eight o'clock to twelve o'clock. Howard's first platoon had from four o'clock to eight o'clock.

"This is my last one," England said under his breath.

Five paces to the right of England's last man, George and I positioned the first three Bodes from our platoon. By positioning them in groups of three we would be able to maintain 30 percent security during the night. When it was time to change guards, the one on duty had only to reach an arm's length to wake his relief.

While Sanh positioned the remainder of the platoon, I found a spot for us to set up our platoon headquarters. It was located in a bamboo thicket just inside the perimeter.

"This looks good," I told George as I cleared away a

few sections of dead bamboo. George, Ly, Rinh, and I lowered our rucks to the ground and looked for places to string our hammocks. It felt good to have the weight off my back.

"Jim," George grabbed my arm, "I'll set up the LP."

"Okay."

After I tied my hammock between two green stalks of bamboo I removed a canteen from my rucksack and swallowed a couple of salt tablets with a long drink of water.

"Donahue." It was Montgomery.

"Yeah?"

"Wagner's running a fever, coughing, and shaking like hell."

"His lungs clear?"

"No," he shook his head.

"Could be pneumonia," I said.

"I loaded him up with penicillin 'G' and APCs. He says he's okay, but you know he's fulla shit."

"He wouldn't tell you if he was dying," I agreed.

"Gritz wants to give it a day. He's gonna have the C-Team put someone on standby, just in case."

"That's about all you can do," I nodded. "Your Bodes holding up?"

"Sent three back to Hal Slusher at Duc-Phong. Looked like falciprium malaria."

"Yeah, latent malaria's gonna be a problem."

"Look, I'll catch you later."

After Montgomery left, Sanh and I checked the perimeter to make sure that our Claymore mines were properly placed. When we returned we found George sitting in his hammock.

"LP in position?" I asked.

"Yeah." He dug into a can of ham and lima beans with a plastic C-ration spoon. "A hundred meters out."

"Perimeter's squared away," I said.

"Good. I want the machine gun manned at all times. That means wide awake and finger on the trigger."

"They got the word."

When George finished eating he went to talk to Gritz. Sitting in my hammock I opened a can of C-ration bread and a tin of peanut butter. For some reason it always took me a day to acclimate when I went on an operation. I never got all that hungry the first day.

Then I positioned my rucksack under my hammock, my ammunition harness on top of my ruck, and my M-16 on top of my harness. If needed, everything would be within reach. Attention to detail was important: everything had its place, and survival dictated that everything be in its place. While I was applying fresh mosquito repellent, George returned. It was almost dark; the once bright colors of the jungle were reduced to dull shades of gray.

"If we get hit during the night, we RV a thousand meters to the east," George whispered in the shadows.

"They translate the documents recon captured?" I asked.

"Yeah. Both contacts were from the 105th VC company."

"Local VC," Sanh said from his hammock. "They under command of Phuoc-Long Province committee. Now all VC know we here."

I removed my boots and placed them on the ground next to my ruck.

Karoumph. Karoumph. Two loud explosions north of our perimeter.

"Artillery from Duc-Phong," offered George.

"Yeah, H and I [harassment and interdiction] fire," I concurred. "Every night they fire a few rounds where they think the VC might have set up camp."

I reclined in my hammock and made a quick mental note of where everything was, then I looked up and saw a few stars through a hole in the canopy.

"One down," George murmured.

"Yeah. It's good to be outta Dodge. How do you want to work security?"

"I'll take the first watch," he responded. "You take 2200 to 2400."

"Okay."

"Sanh, you got midnight to 0200."

"*Oui*, Trung-si."

"Ly," George whispered, "0200 to 0400."

"I do, Trung-si."

"Rinh, 0400 to first light."

"I understand," he answered in the darkness.

"See you turkeys in the morning," George whispered.

Watching the fireflies glow intermittently among the branches, I listened to the sound of the jungle and quickly drifted off to sleep.

CHAPTER NINE

CARRYING SEVENTY-POUND RUCKSACKS on our backs, we were making good time on an elephant trail littered with pieces of crushed bamboo and leaves that had been stripped from the surrounding trees. Slipping in and out of the shadows of those great trees, our green-and-black column was stretched out over three hundred meters. Our order of march: 2-3-1 (that is, second platoon, third, headquarters section, and first). A few paces ahead of me, Danh moved with his silencer-equipped British Sten gun at the ready, and behind me George had the radio handset pressed to his ear.

Whump. A shot fired to our rear—maybe .30 caliber. A surge of adrenaline shot into my system. Whump. Another shot, off to our right.

George closed the gap between us. "Trail watchers."

"Yeah, warning shots. They got a fix on us now."

Whoomph. Whack-whack-whack. A loud explosion, followed by a burst of M-16 fire, not more than two hundred meters behind us.

"Tail gunner porked a tracker," George informed us. "Four got away." I flashed him a thumbs-up. "Blue uniforms," he told me.

"Either main-force VC or NVA," I said.

A hundred meters farther down the elephant trail we cut back into thick underbrush, and for two hours we changed direction every ten to fifteen minutes. If the enemy was still tracking us, we weren't going to make it easy for him.

Whack-whack-whack. Poing . . . whumph. Whump-whump-whump. An intense exchange of fire less than a hundred meters behind us. A few rounds cut through the foliage above our heads. I looked to the rear, and George signaled me to keep moving. A few minutes later he caught up with me.

"Four Cong hit the first platoon," he related.

"Any casualties?"

"Yeah, Montgomery and Jarvis greased three of them. One got away."

I didn't think the contact was intentional. Their earlier run-in with our tail-gunner section should have convinced them that tracking us could be hazardous to their health. To avoid contact with our tail gunners, they likely tried moving parallel to the trail we were leaving in the soft, moist earth. To make sure they didn't lose us, they had to cut across our trail every ten to fifteen minutes and then resume paralleling us on the opposite flank. It was an effective technique, but they got ahead of the game and paid the price.

Two hours later we slowed our blistering pace when Yedinak radioed that our MGF had reached the new support site. It was an area of tall trees whose trunks were covered with moss and white flowers. Between the trees grew shoulder-high plants with large oval leaves. When the third platoon arrived at headquarters, we found Gritz—face dripping with sweat—talking over the PRC-25 radio. Wagner was pale and trying to suppress a cough as he set up the PRC-74 radio.

"Jimmy, check those VC medical supplies." The captain pointed to a canvas bag lying on the ground. "Sidewinder, this is Swamp Fox. Can you give me two strikes? Over."

I lowered my rucksack to the ground. Kindoll directed George to our sector of the perimeter.

"That's a Roger, Swamp Fox," the FAC responded. "I've got a flight of F-4s one zero minutes out. Where do you want it? Over."

"Sidewinder, this is Swamp Fox. From the RP [a reference point on the map], put the first one in at right 0.1, down 0.6, and the second at right 0.7, down 0.8, over."

The reference point system was used when reporting map coordinates because it could not be broken by enemy radio intercept operators. Grid lines on the map were one thousand meters apart and ran north-south and east-west. Every morning we were given a new point where two grid lines crossed, and we marked the location on our maps with a grease pencil. If I wanted to report a location that was a thousand meters east and twelve hundred meters south of the reference point, I would pinpoint it as right 1.0, down 1.2.

I pulled my map from my pocket and saw that the captain was calling the air strikes in on the north-south trail six hundred meters southeast of our support site. After slipping the map back into my pocket, I squatted down and unzipped the blood-soaked VC medical kit. It contained a few glass syringes and an assortment of Vietnamese, Russian, and French medical supplies and vitamins.

"Hey, Jim, what d'ya got there?" Kindoll plopped down next to me and removed a small brown bottle from the kit. It was labeled Spartemie.

"What's this?"

"Got me. I never heard of it."

He picked up a Biere '33 bottle that had a cork stuck in its top. It was labeled Sargactyl.

"Nothing here I'd wanna use," I said.

"I'll have Jarvis booby-trap it."

By the time I finished checking the bag, Wagner was busy tuning the PRC-74 radio and Howard's first platoon was passing by as they moved to their sector of the perimeter. To the south, the whine of a jet engine rose to a banshee-like scream.

Karoumph. Karoumph. Karoumph. The ground shook as a string of bombs exploded south of our perimeter.

"How ya feeling?" I asked Wagner as his trembling fingers attempted to calibrate the radio.

"I'll tell you what," he coughed as a second series of bombs shook the earth. "Monty gave me enough medicine to kill an elephant."

Soon afterward I found George and strung my hammock next to his. Even though it had been a long day, I was quickly acclimating to humping a ruck and felt a lot better than I had at the end of the first day. That night I lay in my hammock listening to the sounds of the jungle. Every few minutes a nearby lizard made the sounds "phuc-yoo, phuc-yoo." After listening for a while I discovered that it always made the sounds an even number of times—never an odd number. The jungle could be predictable after all.

At 0645 on 11 January, Gritz held a team meeting at the headquarters. He explained that one of the weaknesses of patrolling was that your range of vision was generally limited to a few meters of your path through the jungle. Because of this limitation, patrols often missed enemy units, base camps, and trails. The captain suggested that by patrolling in cloverleaf patterns from each of our mission support sites, we would increase the effectiveness of our operation. By sending patrols north, south, east, and west from each support site, our path through the jungle would be measured in kilometers rather than meters.

When Gritz finished, he placed his acetate-covered map on the ground and assigned missions to each of us. I was to take Thach's third squad twelve hundred meters north to booby-trap a trail; George was assigned a reconnaissance mission two thousand meters to the west. We left one squad and the machine-gun section to provide security for the headquarters section.

After hiding my rucksack in thick undergrowth, I led the

third squad north past fifty-foot-tall palm trees and clumps of scrub brush. We reached our objective at 0815 and found it to be a well-used east-west trail that measured a meter across. Thach sent two-man ambushes one hundred meters up and down the trail; once they were in place, I was ready to go to work. I had planned to place a few M-14 "Toe Popper" mines along the trail, but when I saw that a branch had naturally fallen across the path I decided instead to attach an M-26 fragmentation hand grenade—rigged for instant detonation—to the branch. If someone came down the trail and moved the branch, the explosion would kill or wound everyone within ten meters.

With Thach standing over me, his M-16 at the ready, I used green tape to attach the grenade to the base of a sapling. I then tied the grenade's pin to the branch with a piece of fine wire.

Karoumph. Karoumph. Karoumph. A string of bombs exploded far to the south. After straightening the bent-over ends of the pin, I made sure it would slip out of the grenade when the branch was moved. With everything set, I covered the grenade with leaves and Thach recalled security. Ten minutes later we headed southwest for two hundred meters and then shot an azimuth back to the MSS.

We made it back to our perimeter by mid-morning, and while Thach put the Bodes back into their positions, I went to headquarters to check on Wagner. I found him sitting in his hammock; Glossup was squatting in front of him. He had ignited a small piece of C-4 and was using it to heat a canteen cup of water and dried minnows. Gritz was kneeling on the ground with his map spread out in front of him and was talking to Chilton and the FAC over his PRC-25 radio.

"The FAC just fixed the cache site for Chilton," Glossup said while adding salt and pepper to a canteen cup.

"What cache?" I asked.

"Winh died," Gritz said. "They're gonna wrap his body

in a poncho and cache it in a tree. We'll pick him up after the operation.''

"Wanna make sure he gets a proper burial.'' Glossup added a few drops of Tabasco sauce to the brew.

"Winh?'' I didn't place the name.

"The Bode that got hit the first day out,'' Glossup said. "Y'all remember the one at the pool hall in Song-Be? The one with the flak jacket?''

"Oh.'' The news sunk in. "He was a good soldier.''

"They're all good soldiers,'' Gritz said.

"I thought he got hit in the arm,'' I puzzled as Gritz gave Chilton an azimuth and distance back to the support site.

"He did,'' Glossup said. "Best we can figure, he got morphine from two or three medics and died of an overdose.''

"Damn.'' I found it hard to believe.

"Here you go, buddy.'' Glossup handed Wagner the steaming canteen cup.

"This gonna kill me?'' Wagner asked.

"It's my specialty,'' Glossup grinned. "War Zone D fish chowder.''

"Hey, Glossup,'' Gritz said.

"Yes, sir?''

"How on God's good earth did you pick up a name like Lowell?''

"Well, sir, my momma gave it to me. Named me after her favorite radio announcer—Lowell Thomas.''

"Wasn't he a World War II correspondent?'' I asked.

"Yup, that's him.''

While we were talking, George and Sanh arrived and reported that they hadn't found any sign of the enemy to the west. When George finished his report, Gritz assigned us the mission of setting up a squad-size ambush on the north-south trail three kilometers to the south-southeast. We left Sanh at the support site with two squads and the machine-gun section, then we departed with Thach's third squad. At 1210 we were moving through giant shoulder-high, heart-shaped leaves that grew from red stems.

Whack-whack-whack. Whoomph. Whoomph. M-16 fire and explosions to the southeast. George and I stopped and listened for radio transmissions.

"Swamp Fox, this is Fox One, over." Howard was attempting to contact Gritz.

"Fox One, this is Swamp Fox, over," Gritz responded.

"Swamp Fox, this is Fox One. We're in a company-size base camp with eleven structures at down 3.2, left 1.2. Estimated squad withdrew north, negative casualties, over."

"Keep moving," George said.

Fifteen minutes later we came to the edge of a sunny oblong clearing that was a good fifty meters across. The entire area was under cultivation; growing from recently hoed furrows were lines of short, green sprouts. On the far side, a thatch hut was set back under the trees.

After Thach put security in place, he, Danh, Ly, George, and I approached the hut. George and I positioned ourselves at each side of the entrance and, on his signal, looked into the darkened hut. Sleeping on a bamboo mat with his head elevated against a rucksack was a man wearing black pants and Ho-Chi-Minh sandals. His hand was holding his pajama top against the side of his face. I didn't see a weapon, but there were two additional mats on the floor next to him. Along the back wall were a couple of wooden boxes, two rucksacks, and a water jug.

George pressed his index finger against his lips as we entered the darkened room. It smelled of wood smoke, blood, and vomit. With the muzzles of our M-16s pointed at the man's chest, I kicked his foot. He didn't move, so I bent over to see if he had a pulse—he didn't.

"He's dead," I announced as Thach and Danh entered the hut and began searching through the rucksacks.

George bent over and pulled the bloody pajama top from the man's face. His right eye, cheekbone, and nose had been shot away, and by the amount of wet blood and vomit on the floor, I figured he hadn't been dead long.

"Nasty wound," George observed, shaking his head.

"Damn, look at his tongue." It was sticking out, and he had chewed half through it.

"Must have been in a lot of pain."

"Probably one of the VC that ran into recon," I reflected. "Looks like they couldn't stop the bleeding."

Thump. "Aahh."

Out of the corner of my eye I saw Thach punch Danh in the chest and say something in harsh muffled tones. It knocked the wind out of him, and he came close to falling to his knees.

"*Kom pas pral.*" Thach extended his hand and Danh placed a lighter in it.

"VC make lighter bomb." Thach pointed to a wooden box that was filled with Zippo lighters and what appeared to be explosive materials, along with a few tools. "They take Saigon and drop on ground."

Whack-whack-whack. Whump-whump-whump. An exchange of fire to the southeast.

Ly was standing at the door and handed George the radio handset so he could monitor transmissions.

"Many VC," Thach said.

"Yedinak and England are in a base camp just north of where Howard's platoon made contact," George told us. "Thach, pass the word to leave everything like we found it."

"Okay, Trung-si." He and Danh left the hut.

"Jim, rig that box of lighters." He handed me a fragmentation grenade with an M-5 pressure release firing device attached to its top.

I leaned my M-16 against the wall and dropped to my knees. While George waited at the door, I used my K-Bar to dig a hole in the hard-packed floor. When the hole appeared just right, I placed the grenade in it and saw that the plate on the M-5 device was flush with the dirt floor. To keep the grenade stable, I packed some of the dirt back in around it and then pulled the wooden box over most of the release plate.

"Yedinak says the base camp's 150 meters long and has fifteen structures," George advised.

"That's at least company size, maybe battalion," I commented as I continued working.

With everything ready, I carefully pulled the safety pin from the device and slid the box over the remainder of the exposed release plate. If the box was moved, a swing lever within the M-5 device would be released. When it struck the percussion cap, the grenade would explode and kill or wound everyone in the hut.

I stood up, slipped my K-Bar back into its sheath, and wiped my hands on my trousers. When I bent over to put the pajama top back on the dead man's face, I spotted a piece of paper sticking out of a pocket. It was a sheet of notebook paper crowded with Vietnamese writing. I slipped it into my breast pocket, walked back out into the light, and found George talking to Gritz over the radio. "Gritz wants us to return to base."

From the clearing, we headed north for eight hundred meters and stopped to take a break under the spreading branches of a guava tree. Whoomph. I grabbed my compass and took an azimuth on the explosion.

"Hundred eighty degrees," I told George.

"The booby trap." George gave me a thumbs-up.

"Yeah, someone was probably watching and waited for us to leave."

We then shot an azimuth back to the MSS and, at 1500, hit the Da-R'Lah, an intermittent stream that flowed to the west of our perimeter. The water was clear but only an inch deep. To fill our canteens, we had to dig holes in the streambed. After the mud cleared we submerged our canteens into the holes and they bubbled full of cool, clean water.

We broke camp around 1830 and moved south-southeast to set up another support site near the abandoned village

MOBILE GUERRILLA FORCE 107

of Bu-Bitt. It was a mosquito-infested area of scrub brush and bamboo. While George set up our listening post, I checked on Wagner. When I got to headquarters it was almost dark; Gritz was sitting next to the PRC-74 radio with the Morse code key clamped to his thigh. He held Wagner's "Diana Onetime Pad" (a cryptographic system used to encode and decode messages) and was attempting to send a coded message to the C-Team in Bien-Hoa. To Gritz's left, Wagner was sitting in his hammock while Montgomery stood taking his temperature.

"One hundred four," Montgomery said while shaking the thermometer down. "A chopper's gonna pick him up after the resupply drop on the thirteenth."

"I'm not that sick," Wagner coughed.

"Bullshit," retorted Montgomery. "You can hardly walk."

"Don't wanna fool with pneumonia," I advised.

"Good chance he's also got malaria and black water fever [a complication of malaria]," Montgomery gave his diagnosis.

While Montgomery and I talked to Wagner, I had one ear cocked to what Gritz was doing. The operator on the other end was sending him repeated three-letter transmissions: Dah-dah-dit-dah, dit-dit-dah-dit, dit-dah. Dah-dah-dit-dah, dit-dit-dah-dit, dit-dah.

"He sending you QFAs [quit fucking around], sir?" I smiled.

"That he is."

"Doesn't he know he's making commo with an officer?" Montgomery joked.

"Hell, he's gotta know. Only an officer would send code that bad," Wagner laughed.

"You sure it's calibrated?" Gritz asked Wagner about the radio.

"Yes, sir; 3.540 megacycles. If you wanna switch to the first alternate, it's 4.464 megacycles."

"I'll stay on the primary."

"Yes, sir."

"What about the azimuth on the antenna?" Gritz asked.

"Double-checked it, sir."

"Hell, I'm gonna send in the clear," Gritz said as he continued to tap out Morse code on the key.

When I returned to the perimeter, I found George and Sanh sitting on the ground sharing a bag of cold rice and dried minnows. Our dehydrated indigenous rations came in plastic bags; before eating them you had to add water and wait about fifteen minutes for it to be absorbed.

I sat between them, and with birds chirping in the branches above us, I brewed a cup of hot tea and opened a can of pork and beans. At last light the music of the birds faded and was replaced by the grunts, groans, and growls of the night. With fireflies flickering from branch to branch, we sat in the dark and whispered about the events of the day. When we finished talking, George and Sanh crawled into their hammocks and I took the 2200-to-2400 watch. It was an uneventful two hours, but a short time after Rinh relieved me, I was jolted awake by the exploding bombs of a Sky Spot air strike.

The Sky Spot was a technical innovation that provided us with the capability of calling in air strikes at night and during bad weather. After we radioed a target's eight-digit coordinates to the Special Forces air liaison officer in Bien-Hoa, he telephoned them to the III Corps Direct Air Support Center at Ton-Son-Nhut Air Base. The coordinates were then fed into a computer that controlled the aircraft's course and bomb release point. The program was still considered experimental and, for safety reasons, could only be used on targets that were more than six hundred meters from friendly forces.

At 0700 on the morning of 12 January, George and I departed the MSS with three squads. Our mission: check out a possible enemy base camp at map coordinates 294 851—four kilometers south-southeast of the support site. A few days earlier the FAC had spotted morning smoke coming from the area; it was also where the north-south trail crossed the Da-Cok, a stream that flowed east and emptied into the Dong-Nai River. Whenever you had a major trail, a year-round water supply, and overhead cover, you also had the ideal location for an enemy base camp. In the early afternoon we crossed a clear stream and stopped on its bank to take a break. Once security was in place, we took turns filling our canteens.

Whack-whack-whack. Whump-whump-whump. The silence was broken by an intense firefight a short distance to the northeast.

"Swamp Fox, this is Fox Two," England radioed Gritz.

"Fox Two, this is Swamp Fox, over."

"Swamp Fox, this is Fox Two. We got a firefight in progress a few hundred meters south of our location. Sounds like it's coming from the base camp we were in yesterday, over."

"Swamp Fox, this is Fox Four," Cawley broke in. He sounded winded.

"Fox Four, this is Swamp Fox, over."

"Swamp Fox, this is Fox Four. Made contact with at least a squad. One Victor Charlie KIA [killed in action]. They withdrew south. We're in pursuit, over."

"Roger, Fox Four," Gritz said.

"This place is crawling with Cong," I told George.

To the northeast I could hear the hum of the FAC. Following a short break, we continued toward our objective. We were moving downhill through triple canopy and thick undergrowth when Danh suddenly stopped and dropped to one knee. I crept forward to his position.

"Fire, Bac-si," he whispered.

"Yeah." The faint odor of wood smoke was in the air. "Keep it slow."

When we reached the bottom of the hill, the crow of a rooster broke the silence. Danh stopped and I again closed to his position. Looking ahead, I could see that the jungle was beginning to thin. I waved George and Sanh forward. "Got something up ahead," I whispered.

"VC *chroen*." Danh warned that there may be many Vietcong.

"Okay," George said softly to Sanh, "tell Danh to take a look."

Danh nodded, and with feline grace, he slinked forward and disappeared into the green.

"If we're talking big numbers, we'll wait for Gritz to bring in the rest of the company," George murmured.

I nodded my agreement but was worried. Because of the firefights that had taken place to the northeast, whoever was up ahead had to be on a high state of alert.

Ten minutes later Danh returned. "Five VC," he reported. Sanh questioned him in Cambodian.

"He see four building but he not see many VC," Sanh said. "He say three VC play card, one wash clothes, and one take shit." Danh said more to Sanh. "He say many tree. Maybe more VC he cannot see," Sanh reported.

"Okay," George said, "let's hit it. If there's more than we can handle, we'll break contact and run like hell."

"How close can we get without being seen?" I asked Danh.

"Fifty meter, Bac-si."

"Sanh, get 'em on line, five meters apart," George whispered. "Leave half of the third squad here to cover our rear."

"*Oui*, Trung-si."

Sanh stood up and, by extending both arms parallel to the ground, gave the signal to deploy on line. Once the squad leaders had everyone on line and properly spaced, George raised his hand over his head and, by lowering it forward, gave the signal to advance. Slipping silently through the last of the leaves, vines, and brush, we soon entered an area where much of the lower levels of foliage had been cleared. Only the great trees remained, and they supported an umbrella that screened out much of the light and effectively hid the camp from aerial view. While stepping over a foul-smelling slit-trench latrine, I spotted two bamboo-and-thatch huts fifty meters ahead of our advancing line.

"*Linh.*" A shrill Vietnamese voice sounded a warning and my heart shifted into high gear.

Whack-whack-whack. Poing . . . whumph. We opened up and our line surged forward at a slow run. With red tracers cutting through the camp at waist level, exploding M-79 rounds tore gaping holes in the thatch huts.

Over everything, the battle cry Tay-yoo echoed beneath the canopy. To the rear of the huts we jumped over an unoccupied trench. Once past the huts, we saw that the camp and additional huts continued south along the creek for a good one hundred meters. With Sanh and the squad leaders yelling orders to stay on line and to slow their rate of fire, we advanced at a full run. I fired a burst at a retreating black-clad enemy soldier. His head exploded like a ripe melon that had been hit by a speeding truck. Near the center of the camp, George and I jumped over an unoccupied mortar pit and the shooting slowed.

"*Thov tiet.*" Sanh yelled for the Bodes to keep moving forward.

We didn't want to give the enemy the chance to regroup. Still farther into the camp we passed two sets of bleachers and a podium. It was an outdoor classroom. On the far side of the bleachers we reached a second trench.

Whump-whump-whump. From up ahead a long burst of green tracers cut through the foliage a few feet over our heads.

Whack-whack-whack. Poing . . . whumph. We continued to return fire.

"Hold it up," George raised his arm over his head.

"*Chop.*" Sanh yelled to the Bodes to stop.

"First squad, set up security in the trench," George ordered Sanh. "Second squad's got flank security. Take what's left of the third to conduct a search." Sanh barked orders to the Bodes, and George and I ran back to the mortar pit.

"British eighty-eight millimeter," I said as we jumped into the pit.

George lifted a canvas cover from the entrance to an attached ammo bunker and moved inside. I removed the aiming device from the side of the mortar tube and stuck it in my pocket. We didn't have any use for the mortar, so I removed a thermite grenade from my web gear, pulled the pin, and let it slide down the tube. It hit bottom with a "clunk"; a caustic smoke immediately began pouring from the tube. Within seconds, I could feel its intense heat. I remembered seeing a thermite grenade burn through a Russian truck's engine block and knew it would do an equally good job on the mortar.

"Jim," George said, "look at this." I stuck my head inside the dark bunker.

"Two-hundred-gram Chicom [Chinese Communist] blocks of TNT," he gasped while pointing to a stack of rectangular-shaped yellow blocks that were wrapped in wax paper. They were labeled with Chinese characters and the number two hundred.

Looking up again I saw green and red tracers cutting through the camp and the Bodes running from hut to hut carrying pieces of burning thatch. Flames and thick gray smoke poured from the roofs of at least a dozen structures. To the south the first squad was on line—about five meters between each man—laying down a base of fire as they walked backwards toward us. Off to our right Danh and Rinh carried bags of rice from the mess hall and were dumping them in the stream.

Whoomph. An explosion at the top of a nearby tree left my ears ringing. "What was that?" George asked as thousands of leaves floated through the smoke.

"RPG [rocket-propelled grenade]," I yelled. "We'd better get our butts outta here."

"Ever see one of these?" he inquired, tossing me a

Coca-Cola can that had been made into a hand grenade. It weighed a couple of pounds and came to a point on top. Its pin was attached to a thin trip-wire that was wrapped around the can. "There's a bunch of them in here."

"You gonna blow it?"

"Yeah, I got a grenade with a time pencil [time-delay fuse] hidden under the boxes."

"Let's move it," I said, coughing from the smoke. "If we get pinned down, they'll kick our ass."

By the time we finished with the mortar pit the first squad leader had moved his line of security back to our position. Every structure in the camp was engulfed in flames, and a cloud of thick smoke was trapped beneath the canopy. George jumped out of the pit and gave three long blasts on his whistle—the signal to break contact. The Bodes immediately stopped what they were doing and ran through the smoke to the northern end of the camp. To our rear the first squad remained on line and continued to fire as they walked backwards at a fast pace.

When we got back to where Thach's squad was waiting, we jumped over the trench and followed Danh back up the hill. My eyes were watering from the smoke. With everyone out of the base camp the shooting suddenly stopped; the only remaining sound was the cracking and popping of burning bamboo. Halfway up the hill we stopped and waited while Thach strung a trip-wire attached to a Claymore mine across the trail we were leaving. The mine was double primed with a time pencil and would automatically detonate if the enemy didn't trigger it within four hours.

Whoomph. The mortar pit exploded to our rear and pieces of debris fell through the foliage around us. As soon as we cleared the area, we could hear the hum of the FAC far to the north.

"Sidewinder, this is Fox Three, over," George said into the radio handset as we navigated around clumps of bamboo.

"Fox Three, this is Sidewinder, over."

"Sidewinder, this is Fox Three. We got a battalion-size base camp at down 4.8, left 2.7. We need heavy ordnance to take out the bunkers and tunnels, over."

"Roger, Fox Three. I see the smoke. I'll have a flight of 105s on target in one five minutes."

As we continued northeast, the FAC passed over our position. A few minutes later we could hear the more powerful engines of the F-105s. Karoumph. Karoumph. Karoumph. The earth shook as the 105s dropped 500- and 750-pound bombs on the base camp. A few seconds later a jet screeched over our position at treetop level. The sound gave me a secure feeling.

"In the next war I'm gonna be a fighter pilot," I told George as I looked up at the sky through a hole in the canopy.

"Yeah," he said, "three hots and a cot. That's the way to go."

We made it back to the MSS at 1830, and at our debriefing Gritz told us that during the night all of the enemy base camps in the area would be hit with Sky Spots. Following the debriefing George checked the perimeter while I recovered our rucksacks from the underbrush and strung our hammocks next to a fallen tree.

I was in no mood for C rations so I removed an indigenous instant rice ration from my ruck. After tearing open the top of the plastic bag, I poured in two packages of dried milk and shook it up before adding water. I then tied it off at the top with a rubber band and laid it on the tree trunk. While the water was being absorbed I broke off a small piece of C-4 from my two-and-a-half-pound block and brewed a large cup of hot tea. By the time George returned I had dinner ready.

"Chef's specialty," I said. "Rice à la Phuoc-Long." I pulled two large leaves from a nearby branch and, after placing them on the fallen tree, emptied half of the contents of the plastic bag onto each of them. I then sprinkled some sugar on the rice. "This is a sweet dish," I explained as I opened a can of C-ration peaches and spooned a few on each of the leaves.

"I'm starving," he said.

"Dinner is served, sir." I poured half of the tea into his C-ration cup.

"Very good, James," he laughed as we both straddled the trunk and began to eat.

"This is good." I swallowed some rice and sipped the steaming tea.

"Jim, let me ask you something." George's face turned serious. "You getting as attached to these guys as I am?"

"Yeah. Some of the best men I've ever known. Don't make them any better."

As George and I whispered, the light of day quickly faded, and by the time we finished our meal Sanh, Rinh, Ly, and Danh had returned. At our nightly meeting we reviewed the events of the day and sat talking quietly well into the night.

CHAPTER TEN

FOLLOWING A MEETING WITH Captain Gritz, we moved south-southwest toward the Drop Zone. Less than an hour later we arrived at a circular, grass-covered clearing that measured seventy-five meters across and was surrounded by tall trees. The third platoon set up security just inside the tree line on its east side. The morning silence was broken by the distant hum of the approaching FAC aircraft. The ground reception committee then moved to the center of the Drop Zone. When the single-engine aircraft was spotted, Yedinak flashed him with his signal mirror, and Kindoll and Fang began laying out five international orange ground panels in the shape of a tee.

Then, minutes later, two A-1E single-engine fighter aircraft arrived overhead. The Skyraiders appeared black, but when the first aircraft made a low-level pass over the panels, I saw that it was camouflaged with patterns of green, brown, and tan, with a gray underside. The pylons under the wings normally carried 250- and 500-pound bombs, but for this mission they were loaded with silver napalm containers. Each container had been modified to carry four hundred pounds of food, supplies, and ammunition in prepackaged sandbags. Once on the ground, these man-portable loads would be quickly distributed to the troops, minimizing our time on the Drop Zone.

"Those are old Navy planes," George said. "We called them flying dump trucks."

Suddenly, a plane was directly overhead; a split second later, seven silver napalm containers attached to camouflaged T-7A reserve parachutes were floating slowly to earth. They hit with a "thud" near the center of the Drop Zone. By the time the ground reception committee reached the containers, the second aircraft was making its approach. When it appeared overhead, I immediately knew that it had dropped early. Seconds later, all but two of its seven parachutes landed in the trees on the far side of the Drop Zone.

While George stayed with the platoon, I ran over to where Gritz and Kindoll were standing.

"Probably the first time he ever dropped anything by parachute," Kindoll said.

"Sidewinder, this is Fox Three," Gritz called. "We gotta do better than that. We've got five in the trees. Would it be possible for me to communicate directly with the pilots? Over."

"Swamp Fox, this is Sidewinder. That's a can do. They're on FM [frequency modulation], over."

"Sidewinder, this is Swamp Fox. In the future, I'll give the command to execute the drop. Also pass the word to Pleiku that someone's bolting the napalm containers together. If they'd use wing nuts or parachute line, we'd reduce our time on the zone, over."

"Tell 'em we don't carry wrenches," Kindoll kidded Gritz.

I ran back to the platoon and found that George had a sandbag waiting for me. It contained four indigenous dried-rice rations and four C-ration meals—a four-day supply.

"Jim, chopper's coming in to pick up Wagner," George said as I stuffed the sandbag into my ruck. "I'm gonna say goodbye."

"Give him my best."

To the south I heard the wap, wap, wap of the approaching chopper. Soon after George left, someone popped a yellow smoke canister. Looking south, I saw the green hull of the Huey coming in over the trees. "Here she comes," I told Sanh as I tied my ruck shut and fastened the straps.

Looking up again, I saw that the pilot had slowed his forward speed. Just before touching down in the grass, he lowered his nose and kicked up a cloud of dust. While the rotors pulsated and waves of heat poured from the chopper's engine, someone with a rucksack on his back jumped from it and ran to the wood line. At the same time, Gritz, Howard, and George accompanied Wagner to the Huey. As soon as they returned to the wood line, the pilot increased the pitch on the blades and the Huey lifted to a few feet off the ground. Black vapors poured from its engine as it tilted forward, transitioned to forward flight, and climbed across the clearing and over the trees.

"That was emotional," George said, shaking his head. "Wagner felt bad about leaving."

"Who's the replacement?"

"Al Doyle. The radio operator from Duc-Phong."

"Good man."

As we headed southwest I felt fortunate that we hadn't been hit on the Drop Zone. Because we were spread out and had so many troops involved in the recovery of the containers, we were especially vulnerable to enemy attack.

By 1800 the heat of the day was beginning to lose some of its intensity.

Whoomph. A distant explosion echoed as we moved past tall palms and banana plants. "Napalm container," George whispered from behind me.

It was almost dark when we arrived at the high ground that would serve as our MSS. The elevation was packed tight with bamboo and thorn-covered brush. When I arrived at headquarters, Doyle was setting up the PRC-74 radio.

"Al," I shook his hand, "glad you volunteered to join us."

"Volunteered?" He pulled me aside. "Hey, I was down in Saigon on the best R and R of my life when they Shanghaied me. Word has it that Kindoll volunteered me."

"That's what I call a friend," I snorted. By the time I finished talking to Doyle, he had me doubled over with laughter.

On the morning of 14 January we were on the move at first light. Our objective: to evaluate an old French fort as the possible future location for a Special Forces camp. At 1000 we arrived at the fort. All that remained were three earthen walls laid out in the shape of a triangle. The mounds were overgrown with weeds and tall grass, and here and there rusted sections of barbed wire twisted above it all.

The fort had been built on a ridge that provided excellent fields of fire and a commanding view of the surrounding terrain. We concluded that it would be an ideal location for a camp. From here troops could patrol west to Bunard and east to the Dong-Nai River. There was also something magical about the place; I found myself wondering about the men who had fought there and what had become of them. With a little imagination, I pictured the tri-colored French flag flying at its center and a garrison of the Foreign Legion fighting to the last man. In eerie silence it stood as a memorial to another war.

Our mission completed, we departed; the third platoon was leading the column. Danh was the point man and I followed ten paces behind him. With my map in one hand and my compass in the other, I kept us moving in the right direction and, when necessary, used hand and arm signals to adjust Danh's course to the left or right.

A short time after departing the fort, Danh suddenly stopped, dropped to one knee, and motioned me forward. When I arrived at his position, I saw that he had stopped a few meters short of the north-south trail. Before making the crossing, we would put security one hundred meters up and down the trail. We didn't want to chance making contact with a large enemy unit while we were in the process of crossing.

While Sanh and George got the security units ready to move out, Danh inched his way to the edge of the trail. Using his hands to part the last of the leaves, he extended his head out over the trail and looked to his left. Whump-whump-whump. An automatic weapon opened up and rounds tore into the dirt trail in front of Danh. "VC!" he yelled as he jumped out onto the trail.

Chunk-chunk-chunk. He returned fire with his silencer-equipped British Sten. I flipped my selector switch to automatic. When I reached the trail, I spotted the backs of two black-clad Vietcong seventy-five meters down the trail. I fired a quick burst a split second before they disappeared around a bend in the trail. Danh and I dropped our ruck-sacks and ran to the bend; the enemy had disappeared into the jungle. We found no evidence that we had hit anyone, but we did find a piece of shattered rifle stock lying on the trail.

With our hearts pounding in our chests, we jogged back to the platoon. After Sanh positioned the security units we crossed the trail and continued west. Six hundred meters past the trail we crossed a shallow stream called the Da-Pembeu, and at 1515 we reached the high ground that would serve as our support site. At a last-light meeting, Gritz informed us that he had requested a Sky Spot on a major trail junction a short distance south of our perimeter.

That night, the third platoon was assigned much of the western half of the perimeter, and shortly after dark, our listening post reported hearing chopping farther west. By the time they settled down it was time for me to take the 2200-to-2400 watch. Except for the crunching of elephants feeding in a nearby bamboo thicket, it was a quiet two hours. After Sanh took over at midnight I quickly fell asleep.

Karoumph, karoumph, karoumph. The ground beneath my hammock shook as a Sky Spot hit to the south. I checked my watch—it was 0105—then I fell back to sleep.

Whoomph. An explosion jolted me awake. It was 0400.

"Claymore we left on the trail," George mumbled.

"If Mister Charles is moving at night, he's gotta want us bad," I commented.

At first light on the morning of 15 January, Gritz assigned the third platoon the mission of conducting a recon two thousand meters to the west. The map showed a stream a few hundred meters north of a trail that led to Bunard; Gritz suspected it was a likely area for a base camp. We also wanted to check out the chopping that our listening post had reported. We were eight hundred meters west of the MSS by 0740. We were moving uphill through thick underbrush when Danh stopped and pointed to two light brown patches surrounded by green. They were about fifty meters ahead.

"What d'ya got?" George asked softly.

"Looks like a couple of hooches."

"Check it out," he told Danh, who pushed the leaves aside and slowly moved forward. Five minutes later, he returned.

"Big base, many bunker," he reported. "No VC."

"Did you go into it?" I asked.

"No, Bac-si."

"Sanh, give Danh a radio and have him and Thach check it out. One around the left side and the other around the right," George ordered. "Make sure no one's in the bunkers."

As Sanh got them ready to go, George and I discussed the situation. "You're right about the bunkers," I said. "A couple of automatic weapons would have us for lunch."

We deployed the platoon on line and moved to the edge of the camp. From behind a large tree I could see a short distance into it. Hidden in the shade of the great trees were seven thatch structures. Twenty meters into the camp, a chicken-wire pen confined a few ducks. Our presence must have spooked them because they were pacing and quacking with excitement. In some ways ducks were better than dogs when it came to sensing unwelcome visitors.

Danh and Thach returned fifteen minutes later. Both were dripping with sweat. "Maybe twenty building," Thach panted.

"Much rice," Danh said. "No VC."

"Wonder where they went?" George muttered.

"Probably out looking for us," I quipped. "What d'ya wanna do?"

"Let's hit it," he said while looking at his map. "Sanh, have the first squad move through and set up on the far side."

"*Oui*, Trung-si."

"Second's got flank security on both sides; third's got rear security." Sanh nodded. "Okay, let's do it." George folded his map and slipped it into his pocket.

After a short meeting with the squad leaders, the first squad lined up and moved out. As soon as they were into the camp, the second squad deployed to the north and south sides of the camp. With security in place, George, Ly, Sanh, Danh, Rinh, and I entered the camp. Just past the ducks, we found the rice—more than a dozen fifty-pound burlap bags stacked on an elevated bamboo platform.

"Sanh!" George tossed him a white phosphorus grenade with a time pencil attached and pointed to the rice. As we continued into the camp, Sanh climbed on top of the bags and wedged the grenade between two of them; it would blow when we were well clear of the area.

"Rinh," George pointed to a row of huts off to our left, "check them out. Danh," George called, pointing to a few others off to our left. Twenty meters past the rice we found the mess hall. "Booby-trap it," George told me as he and Ly continued deeper into the camp.

The mess hall had been dug below ground level and was covered with a thatch roof. I entered by walking down four steps to a mud floor. Dug into the far wall were four fire pits with blackened pots hanging above them. The ashes beneath the pots were still warm. I removed my K-Bar, dropped to my knees, and, on the hard-packed floor in front of the last step, dug a small hole.

When I finished, I removed a plastic M-14 Toe Popper mine from my pocket and placed it in the hole. The hole was a little too deep, so I replaced some dirt and packed it with the handle of my knife. When I put the mine back in the hole I saw that its top was just below ground level. I again removed the mine from the hole and pulled the safety clip from the device.

With everything the way I wanted it, I placed the mine back in the hole and spread a thin layer of dirt over it. I then spit on the dirt to make it wet and smoothed it with my finger. When it dried it would look the same as the surrounding floor. If someone stepped on the mine, twenty pounds of pressure would release a spring that would drive the firing pin into the detonator. Normally, it blew off the victim's toes, broke his leg, and sent shrapnel up into his genital area. When I finished with the Toe Popper, I began looking for a good place to rig a grenade booby trap.

"Jim!" It was George calling.

"Yeah?" I responded, running up the stairs.

"We found the ammo bunker." He motioned for me to follow him. "Hole's too small for me to get in." We ran to where a Bode was waiting in a clump of bamboo.

"Here, Bac-si." He pointed to the ground. A dirt-and-grass-covered square piece of wood had been removed from the entrance and lay on the ground next to the hole. It measured about eighteen inches across, was four inches thick, and, with beveled sides, was tailor-made for this particular entrance.

"I tried but got stuck," lamented George, handing me a Claymore mine with a time pencil. "This should do it."

"Gimme your flashlight." I removed my harness and handed him my M-16.

"Ly's already down there with it," George replied. Looking into the hole I saw the bottom, four feet below ground level. I sat on the edge and, after lowering myself into the hole, saw there was a tunnel leading to my front.

"Ly," I called.

"Bac-si." A beam of light hit my eyes.

"Hand me the light," I said. (George, Sanh, Thach, and I were the only members of the platoon who were qualified to set up booby traps.) He crawled in my direction and, after handing me the flashlight, backed down the tunnel. In its light I could see that the tunnel continued downward at a forty-five-degree angle. There was a bunker at its far end. I crawled feet first down the tunnel and, when I came to the bunker, saw that it measured about twelve feet by twelve feet. It was cool and damp and smelled of mold. I had to stand bent forward because the ceiling was only shoulder high.

Piled on bamboo platforms at the rear of the bunker were a number of wooden boxes. The first one I checked was full of Soviet fragmentation grenades; they were made of serrated cast iron and were painted military green.

"*Russi*," Ly proclaimed. He then showed me a second box. "*Chen.*" He pointed to Chinese characters on the box. I opened the box and found that it contained stick-type fragmentation grenades. To the right of the grenades were six wooden boxes stacked together. They were also labeled with Chinese characters and the numbers 7.62. It was 7.62-mm ball ammunition. Additional ammunition was stored in galvanized metal cans.

"Nothing we can use," I told Ly. I crawled over the top of the boxes and found that there was just enough room to wedge the Claymore between them and the back wall.

"All set." I motioned for Ly to move out ahead of me. The air outside was thick with smoke; every structure in the camp was ablaze. Rinh and Danh were kneeling next to the entrance, fingering through a stack of documents, newspapers, and a much-read *Playboy* magazine.

"Ready," I told George as Ly and Sanh replaced the cover over the entrance.

"One battalion lives here," Rinh reported, pointing to a yellowed document.

"Let's get outta here," George ordered. Sanh raised his HT-1 radio to his mouth and issued the order to withdraw from the camp. With a line of security moving to our rear, we headed back to where Thach's squad was waiting. Danh quickly found our trail, and I followed him east. Three hundred meters from the camp we stopped while Sanh booby-trapped our back trail.

Whoomph. A loud explosion to our rear. "The bunker," George grinned.

When Sanh's booby trap was in place we headed north for twelve hundred meters and then shot an azimuth back to the support site. When we reached the perimeter, George and I headed for headquarters to brief Gritz and then returned to the perimeter to inspect everyone's weapon, ammunition, and equipment.

Halfway through the inspection, we found Danh sitting in his hammock, crying. After Sanh questioned him we discovered that Winh—the Cambodian who had died—was his brother-in-law. Danh had just learned of his death. It was a very emotional time for everyone, and in between his tears and Buddhist chants, we did our best to console him. Our assurances that Winh's body would be recovered and properly buried seemed to help. George also promised that Captain Gritz would see to it that everything possible would be done for Danh's sister and her children.

By the time we got to our hammocks it was almost 2200, and as I lay in the darkness, I found myself thinking about Winh's family. I felt bad about having to cache his body because I knew that his religion required that he have a proper Buddhist burial. I also knew that after a couple of days, his decaying body would attract every wild pig in the area. I only hoped that there would be something left to bury. After tossing and turning for almost an hour, I finally fell asleep.

Karoumph, karoumph, karoumph. Bombs exploding to the west woke me from a sound sleep.

"Jim," hissed George from a few feet away. I was wrapped head to toe in my piece of parachute nylon and pulled it away from my face.

"Yeah?" I leaned over the side of my hammock and found the damp night air unusually cold.

"That was the Sky Spot going in on the camp."

"Might catch 'em at home," I whispered. "Boy, it's cold." I could hear George searching through his rucksack.

"You want my sweater?"

"I'm good." I was moved by his offer. George was like that.

"Never thought I'd get cold in Vietnam," he mused.

"Yeah, your blood thins. Aren't you from Minnesota?"

"Well, I was born in North Dakota. After Mom died, my brothers John and Dick and sister Vonni and I moved to Frazee, Minnesota, to live with my Uncle John and Aunt Ann. The other kids, Will and Joanne, moved in with other relatives."

"Live with them until you joined the Army?"

"Well, Uncle John got killed in a packing plant accident in '47. Ann took care of me until I joined the Navy when I was seventeen," he said in the darkness. "I loved her like a mother."

"You part Indian?" I asked.

"Bohemian and Irish. But people tell me I look Indian. Back in school I got a Mohawk," he chuckled. "The priest made me sit in the back of the church until it grew in."

"You went to Catholic school?"

"For a few years."

"So did I," I said. "The nuns beat the hell outta me. Said I was a nonconformist."

"Nuns are very perceptive," he laughed. "You play any sports?"

"I went out for football but only weighed ninety pounds."

"Ninety pounds?"

"We won the city tennis championship in '60." I ignored his disbelief.

"Tennis? Your family got money?"

"No," I objected, "I was raised on welfare. One place we lived had nothing but cockroaches and displaced persons. We had one bathroom for three or four families."

"I hate roaches," he shuddered, "especially when they get into food."

"When I poured milk on my cereal, they'd float to the top and I'd flick them out with my spoon."

"Yuk."

"Were you into sports?"

"Football and basketball," he said, "and some boxing."

"Oh, yeah, I boxed at the Butler Mitchell Boy's Club," I told him. "You any good?"

"Only lost once, and that was a close decision to Ralph Cousey, a kid from Detroit Lakes."

"My friend Red Fenton and I had some good matches," I told him. "Last I heard, old Red was in the Navy."

Karoumph, karoumph, karoumph. Bombs from a second Sky Spot exploded to the south. It was 0105.

"Hey, buddy," George said, "better get some sleep."

"Wait one." I reached out into the darkness and yanked the side of his hammock. "Did you tell me I'm out here in the middle of War Zone D with a sorry-assed swabbie?"

"Hey," he laughed, "come morning, this swabbie's gonna kick your butt."

CHAPTER ELEVEN

0830, 16 JANUARY 1967

THE THIRD PLATOON WAS moving uphill through bamboo and a tangle of vines. We were less than a hundred meters east of the enemy base camp we had found the day before. Our mission: to conduct a bomb damage assessment of the Sky Spot that had been directed against the camp during the night. If the Sky Spot proved to be accurate, we could rely on it as a direct support weapon at night and during the hours when the FAC wasn't available to direct air strikes against enemy targets.

Danh was leading on point and stopped when he came to the edge of a bomb crater that measured ten meters across. At its bottom, trails of steam drifted in the morning calm. The bamboo around the rim had been blown flat; beyond it, the tops of the trees were snapped like matchsticks. Their bare trunks were silhouetted against a clear blue sky, and an area that once was shaded by a canopy of leaves was now bright with sunlight and smoke. Standing at the edge of the crater we strained for a sound.

Quack. A duck broke the silence. I gave George a thumbs-up.

"Sanh, leave the third squad here," George whispered. "We'll move through with the first and second."

While George radioed Captain Gritz, Sanh and I deployed the two squads on line. Skirting the rim of the crater, my feet sank ankle deep into the soft, loose dirt. On its far side we crawled over splintered tree trunks, branches, and the black smoldering remains of a hut. Just beyond the hut I spotted a head lying on the ground. It must have been severed during the air strike.

Chunk-chunk-chunk. Danh fired a burst from his silencer-equipped Sten. The head rolled across the ground like a basketball on a gym floor.

"I see face, Bac-si. I think he VC in hole," Danh said under his breath as he bent over and picked the head up by the hair.

The dead man's skin looked waxy, and his lips formed a haunting smile. He appeared to have been in his late teens. Danh's 9-mm slug had left a small hole above his right ear and a fist-sized exit wound on the left side of his head. Danh placed the head on a tree trunk.

After skirting a few more craters, I came to the mess hall. Its roof had been blown away, but the underground section remained intact. Looking down its steps, I saw a small hole where I had placed the M-14 Toe Popper the day before. The area around it was streaked with dried blood.

Only a blackened pit remained of what was the ammo bunker, and a trail of blood and undigested food led to a man sitting against a tree with his intestines lying between his outstretched legs. He had straight black hair, wore a khaki uniform, and stank of death. When I bent over to check his pockets, I found his hands red with dried blood. It appeared he had been attempting to push his intestines back into his abdominal cavity when he died.

Whump-whump-whump. Green enemy tracers cut through the air, thumping into the tree trunks around us.

I fired a burst, and Sanh and I hit the ground behind a mound of dirt. Looking over it I saw the muzzle flashes of enemy troops firing at us from about seventy-five meters away. Everything between us and them had been blown flat by bombs. I returned fire in quick three-round bursts and ducked to change magazines. Sanh was on his radio giving orders to the squad leaders.

Whoomph. An explosion on the far side of the mound showered us with dirt. "Jim!" George and Ly hit the ground next to me. "Take Thach's squad around and hit them from the south," George ordered. "We'll lay down a base of fire."

"Okay. Two blasts on my whistle and you stop firing. Let the Bodes know we're gonna be out there."

Running zigzag in a low crouch, I returned to the eastern end of the camp. "Let's go," I motioned for Thach and his squad to follow me.

With a cacophony of fire building to our right, we ducked under the trunk of a large fallen tree. While crawling over its branches I stepped on a dead man's stomach. His mouth and eyes were wide open.

"*Suttrov!*" Thach kicked the body.

Moving as fast as possible, we worked our way around a few more craters before stopping. I took my compass and shot an azimuth to the north. If we didn't assault at just the right angle, our rounds could pass through the enemy ranks and hit our own men.

"Psst," I motioned Thach forward and used my scarf to wipe the sweat from my face. "Get 'em on line," I said while pointing north.

"Okay, Bac-si."

"Make damned sure they know the platoon's off to our right."

He spoke in an undertone to each man as they deployed on line. Advancing at a slow pace, we left the craters behind and soon found ourselves in waist-deep grass as we moved past tall trees and clumps of bamboo. Fifty meters ahead of our line a firefight raged and red tracers streaked above the grass.

Whack-whack-whack. Poing . . . whumph. The squad

opened fire and I gave two long blasts on my whistle.

Tay-yoo echoed beneath the canopy as our line surged through the grass at a slow run. Thach yelled for his men to keep on line.

I kept one eye on the Bodes and the other to my front as I fired quick bursts at momentary glimpses of fleeing Vietcong. While jumping over an unoccupied foxhole, I spotted a black wire leading in the direction of the camp. Twenty meters beyond the hole we came to a natural wall of thorn-covered vines and tangled undergrowth.

Thach ordered his troops to stop. Suddenly, everything was silent; I could hear my pulse pounding in my ears.

"We got everyone?" I asked Thach. He nodded. Whoomph. A muffled explosion off to our left.

"*Kang!*" Binh yelled that they had blown a bunker.

"Tell Sanh we've cleared them out," I told Thach. He raised his HT-1 radio to his lips and spoke a few words into it.

"Okay, Bac-si."

"I saw a wire," I told him. "Get security in place while I check it out."

Thach spread his squad out to the west of the foxholes. When I arrived at the hole, I found the wire attached to a battery pack held together with black tape. I disconnected the wire and followed it toward the base camp. At the end of the wire I found a round Claymore-type mine. The military green device measured a good foot in diameter and was supported by a metal stand.

"What is it?" George yelled from the other side of a bomb crater.

"Claymore." I pushed it face down in the grass.

"It disarmed?"

I flashed him a thumbs-up. He and Sanh ran to where I was standing. "Chinese," Sanh said.

"DH-10 model," I told him. "An ass-kicker."

"Bac-si." Ten meters to our right, Thach held up a second mine for us to see.

"Damn," George grunted. "If they'd waited and opened up with these, we'd be dead."

"Yeah, they got a range of two hundred meters."

"Jimmy, go ahead and blow 'em," George said.

"Bring it over here," I shouted to Thach as I carried the mine back to the foxhole and tossed it in. Thach placed the second mine on top of the first; after rolling the wires up, I tossed them and the battery packs into the hole. With everyone clear, I removed a fragmentation hand grenade from my harness, pulled the pin, and held the safety lever tightly.

"Fire in the hole!" I bellowed as I dropped the grenade into the hole and ran in the direction of a nearby tree.

"One, one thousand, two, one thousand, three, one thousand," I counted before hitting the ground behind the tree.

Whoomph. Black smoke poured from the hole. I jumped to my feet and ran to where George was waiting.

"Sanh, have Thach's squad cover for him while he rigs a few Toe Poppers in the clear areas," George directed.

"*Oui*, Trung-si," Sanh agreed before speaking into his HT-1 radio.

I followed George back to the eastern edge of the camp. Once past the first bomb crater, Sanh started lining up the troops. "VC bugged out as soon as they saw you," George said.

"Yeah, movement on their flank spooked 'em."

While waiting for Thach, Kien gave me a cold, stiff hand and showed me a gold wedding band he had removed from it. I dropped it into a hollow tree stump. Five minutes later, Thach's squad made it to the rendezvous point and we headed back to the support site. When we arrived, we found Howard's first platoon and the headquarters section ready to move. At a quick meeting, Gritz informed us that we would be linking up with recon and the second platoon later in the day. We recovered our rucksacks and departed, with the first platoon on point. At noon we crossed a slow-moving stream called the Da-Miehn and stopped to take a break.

As I sat drinking from my canteen, the distant sound of gunfire broke the silence.

"Swamp Fox, this is Fox Four, over," Chilton radioed.

"Fox Four, this is Swamp Fox, over," Gritz responded.

"Swamp Fox, this is Fox Four. Made contact with two Victor Charlie at right 1.5, up 2.7. One VC, KIA; one withdrew south, over."

I pulled out my map and saw that Chilton was a little more than a kilometer to the northeast. We continued southeast and were making good time moving past clumps of bamboo when the column suddenly stopped. It was 1300.

"Got a trail up ahead," George whispered. Seventy-five meters farther on we hit a well-used trail and began following it southeast, a calculated risk on Gritz's part. He was convinced that if we made point contact on the trail, we could outshoot and outmaneuver the enemy. If we overtook an enemy unit moving in the same direction, we would deploy on line and overrun them from the rear. It was a calculated risk.

Three hundred meters down the winding trail, we passed a black-clad Vietcong lying beside it. The side of his head had been blown away, and the ground beneath it was wet with blood and cerebral fluid. He hadn't been dead for more than a few minutes, the likely victim of a British Sten gun.

Moving down the trail at a fast pace, we passed a half-dozen enemy way stations. Each had been cleared of brush and had one or more fire pits. Way stations were maintained by local Vietcong and were used as overnight stops by VC and NVA units when they were on the move. We knew that they were Vietnamese and not Montagnard because three poles had been pushed into the ground and tied together above some of the fire pits. The Vietnamese used the poles to hold their cooking pots when they prepared rice. When Montagnards cooked in the jungle, they filled sections of green bamboo with rice and placed them on a bed of hot coals. The green bamboo wouldn't burn, and its moisture steamed the rice.

"Jarvis booby-trapped a few of the pits," George said as he held the handset to his ear. "Some were used last night."

At 1600 we linked up with recon and the second platoon and then moved back into the jungle. Two hours later we arrived at the bamboo thicket that would serve as our MSS. As soon as we had the Bodes in place, I set up a three-man listening post one hundred meters to the east. When I returned, I found Howard checking the perimeter.

"Hey, Jim, how's it going?" I shook his hand.

"That's Jim 'The Trail Runner' Howard," Jarvis said from behind a nearby tree. "The fastest man in the east."

"Okay, what happened?" I smiled.

They both moved close enough to whisper. "When we were on the trail, Hout spotted a VC moving in the same direction," Jarvis began.

"Hout was on point and I was behind him," Howard added.

"So 'The Trail Runner' here drops his ruck and takes off after him," Jarvis laughed.

"That VC took off like a jackrabbit," Howard confirmed.

"Clyde was the *second* fastest man in Vietnam," Jarvis scoffed.

"He wasn't armed?" I asked.

"He had an AK but didn't use it," Jarvis answered. "Probably panicked when he saw the ugliest man in the world was after him."

"Can't say I blame him," I joked.

"Clyde was fast," Howard shook his head, "but he ran outta gas."

"What happened?" I asked.

"When I caught up with him, I grabbed his collar, he tripped, and we both went flying," Howard explained. "Just as I got to my feet and was about to butt stroke him,

Hout and Jarvis got there, and Hout shot him with his Sten.''

''What!''

''Hey, Hout thinks he saved Howard's life,'' Jarvis protested.

''What could I say?'' shrugged Howard.

Soon afterward, I returned to where George had set up our hammocks. He was kneeling on the ground brewing a cup of tea.

''Gimme your cup,'' he said.

I removed my cup from my ruck, and he half filled it with steaming tea. ''Thanks.''

''We got a prisoner,'' he said. ''Recon picked him up in a base camp. Fang says he's a guide.''

''Donahue.'' I turned and Rinh motioned for me to follow him.

''What's up?''

''Chote is very sick,'' he said as we headed for the perimeter. ''He had diarrhea all day.''

''You see his stool?''

''Yes, it had some blood and mucus.''

''It look like rice water?''

''No.''

''Well, at least it ain't cholera,'' I said.

We found Chote—a teenage rifleman with the second squad—lying in his hammock with a normal saline IV plugged into a vein in his arm. His hair was matted with sweat. I put my hand on his forehead.

''102.8,'' Rinh said.

I pinched the skin on the back of his hand and saw that it had lost much of its elasticity. ''He's dehydrated,'' I observed. ''Good thing you got an IV going.''

Chote leaned his head over the side of the hammock and had a bout of the dry heaves. When he finished gagging I opened his fatigue jacket and checked his stomach. It was distended and felt like a bowling ball. He moaned, and something splashed beneath the hammock.

"I cut a hole in his hammock," Rinh said. "He won't have to get up to shit."

I looked and saw that a round, three-inch hole had been cut beneath Chote's butt. Rinh had also dug a small hole beneath the hammock.

"What do you think?" Rinh asked.

"Without a lab test there's no way of knowing for sure," I said. "Could be bacillary dysentery."

"I gave him paregoric."

"Good, it'll slow his bowel movements."

"Should I put him on tetracycline?"

"Yeah, if it's bacterial, tetracycline will kill it. Put him on Kaopectate. It'll absorb some of the liquid in his intestinal tract. And something for nausea."

"I will stay with him tonight," Rinh said.

"Okay, my friend. You did a great job. Let me know if there's any change in his condition."

By the time I got back to my hammock, only the shadows remained. For the first time, I had mixed feelings about having brought Rinh to the MGF. I knew that as a soldier he would benefit from the experience. But I also knew that if he were killed, the Cambodian people would lose a man of unlimited potential. It was one of life's dilemmas.

At first light Gritz called a meeting of the Americans and informed us that our resupply would be dropped at a nearby clearing at 1300. He also gave us assignments that would keep us busy until the drop. I took Sanh, Rinh, Ly, and Thach's third squad eight hundred meters west to a stream called the Da-R'Naum. We followed it north for a hundred meters and stopped when we discovered a deep, rock-bottomed pool. Above the pool the water sparkled as it cascaded over moss-covered rocks. A steep bank on the far side was covered with ferns and vines, and at its top, large banana plants grew over the edge. Great cypress trees, giant ferns, and tropical flowers grew along our side of the stream.

Members of the "third herd" recover a napalm container on a Drop Zone in War Zone D. Each container was packed with four hundred pounds of food, ammunition, and supplies.

A Cambodian, armed with an M-16 rifle, stands guard over a Vietcong prisoner.

An aerial view of the star-shaped Special Forces camp at Duc-Phong. The end of the runway can be seen to the far right.

At George's suggestion, he and the author pose in a Vietcong base camp in War Zone D.

Silent weapons specialist Danh (*left*) with senior Cambodian medic Rinh.

A Cambodian from the recon platoon is armed with a Soviet 7.62-mm light machine gun and plays the role of a Vietcong during training at Ho-Ngoc-Tao.

Sgt. 1st Class George Ovsak (*left*) and the author oversee training on the rifle range at Ho-Ngoc-Tao. The Cambodian is firing a .30 caliber M-2 carbine.

The "Bodes" undergo training in setting up Claymore mines at Ho-Ngoc-Tao. Sandbags were placed over their heads to simulate nighttime operating conditions.

Capt. Jim Gritz inspects a Cambodian's weapon at Ho-Ngoc-Tao in November 1966.

Staff Sgt. Dale England holds an M-16 rifle with a scope.

Capt. Steve Yedinak leads members of his second platoon.

Staff Sgt. Dick Jarvis stands in a field cleared for slash-and-burn agriculture by local Montagnards.

Rinh (*right front*) accompanies Sgt. 1st Class Al Doyle and other members of the MGF's headquarters section.

Gen. William C. Westmoreland, commander, U.S. Military
Assistance Command, Vietnam, with Colonel Kelly at the
Special Forces compound in Nha-Trang in 1967.

Col. Francis Kelly presents the Army Commendation Medal
to the author in Bien-Hoa following Blackjack-31.

"Let's take a quick bath," I told Sanh as we stood on a large flat rock at the edge of the stream.

Sanh sent one-man patrols to the north, east, and west, and when they returned, we set up a small perimeter.

"Here." I handed Sanh a bar of white surgical soap. "Two at a time. I'm gonna take a shit."

I dug a hole in the soft earth with my heel, then dropped my drawers and squatted. When I finished, I found I was out of C-ration toilet paper. As a substitute, I pulled a few leaves from a nearby plant. I then covered everything with dirt. While pulling up my trousers, I detected movement in the grass a few feet in front of me. A six-foot gray snake was slithering in the direction of the creek.

"Sanh," I whispered, "gimme the machete."

"What is it, Bac-si?" He handed it to me.

"Snake!" I raised my arm to take a swing at it.

"No, Bac-si." He grabbed my arm. The snake's head lifted a couple of feet off the ground; with its hood flared, a golden chest and long white fangs came into view.

"Cobra!" I jumped back to avoid being bitten.

"Do not hurt him," Sanh said.

"What?"

"Bac-si, this is good snake. He close to holy one."

"Who?"

"Buddha, Bac-si," Sanh told me as I watched the snake's every move. "Once Buddha almost drown and cobra lift him above water and save him." He picked up a branch and carefully nudged the snake away from the stream.

I moved back to the flat rock at the edge of the stream. As Rinh and Ly sat combing their wet hair, I removed everything from my pockets. While emptying my breast pocket I discovered the piece of paper I had found on the dead Vietcong in the hut. It was wet with sweat but could still be read.

"This anything important?" I asked Rinh as he sat lacing his boots.

"I don't know the word," he said. "It is when you write words in a beautiful way."

"Poetry?"

"Yes, Donahue. It is poetry."

"Would you translate it for me?"

I removed my boots and lowered my feet into the water. "Ahhh." I quietly slipped into the cool, waist-deep stream and allowed myself to sink to the bottom. Suddenly, I was lost in another world. The cool water pulled at my fatigues as I swam the breaststroke against the current, and colorful minnows drifted downstream. When I couldn't hold my breath any longer I came to the surface. "This is the life."

I removed the bar of soap from the rock and began washing my filthy hair and face. Just the smell of the soap made me feel clean. Looking up I saw a narrow strip of blue sky high above the stream. There, everything that lived seemed to compete for the few rays of sunlight that penetrated to the stream. Creeping vines twisted around the tree trunks as they grew toward the light, and leaf-filled branches reached high over the stream. Butterflies and other insects drifted in and out of the bright shafts; colorful orchids grew where the rays touched the soft moist earth.

"A beautiful place," I remarked in awe as Sanh slipped into the stream next to me.

Only a few feet away sat the radio, and as I unbuttoned my trousers to wash my crotch, it crackled to life.

"Swamp Fox, this is Fox Two," England radioed.

"Fox Two, this is Swamp Fox," Gritz responded.

"Swamp Fox, this is Fox Two. We're at our objective. We've got two structures and fifteen hundred kilos of rice, over."

"That's a lot of rice," I said as I noticed a half-dozen festering sores where leeches had attached themselves to Sanh's back.

"Let me get your back," I said. He turned his back to me and I lathered it with soap.

"Swamp Fox, this is Fox One, over," Howard radioed Gritz.

"Fox One, this is Swamp Fox, over."

"Swamp Fox, this is Fox One. We're in a large base camp at right 3.1, down 0.9. We've got sixteen hooches and, would you believe, a two-story house with blue-and-white-tile floors and a veranda? Someone important must live here."

"Thach, where is that from here?" I asked as he squatted next to the radio.

"Roger, Fox One. Any sign of Clyde? Over," Gritz asked.

"Swamp Fox, this is Fox One. The place is empty, but I'd say there was at least a company here earlier in the day. A few of the hooches are filled with bottles of water, and it looks like they left in a hurry. We left a package for the homeowner, over."

"Roger, Fox One. Swamp Fox, out."

Thach moved to the edge of the stream and used a pen to point to the spot on the map.

"Base camp 350 meter south, Bac-si," he said.

"Wonder where they went?" I said as Sanh washed his armpits.

"Fang tell me prisoner say all VC look for us," he volunteered. His words scared me; I worried they would spook the Bodes.

"A lotta scuttlebutt," I brushed his answer aside as I crawled out of the stream and squatted next to Rinh. While using my scarf to dry my face, I realized how fast moods and situations could change. One minute you could be bathing in a tropical paradise and, a squeeze of the trigger later, lying dead on the bank with a bullet through your head. Death was never more than a heartbeat away.

"Donahue." Rinh handed me his translation; Ly slipped into the stream.

"Let's see what we've got here," I mused, reading aloud what he had written.

There are minutes which build up the history of a
    nation.
    There are deaths which are beginnings.
There are some words which are more exciting than
    songs.
    There are some people who are born from the truth.
Nguyen Van Thoi, you have died.
    But you are still alive in everyone's heart.
Remember my words, Nguyen Van Thoi.

"Bullshit," Thach growled with anger in his voice.

"You gotta admit it's good poetry," I countered.

"Sometimes fish look good to eat," Sanh said as he
crawled out of the water, "but when you cut fish, you see
it rotten. Communism same, Bac-si. When I was Viet-
Minh, Communist Party cadre say after we defeat French,
all people live in peace and freedom. But one day I see I
only free to do what party tell me; I only free to say what
party tell me; and I only free to think what party tell me.
This is not freedom, Bac-si."

"Communist must die," Thach ran his finger across his
throat with a slashing movement.

"Thach, you shoulda been a diplomat," I joked.

"When I was Viet-Minh, cadre kill many Cambodian
because they question party," Sanh said as he dried his
face. "Marx and Lenin promise many thing, but they give
only fear, oppression, and death."

I laced my boots, and at 0945 we departed and followed
the stream north for a few hundred meters. From there we
shot an azimuth back to the MSS and arrived there two
hours later. After recovering our rucksacks from the underbrush we moved the short distance to the Drop Zone:
an oblong clearing that measured 75 by 150 meters.

By 1240 we had security in place and the FAC overhead.
As soon as Gritz had contact with the Skyraiders, the FAC
left the area and began directing an air strike against the

enemy base camp Howard's platoon had discovered a few hours earlier.

Karoumph, karoumph, karoumph. Bombs pounded the enemy base camp as the first Skyraider was making its final approach to the Drop Zone. When the aircraft was overhead, the pilot released the napalm containers on Gritz's radio command and five camouflaged parachutes popped open. Two chutes failed to open and their attached containers slammed into the ground just a few feet from where the captain was standing.

It took us less than thirty minutes to recover and distribute the supplies. We left a stay-behind ambush on the Drop Zone, and the remainder of the company headed east to conduct a bomb damage assessment. When we arrived at the base camp, we found a few dead pigs and what appeared to be a trail of human blood. Most of the structures had been flattened by bombs.

A short distance east of the camp we reached a stream called the Da-Riek. After crossing it, our movement was slowed to a near crawl by thick undergrowth; it took us until nearly 1800 to move the two kilometers to our new support site. It was located in a tangle of vines and leaves a few hundred meters inside the southern border of Phuoc-Long Province.

A still, hot night passed, and on 18 January we were up and moving well before first light. Our order of march: 3-1-2. With Danh leading on point and heavy rucksacks on our backs, we followed an elephant trail under a star-filled sky. We were making good time on the trail, but soon after first light, we had to cut back into the jungle when the trail suddenly turned northeast. A short while later we entered an area of almost impenetrable thorn-covered vines and thick scrub brush. We had to chop, climb, and crawl every inch of the way.

With little overhead cover and a tropical sun beating down on us, we continued to cut our way through the tangle. When we finally reached the high ground that would serve as our MSS, our uniforms were streaked white with dried salt. Once our perimeter was in place we passed salt tablets out to everyone and discovered three Bodes who had to be treated for heat exhaustion.

On the morning of 19 January we departed the support site at 0730. In a single column we moved down into a deep gorge that was thick with trees. At the bottom of a narrow ravine we crossed a fast-moving, waist-deep stream and slowly climbed the far slope. Once on top we began following a ridge line to the south-southeast. Bamboo growing at the higher elevations was relatively thin, making our movement easier.

During the morning hours my entire body started to itch. When we stopped for a midday break I saw that my face, hands, crotch, and butt were covered with poison ivy. I must have grabbed poison ivy leaves when I ran out of toilet paper. It was a mistake I wouldn't make again.

At 1500 the FAC passed overhead and dropped a canvas message bag attached to a red streamer. Three hours later we stopped in a bamboo thicket and set up for the night. As soon as everyone was in position, Gritz called the Americans to the headquarters. I arrived at the same time as Chilton and Cawley. It was the first time I had seen them since Duc-Phong.

"Hey, Jim." Cawley reached to shake my hand but recoiled when he saw its pink color.

"Just calamine lotion," I said. "A good case of poison ivy."

"Sir, I wanted to talk to you about Winh," I addressed Chilton. "He was related to one of the guys in my platoon."

"Everyone feels bad about it." He shook his head.

"What happened?"

"We hit a high-speed trail on the way to a target," he explained. "I didn't want to pass up the opportunity, so I left Winh's section to set up an ambush. We were going to pick them up on the way back."

"They weren't in position more than fifteen minutes when Charlie came rolling down the trail," Cawley said.

"One of the Bodes opened up before they were in the killing zone," chimed in Chilton. "The VC broke contact, swung around, and hit them from the rear."

"The round caused a nasty compound fracture," Cawley continued. "By the time we got there, they'd already overdosed him."

"Okay, fall in," Howard ordered.

With Yedinak on our right, we formed a line in front of Gritz and Howard. "Staff Sergeant Cawley, front and center," Gritz ordered. Cawley stepped out of line and moved to a position a couple of paces in front of Gritz. "A couple of hours ago the FAC dropped a message that Staff Sergeant Cawley has been commissioned a second lieutenant in the United States Army," Gritz smiled, removing two gold bars from his pocket. Howard handed Gritz his Bible.

"Sir," Glossup interrupted, "with Cawley becoming an officer, this might be our last chance to hymn him."

"By God, you're right," Gritz nodded his approval.

Glossup stepped forward and did an about face. "Okay, let's get tuned up." He smiled as he raised his arms like an orchestra conductor.

"Hymmm," everyone joined in as he lowered and then raised his arms.

"Y'all can do a lot better than that. One more time."

"Hymmm," everyone joined in as he lowered and raised his arms a second time.

"Much better," he said. "All together now."

"Hymmm, hymmm, fuck hymmm."

"Now, that's what I call a hymn," Glossup chuckled as he returned to his position in line. I noticed puzzled expressions on the faces of the Bodes who were watching, and I wondered what they might be thinking.

"Now that you've been properly hymned, we can get on with the ceremony," Gritz told Cawley. "Raise your right hand, put your left hand on the Bible, and repeat after me,"

Gritz paused. "I, Joseph J. Cawley, do solemnly swear that I will support and defend the Constitution of the United States against all enemies, foreign and domestic."

Cawley repeated the captain's words.

"That I will bear true faith and allegiance to the same; and that I will obey the orders of the president of the United States and the orders of the officers appointed over me. So help me God."

Cawley again repeated Gritz's words. Gritz then pinned the gold bars on Cawley's collars. "Congratulations! Lieutenant." They exchanged salutes and handshakes.

After Howard dismissed the formation, everyone gathered around Cawley. "Sir," Montgomery snapped the lieutenant his first salute, "you owe me a dollar."

"Hey," Cawley smiled, "I know the tradition, but I'm broke!"

CHAPTER TWELVE

LOWELL GLOSSUP'S RECON SECTION led on point, our order of march: 2-1-3. Moving east through thick secondary growth, we advanced at a slow pace until we stopped for a needed break at 1300. Whump-whump. Two shots fired to the northeast.

"Warning shots," George whispered as we lowered our rucksacks to the ground.

"Yeah, they know we're in the area."

After the break we moved southeast for two hours. Suddenly, the column stopped. "Swamp Fox, this is Fox Four," Glossup called softly over the radio.

"Fox Four, this is Swamp Fox, over," Gritz responded.

"Swamp Fox, this is Fox Four. We've got voices up ahead. They're moving in our direction, over."

"Roger, Four. I'm advancing to your position."

While George continued to monitor the radio, I moved down the line and signaled for everyone to remain silent. Whump-whump-whump. Whack-whack-whack. A volley of heavy fire erupted a short distance ahead. I ran back to where George was standing.

"VC broke contact," he said.

"How many?"

"Don't know. Made contact with their point element."

"Any casualties?"

"Killed one, wounded one. No friendlies."

George continued to monitor the radio. "Picked up a few Montagnards," he said. "Two men, three women, and two kids. They may be VC guides."

"Any info on the VC?" I asked.

"Locals," he said. "Mixed black, blue, and khaki uniforms."

After the column began moving again, we soon passed Glossup and a few Bodes waiting at the point of contact—a north-south trail. Once everyone was across, Glossup would set up a stay-behind ambush and remain there until we were out of the area.

We continued east until we reached a bamboo thicket at 1700. "We're there," George announced. When we arrived at headquarters, Doyle was sitting on a fallen tree talking to the two male captives, both of whom wore loincloths. Doyle spoke some Montagnard and appeared to be striking up an amiable relationship with them.

"Hey, Doyle. Where were they headed?" I asked.

"Northeast to the Dong-Nai River. They say there's beaucoup VC up that way."

"Third platoon." Kindoll pointed to the southeast. "One hundred twenty to 240 degrees."

While Sanh and George put everyone in position, I took six Bodes on a water run to a nearby stream. By the time I got back, it was almost dark. That night George, Sanh, and I sat on the ground chatting quietly.

"The Yards told Doyle we're between two major VC base areas," George said. "One's a day and a half south; the other's two days to the northeast."

"You mean the Dong-Nai River valley?" I asked.

"Yeah."

"Many VC there," Sanh said.

"I've heard a lot of bad stories about that area," George confirmed. "ARVN won't go near it."

"If soldier go Dong-Nai, he die." Sanh said.

"Did you find out where we're headed?" I asked.

"Northeast to the Dong-Nai River," answered George.

That night I lay in my hammock thinking about the Dong-Nai and the days to come. As long as we remained mobile and avoided decisive engagements, we had a chance. If we allowed the enemy to find and fix us, however, he would surely destroy us with his superior forces. The more I thought about it, the more I realized that we—not the enemy—would be the masters of our destiny.

At 0700 on the morning of 21 January, Captain Gritz sent two recon sections to set up an ambush on a trail that ran along the edge of the nearby Drop Zone. Cawley's section set up north of the zone, Chilton's to the south. They were in position for about an hour when the radio came to life.

"Swamp Fox, this is Fox Four. Got a blue uniform moving north on the trail. Maybe . . ."

Whump. Whack-whack-whack. There was a long minute of radio silence.

"Swamp Fox, this is Fox Four. VC broke contact and withdrew south. Negative casualties," Chilton reported.

We moved a couple hundred meters east to the Drop Zone at 0900. It measured fifty by two hundred meters and was surrounded by bamboo and trees fifty feet high. A shallow creek ran along its length. The north-south trail ran just inside the wood line on the western side of the clearing, and the third platoon set up security along the trail.

While we waited for the resupply drop scheduled for 1000, Jarvis positioned two captured VC rucksacks on the trail and booby-trapped them. One rucksack was attached to a pull detonating device on a Claymore mine. He also buried an M-14 Toe Popper mine on the trail in front of the second rucksack. Once the booby traps were rigged, George and I moved a short distance up the trail and Jarvis returned to his platoon.

Whoomph. An explosion from the area of the booby-trapped rucksacks scared the hell out of me. George, Rinh, and I ran to see what had happened. We found Kien lying on the trail twisting in pain. Rinh and I knelt at his side and saw that the toe section of one of his Bata boots had been blown away.

"Shit! He stepped on the damned Toe Popper," I told Rinh.

"*Putho!*" Kien swore, as George used his radio to brief Gritz on the situation.

"Wasn't he told about the booby traps?" I asked Rinh as he unzipped our M-5 medical kit.

"He says he wanted the bearskin." Rinh pointed to a rolled-up black animal skin that was tied to the top of one of the rucksacks. "He knew about the Claymore but not the other mine."

To the west I heard the engine of a Skyraider making its approach to the Drop Zone.

"Should I give him morphine?" Rinh asked as Montgomery arrived.

"Yeah," I said, "load him up on penicillin and streptomycin."

"What happened?" Montgomery panted.

"Stepped on a Toe Popper," I explained as Rinh injected morphine into Kien's leg and then attached the empty syrette to his collar.

"Jim," George stood with the handset pressed to his ear, "we'll have a chopper on the ground in twenty minutes. Kien and the women and kids are going out."

"Great," I said, "I was wondering how we were gonna get them out."

"What about the two men?" Montgomery asked.

"They're gonna guide us up to the Dong-Nai," George replied.

As Montgomery used scissors to cut through the top of the boot, Kien said something to Rinh.

"What's he want?" I asked.

''His cigar.'' Rinh looked around and found it lying on the trail a few feet away.

Montgomery and I carefully peeled the boot away from his bloody foot and found that his big toe and the one next to it had been blown off. His center toe was mangled and was hanging by a piece of skin. While Kien chomped on his cigar, Montgomery snipped the piece of skin and tossed the toe over his shoulder. Looking closer, I saw that most of the bleeding was coming from a severed blood vessel. I removed a forceps from the medical kit and clamped it to the end while Montgomery tied a piece of black silk suture thread around the vessel. Once the serious bleeding had been stopped, I held Kien's foot while Montgomery placed pieces of sterile gauze over the wound. Rinh then wrapped the foot tight with an Ace bandage.

''He says his balls hurt very much,'' Rinh interjected.

Montgomery cut Kien's pant leg up to his crotch; we saw that his genital area had been peppered by small pieces of shrapnel. ''Nothing serious,'' Montgomery assured him.

''He wants to know if the hospital will remove his balls?'' Rinh said. ''He says the Vietnamese doctors do not like Cambodians.''

''No,'' I laughed. ''In a couple of weeks he'll be back in Cambode alley chasing women and raising hell.''

''Good, Bac-si,'' Kien smiled. Just then, Gritz and Doyle came down the trail from the north.

''Chopper will be on the ground in five minutes,'' Gritz advised. ''Jimmy, ain't that the guy who got hit on the black box operation?''

''Yes, sir. That's him.''

''Bring him up with the others,'' Gritz said before he and Doyle turned and headed back up the trail.

While Montgomery filled out a med-evac card and attached it to Kien's jacket, Sanh brought George, Ly, Rinh, and me our sandbags of food. To the west I heard the wap, wap, wap of the approaching chopper.

We carried Kien thirty meters up the trail and placed him

on the ground next to where Gritz and Doyle were standing just inside the clearing. Doyle had popped a yellow smoke grenade; Kindoll and Fang were waiting in the wood line with the Montagnards.

Looking north, I saw the green hull of the chopper silhouetted against the clear blue sky. "Kien." I squatted and handed him some money. "Here's a couple thousand piasters."

"Thank you, Bac-si."

Seconds later the nose of the chopper rose slightly and, with the blades slapping the humid air, it rocked as it touched down in the tall grass. Using our arms to protect our eyes from the blowing grass, we carried Kien through the swirling yellow smoke.

"Hurry," the door gunner yelled over the noise.

When we reached the chopper we lifted Kien to its honeycombed aluminum floor. Looking through the cabin, I saw Gritz, Kindoll, and Doyle helping the Montagnards in from the other side. They appeared terrified.

"This one goes to Cong-Hoa Hospital in Saigon," I yelled to the door gunner.

"Good-bye, Bac-si." Kien shook my hand and grabbed me around my neck.

"Take care, my friend."

We ran back to the wood line. Looking over my shoulder, I saw a steady stream of black fumes pouring from the chopper's engine. While it hovered a few feet off the ground, Kien flashed a "V" with one hand and held up the bearskin with the other. He was chomping on his cigar and wore an ear-to-ear grin.

"He's got that damned bearskin," remarked George, shaking his head as the chopper tilted, transitioned to forward flight, and climbed across the clearing.

We finished distributing the supplies and returned to the MSS. Because of the activities and noise on the Drop Zone, Gritz decided to move eight hundred meters east to a new location. We arrived at the bamboo thicket at 1200, and during a meeting with the Americans, Gritz gave us our patrol assignments.

George and I were to take our first squad one thousand meters northeast to a stream called the Da-Bao. Our movement toward the objective was slowed when we hit a swamp. It took us nearly an hour to find a way where the water wasn't over our heads. When we finally reached the Da-Bao we began following it south.

Whack-whack-whack. Whump-whump-whump. An exchange of fire to the north. We continued to skirt the stream to the south, and ten minutes later George closed the gap between us.

"Yedinak made contact with at least a squad," George told me.

"Any casualties?"

Whack-whack-whack. Poing . . . whumph. Whack-whack-whack. Another intense exchange to the north. George and I stopped to monitor radio transmissions.

"Swamp Fox, this is Fox Two, over." Yedinak was out of breath.

"Fox Two, this is Swamp Fox, over."

"Swamp Fox, this is Fox Two. Caught up with them at a way station," Yedinak reported. "Five VC KIA, weapons and equipment CIA [captured in action], negative friendlies, over."

"Roger, Two. Are you in need of assistance? Over."

"That's a negative, Swamp Fox. Fox Two, out."

We shot a 270-degree azimuth back to our support site, and at 1800 we arrived at headquarters. There we found England and Yedinak standing at the base of a great cypress tree talking to Gritz and Kindoll. Lying on the ground next to them was a pile of Vietcong equipment.

"Jim," Kindoll stopped me, "wanna show you something."

"What d'ya got?" I asked as George headed for the perimeter.

Kindoll reached into his pocket and pulled out a black-

and-white photograph of two enemy soldiers holding a Vietcong flag between them.

"England picked it up in a way station. Kimh Ly says the guy on the right's with the Mike Force."

"A VC in the Mike Force?"

"Kimh says he got to know the guy when we were in Bien-Hoa."

"Hate to be him when Old Snake and the Chinamen find out," I shook my head. When I finished talking to Kindoll, I moved to the perimeter and found George standing next to his hammock drinking from a canteen.

"Cut my foot with the machete." He pointed to his right boot. I looked down and saw skin through a slit in the leather.

"Let's take a look." He sat in his hammock and unlaced the boot. I knelt and pulled it from his foot. "Damn." His foot was red with blood and the toe area black with dirt that had entered through the opening. There was a deep incision between his first and second toe. "When did you do this?"

"Right after the drop," he said as Rinh returned and began stringing his hammock.

"What! Why the hell didn't you say something?"

"Didn't want to slow us down."

Rinh placed the M-5 medical kit on the ground to my right and examined George's foot. "It will need stitches," Rinh said as he squatted and unzipped the kit.

"I don't know if you're gonna be able to stay out here with this," I said. "Good chance it'll get infected."

"Let's see what happens."

I cleaned the wound with a fifty-fifty mixture of Phisohex (liquid surgical soap) and hydrogen peroxide and deadened the area with injections of lidocaine hydrochloride. While George used his fingers to keep his toes spread wide, I closed the gash with six stitches.

"That should do it," I said as I covered the stitches with

a piece of sterile gauze. "Rinh, go ahead and load him up with procaine penicillin and streptomycin."

"Feels good," George said as I covered the gauze with a strip of surgical tape.

"We'll see how it looks in the morning," I said. "If it swells up, you may have a problem getting your boot on."

"I'll get it on," he said.

Whoomph. An explosion boomed far to the north.

"Look," I said. "Under ideal conditions this would take a week to heal. You've gotta keep off your feet as much as possible and try to keep it dry."

"No problem," George asserted as Rinh reassembled the suture set and put it back in the medical kit.

With the last light of day quickly fading, I strung my hammock, positioned my gear for the night, and wiped down my M-16. By the time I finished applying mosquito repellent to the exposed parts of my skin, only shadows remained. I had the first watch so I removed a bag of instant rice and dried carrots from my rucksack.

"Jim," George whispered, "Glossup and I wear the same size. I'll trade boots with him so the dirt won't get in."

"Good idea. Let me know if you need anything for pain."

"I'm fine, buddy. See you in the morning."

I sat eating my rice and listening to the sounds of the night. Within a few feet of my hammock I could hear the buzzing of mosquitoes, the chirping of crickets, and the croaking of a frog. Outside the perimeter something was making "hoot" sounds, and from a distance came an occasional scream, grunt, or cry. The jungle never slept.

CHAPTER THIRTEEN

0900, 22 JANUARY 1967

A FLASH OF LIGHTNING lit the area beneath the canopy, and thunder rumbled across a steel-gray sky. It had been raining since first light, and we were moving east through thick undergrowth. Our order of march: 2-3-1.

Whoomph. A distant explosion muffled by the rain. Using a compass I took an azimuth on the explosion. "Twenty degrees," I told George as we continued to push through large dripping leaves and wet vines. I had been cold, but with the heavy rucksack on my back, I was beginning to sweat. The drenching rain suddenly felt cool and refreshing.

"Cawley's on the radio," George whispered from behind me. "They killed two VC on a trail. They're thirty-two hundred meters north-northeast."

George had a plastic, indigenous meal bag over the radio handset to protect it from the rain, and it was difficult to hear what was being said.

Lightning cracked against a nearby tree, and a large branch creaked before crashing to the ground. I turned to George. "Everyone take the electric blasting caps outta their Claymores?" I was concerned that lightning might detonate them.

"Yeah."

At 1200 we came upon a gravel streambed and began following it to the northeast. Both sides of the rocky bottom were packed tight with leaves, ferns, and vines, and it reminded me of a walkway through a botanical garden. After following it for a thousand meters, we cut back into the jungle and headed north through thick undergrowth. It was almost 1500 when we stopped. While standing among waist-high ferns, I noticed some of the strangest trees I had ever seen. They grew at such odd angles, their gnarled trunks appeared ready to fall to the ground. At their higher elevations they disappeared into a thick mist. "The leaning trees of Pisa," George joked while waiting to move.

With the rain coming down heavier than ever and thunder rumbling overhead, we received word that we had reached our MSS. When we arrived at headquarters, Kindoll assigned us our sector of the perimeter. Once we had the Bodes in position and tied in with the other platoons, we found a spot where we would set up our hammocks for the night. While George, Rinh, Ly, Danh, and I strung our ponchos, Sanh led a patrol to the west.

"How's that foot doing?" I asked George as I tied my hammock beneath an outstretched poncho.

"Feels good." He sat in his hammock and began unlacing his boot as large drops drummed on the poncho above his head.

"Rinh," I called, ducking under George's poncho, "bring the M-5 kit over here."

When George pulled off his boot, I saw that his dressing was wet, but clean. Kneeling on the soft ground in front of him, I carefully removed the tape from between his toes.

"Looks good," I said as Rinh came in under the poncho and placed the medical kit at George's feet.

"Do you want me to clean it?" Rinh asked.

"Yeah, clean it up with some hydrogen peroxide and put on a clean dressing." While Rinh worked on George's foot I took two plastic bags of dehydrated rice and poured in some C-ration cocoa. Before adding water to the bags I shook them up.

"How's Chote's diarrhea?" I asked Rinh as I tied rubberbands around the tops of the plastic bags and placed them on the ground next to me.

"The diarrhea has stopped," Rinh reported as the hydrogen peroxide bubbled when it came in contact with George's wound.

"Gimme your cup," I said to George. He reached under his hammock and removed it from his rucksack.

"Here you go."

"Nothing like rainwater." I filled both canteen cups with water that was cascading from the edge of the poncho. Using my finger, I then dug a six-inch trench in the wet ground and broke off a couple of small pieces from my block of C-4. I put a small piece of the explosive material at each end of the hole and lit them with a match. When I was sure that they were both burning, I placed the canteen cups over them and added a teabag to each cup.

"Hey, Jimmy," George kidded, "I'm gonna order a couple of pizzas. What do you want on yours?"

"Double cheese and pepperoni." I used a twig to stir the tea.

"You like pizza?" George asked Sanh.

"I like hot dog, French fry, and Pepsi-Cola," he grinned.

"There's a place in Saigon where you can get pizza," I said.

"There is?"

"Yeah, but they use sliced hot dogs instead of pepperoni. What are you grinning about?"

"Every time I think about that damned Kien I have to laugh." George rested his head on his hand.

"You mean the bearskin?"

"Yeah. Can't figure how that turkey got it on the chopper."

"Old Kien's a little light-fingered," I laughed.

"He is KKK," Rinh explained as he prepared injections

of penicillin and streptomycin. "Some were bandits before they came to Ho-Ngoc-Tao."

"What was he?" George asked.

"Khmer Kampuchea Krom," Rinh continued. "Kampuchea Krom is the part of Vietnam you call the Mekong Delta. To the French it was Cochinchina, and to us it is Kampuchea Krom, or lower Cambodia. The KKK want the Vietnamese to return Kampuchea Krom to Cambodia."

"Yeah, I remember Sanh telling us how the Delta used to be part of Cambodia," George recalled.

"Kampuchea Krom was part of the Khmer empire until the Vietnamese invaded our country during the 1600s." Rinh finished preparing the syringes. "Ovsak, roll on your side."

"I can understand why there are hard feelings."

"Yes, the Vietnamese are the real imperialists." Rinh wiped a section of George's rear end with an alcohol-soaked gauze. "They took our land and treat us badly. They look down on us just as the Chinese look down on them."

"You guys look more sturdy than the Vietnamese," George reflected as Rinh injected the penicillin into his buttock.

"Yes, also many cultural differences. Cambodia was influenced by India and the Vietnamese by China."

"How many KKK are in the company?" George asked as Rinh injected the streptomycin.

"Only a few. Most are Khmer-Serei, or what you call Free Cambodians."

"They're the ones who wanna kick Sihanouk outta Cambodia?" George pulled up his trousers.

"Yes," Rinh replied, "the rest are *Chams*. They are Muslims who believe in Allah."

"How did we get Muslims in Vietnam?" I tested the tea and smacked my lips.

"Over a thousand years ago Muslim traders sailed to Vietnam," Rinh recounted while zipping the medical kit.

"They converted many people to Islam and formed the empire of Champa."

"Tea's ready," I said as Sanh returned from the patrol and squatted next to his rucksack.

"Get your cup." George motioned for Sanh to join us.

"LP one hundred meter at 270 degree." He squatted near the foot of George's hammock.

"Got commo with them?" George asked.

"*Oui*, Trung-si." Sanh used a green towel to dry his face and the HT-1 radio. I poured some steaming tea into their cups.

"Thank you, Bac-si." Sanh smiled before taking a sip. "When it rain, the tea is good."

I reached out into the rain and pulled four large leaves from a branch. After placing them on the ground, I poured equal portions of cocoa-flavored rice onto each of them. "Here you go." I passed them their meals.

Large drops continued to drum on the poncho above our heads while we sat eating rice with our fingers. Sanh removed a small brown bottle from his pocket.

"You want sauce on rice?" he asked.

"Fish and cocoa?" I questioned the combination.

Sanh reached over and pulled the hair on my chin. "American have too much hair," he smiled.

"Yeah, we look like the Smokey Mountain Boys," I laughed. As we enjoyed the rice, and each other's company, the rain stopped and the mist glowed a dull shade of red as the sun sank slowly into Cambodia. After dinner we field-stripped our M-16s and ran a few patches through the bores before wiping down each part with a thin coat of oil. When we finished with our weapons, Sanh and I made a quick check of the perimeter. It was lined with shiny wet ponchos, under which the Bodes sat in groups of two or three eating or cleaning their weapons. On the highest branches of the trees to the west of our camp sat dozens of monkeys silhouetted against the crimson evening sky.

At 0815 on 23 January we broke camp and headed north

through an emerald forest and fresh morning mist. Everything was wet from the rain and alive with the singing of
birds and the tapping of woodpeckers. On the branches
above our heads, small black monkeys with white beards
and flesh-colored faces sat eating leaves—they appeared
almost human.

Six hours and two thousand meters to the north later we
hit the north-south trail again. It formed a tunnel as it cut
through thick foliage and triple canopy, and its hard-packed
surface was crowded with leeches an inch long. If we
stopped for more than a few seconds, our body heat at-
tracted the bloodsuckers like ants to sugar. Moving at a fast
pace, we followed the trail north; at 1700 we passed Glossup and his recon section setting up a stay-behind Claymore
ambush along the trail. After thirty minutes we cut back
into the jungle and moved to a wooded ridge line two hundred meters east of the trail. It would serve as our support
site.

As soon as our perimeter was in place, Gritz sent Chilton's and Cawley's recon sections on missions to the north.
I took a patrol nine hundred meters west to a stream called
the Bo-Dao, and by the time I returned it was almost dark.

At first light on 24 January, Gritz assigned missions to
each of the platoons and cautioned us that he anticipated
increased enemy activity as we neared the Dong-Nai River.

Whoomph. The morning calm was broken by an explosion to the southwest. The captain also told us that if we
made contact with a large enemy force and were split up,
the Air Force would make an emergency resupply drop of
ammunition and supplies at coordinates 520 697—a clearing forty-seven hundred meters southeast of our location.

When Gritz finished, Sanh and I departed with the second squad. Our mission: to patrol two and a half kilometers
southeast to a stream called the Da-Bitt. Danh led on point;
I followed, and Ly came behind, with the radio. Behind Ly
were Sanh and the remainder of the patrol. George remained in camp. At 0900 we were slipping and sliding

downhill through thick underbrush and soft mud when England radioed Gritz that they were in a company-size base camp two kilometers southwest of our location.

"Many VC this area," Sanh whispered from behind me. At the bottom of the hill we hit a still stream. The smooth water reflected banana leaves and palm fronds like a large mirror. In the shallows along both banks, long-legged blue birds stabbed at insects; just above the water, colorful dragonflies drifted like small helicopters. We followed the stream south for a short distance and stopped when we found a board extending from one bank to the other. In the middle of the stream the board was supported by a pile of rocks. It looked sturdy, so I motioned for Danh to move across.

"*Chop!*" Sanh yelled for Danh to stop. He pointed to three pieces of red twine hanging from a branch above the bridge. "This is warning," he said.

"A warning?"

"Yes, Bac-si. To VC, three string mean danger. Maybe booby trap."

"Danh, check out the other side," I ordered. He quietly slid into the knee-deep water, and an expanding circle of ripples spread to the other side. Once on the far bank, he disappeared into the foliage. As Sanh set up security on our side of the stream, I detected the engine drone of the FAC to the northeast.

"No VC," Danh hissed from across the stream. "Trail go east."

"Stay there while we check this out," I said. He nodded and moved a few meters into the jungle. As soon as he was in position, Sanh slipped into the water and checked out the bank under the board. "See anything?" I asked.

"No, Bac-si." I followed him into the stream. When we reached the pile of rocks at the center, he stopped to examine them. A long-legged black insect with bulging eyes stood on the board watching our every move. "Booby trap," he whispered.

He carefully removed a few rocks from the top of the pile. "What d'ya got?" I looked closer. An inch under the board I saw what looked like the top of a brass 105-mm Howitzer artillery shell. Sticking out of its top was part of an olive-drab detonator. The area around the detonator had been waterproofed with tar. My knees suddenly felt weak when I realized what would have happened if Danh had stepped on the board.

"American 105 with Russian MV-5 detonator," Sanh whispered. "If soldier walk on board, it hit detonator and everyone die."

"For an old fart, you do good work," I smiled.

"We blow it?" he asked.

"No, leave it." As he replaced the rocks, I moved to the far bank. Hanging above the board I found another three pieces of red twine. I untied them and signaled Ly to do the same on the other side. There weren't going to be any friendly troops in the area; with the warnings removed, the VC might just use the bridge. When Sanh finished, the remainder of the squad crossed the stream and we continued moving southwest.

"Swamp Fox, this is Fox Two, over." It was England.

"Fox Two, this is Swamp Fox, over," Gritz responded.

"Swamp Fox, this is Fox Two. We're at the way station we hit yesterday. Someone stepped on two of our Toe Poppers and left two rucks, over."

"Roger, Two. Any signs of the owners? Over."

"That's a negative, Swamp Fox. But the place smells of death. Both mines were wrapped with det [detonating] cord, so they did a job on whoever stepped on them, over."

"Roger, Two . . ."

"Swamp Fox, this is Fox Two. We've got voices up ahead." The radio went silent.

"They're three and a half klicks southeast of the MSS," I said to Sanh as I used a grease pencil to mark their location on my map.

A few minutes past noon we hit the Da-Bitt. The stream

measured a good ten meters across, and its deep, swiftly moving waters were too hazardous to cross. We took turns crawling down its steep bank to fill our canteens, and as I filled mine, a dozen large birds with white wings floated by on the current. We followed the bank north for a short distance; at 1230 we stopped in a bamboo thicket. Before taking our midday break I sent out short one-man patrols. A few minutes later Danh ran back to where Sanh and I were waiting.

"VC house," he said. Sanh asked him a few questions.

"No VC," Sanh relayed.

"Okay, let's check it out." We continued along the bank for fifty meters and stopped when we smelled wood smoke and spotted a thatch hut in the sunlight near the edge of the stream. To its right a double-rope bridge was tied to trees on both sides of the stream.

I extended both arms parallel to the ground and the squad quickly deployed on line. With everyone spread out, I gave the signal to move forward. In front of the shelter we found a smoldering fire pit and a gutted deer hanging from a branch. To the left of the hut a thatch lean-to was piled high with firewood.

"Check the hut," I told Sanh. As Ly and I waited, Sanh entered the hut. A few seconds later, he came out.

"Maybe one squad live here," he said. We moved to the rear of the hut and found a bamboo rice bin and a large fishing net hanging from a branch.

"Get security in place and don't touch anything," I told Sanh. He spread the squad out in a large circle and sent Danh across the bridge to check out the other side. We wanted to make sure we weren't on the edge of a base camp.

Suddenly, an exchange of fire erupted to the northwest. A minute later, Chilton radioed Gritz that his section had killed a Vietcong two and a half kilometers north of our location.

"Many VC," Sanh whispered as I marked the location on my map.

"I wish you'd quit reminding me," I joked.

"How far Song Dong-Nai?" he asked.

"Seven or eight klicks."

"I think this security unit for VC who live by Dong-Nai," he speculated.

Danh appeared at the far side of the rope and signaled the all clear. Sanh, Ly, and I entered the hut. It contained a half-dozen sleeping mats, food, clothes, and a couple of canvas rucksacks. On one of the mats was a teak chess-board with hand-carved pieces. The players had stopped in the middle of a game.

"NVA." Sanh picked up a khaki belt with a brass buckle.

"You're probably right about a security unit operating outta here," I concurred as we left the hut and moved to the rice bin. A volley of automatic fire erupted to the east and Ly handed me the radio handset.

"Sidewinder, this is Fox Two, over." Yedinak sounded excited.

"Fox Two, this is Sidewinder, over." The FAC responded.

"Sidewinder, this is Fox Two. Made contact at left 0.2, up 1.5. We counted twelve. There may be more. They were digging graves in the clearing just up the hill from the way station. We're getting heavy fire from the north side of the clearing. Can you get us some air? Over."

"Must've been the voices England heard," I said to Ly. He nodded, but I don't think he understood.

"That's a can do, Fox Two," the FAC replied. "I'm in contact with a flight of fast movers looking to dump unexpended ordnance. I'll have them on target in three to five minutes, over."

"Roger, Sidewinder. We're in the woods at the south end of the clearing. Do you need smoke? Over."

"Negative, Fox Two. I see you. I'll give y'all some support until the F-4s get here."

"You got any grenades rigged for instant detonation?" I asked Sanh.

"I have three."

"Gimme one. You rig the wood pile and the hut; I'll take care of the rice bin." With any luck, three well-placed grenade booby traps would kill or wound everyone living in the hut. Sanh handed me a grenade before leaving.

"Fox Two, this is Sidewinder," the FAC radioed Yedinak. "I see four bad guys just inside the wood line at the north end of the clearing." A confused roar of AKs, M-16s, and explosions resounded through the jungle.

"Fox Two, this is Swamp Fox," Gritz radioed. "Give me a sit rep [situation report], over."

"Swamp Fox, this is Fox Two," Yedinak answered. "Our FAC's dropping grenades and firing out his window, over."

"Roger, Fox Two. You asked for air support," Gritz laughed. "Swamp Fox, out."

The bamboo bin had a hinged lid, was lined with clear plastic, and was half full of rice. "Ly, get the green tape from Sanh." He left and returned a minute later with the tape. Leaning into the bin, I pulled the plastic lining from the bamboo. I then taped the grenade to the bamboo just above the level of the rice. In the distance I could hear the jet engines of the approaching F-4s. As I worked, the radio came to life, and Ly held the handset close to my ear.

"Fox Two, this is Sidewinder. Y'all can give me smoke now."

"Roger, Sidewinder," Yedinak responded. "You've got red smoke ten meters north of our position, over."

"Roger, Fox Two. I see it. We've got heavy ordnance coming your way. Suggest y'all get down."

"Swamp Fox, this is Fox Four, over." It was Chilton.

Having taped the grenade to the wall of the bin, I straightened the bent ends of the safety pin.

"Fox Four, this is Swamp Fox, over." Gritz responded.

"Swamp Fox, this is Fox Four. We found an ID on the VC we killed on the trail. He was NVA political cadre, over."

"Roger, Four. Swamp Fox, out." A chain of bombs exploded to the east, and seconds later a jet screamed over our position.

"Sidewinder, this is Fox Two. You're right on target, over."

"Roger, Fox Two. Twenty Mike Mike on the way." Seconds later, a second jet streaked over the target with its 20-mm cannons screeching.

"Fox Two, this is Sidewinder. That's all we have. Do you need more air? Over."

"Negative, Sidewinder. We're moving forward. You made our day. Fox Two, out."

I removed a section of fine wire from my pocket and tied one end to the grenade's pull ring. Carefully moving the pin up and down, I made sure it would easily slip out if the wire was pulled. I then tore the plastic from the inside of the lid and lowered it until it rested on my arms. Running the wire around one of the sections of bamboo, I took up the slack in the wire and tied a knot. With everything set, I slowly slid both of my arms out of the bin. If someone lifted the lid, the wire would pull the pin from the TNT-filled grenade and it would instantly explode.

As I reached to pick up my M-16, I found something crawling on my lower arm—a six-inch green centipede. "Damn." I brushed it off with my hand and stomped it into the mud. I was lucky it hadn't stung me: the venom of a large centipede could be deadly. Before leaving I scooped up some mud with my finger. As I used it to camouflage the section of wire I had tied around the bamboo, Yedinak radioed that his platoon had killed five Vietcong.

Ly and I returned to the front of the hut and found Sanh sitting on the floor. His black beret was lying on the ground in front of him; in it were a few rounds of ammunition.

"Grenáde under rucksack." He pointed to a canvas rucksack in the corner. "Other grenade in wood pile."

"You need any help?"

"No, I have one more." I watched Sanh use a pair of pliers to pull a white-tipped bullet from its brass casing. As he poured the powder from the casing into his beret, the radio crackled in the background.

"Swamp Fox, this is Sidewinder," the FAC radioed Gritz. "Got two blue uniforms moving northeast at left 1.4, up 0.3. Also spotted fresh graves where we put in the strike on the twentieth, over."

"Roger, Sidewinder. Will move to intercept. Thank you for the intel. Swamp Fox, out."

Once the powder was removed from the shell, Sanh replaced it with a section of detonating cord. He then used the pliers to carefully push the bullet back into the shell casing. "That ball ammo?" I asked.

"*Oui*, Bac-si. Chinese 7.62 millimeter," he said. "White is ball, and red or black is armor piercing." He rose to his feet and returned the ammunition to a galvanized metal ammunition can. If the rounds were fired, they would explode and kill or wound the person firing the weapon. I reached down, removed the black queen from the chessboard, and placed it with a half-dozen other pieces at the side of the board.

"This'll really piss someone off. Let's get outta here."

As soon as Danh was back across the rope bridge, we continued north for three hundred meters and stopped to booby-trap our back trail before shooting an azimuth back to camp. We arrived at 1530. It was a beautiful, sunny afternoon, and I was relieved to find George lying in his hammock with his boot off. "You've got the life."

"Hey, Jim. Glad you made it back," George said as Sanh and I leaned our rifles against a tree at the foot of his hammock.

"Let me see your foot." I lifted the dressing and was

pleased to see that there wasn't any discharge. "Healing nicely."

"Some bad news." He sat up in his hammock. "The prisoners tried to escape. They're both dead."

"Damn, that means we're going to the Dong-Nai without guides."

The last of the patrols returned at 1600, and a few minutes later we departed and followed the ridge line to the northeast. Our order of march: 1-2-3. As we moved along the ridge, the jungle thinned and we were soon moving downhill past clumps of bamboo. At the bottom of the hill we hit flat ground and scrub brush; at 1845 we linked up with recon and set up our MSS on a section of high ground near the edge of a swamp.

CHAPTER FOURTEEN

0800, 25 JANUARY 1967

WE BROKE CAMP AND headed northeast to receive our scheduled mid-morning resupply drop. Thirty minutes later we arrived at a clearing that at one time had been swampland. It was a good two hundred meters across and was littered with rotting stumps and fallen trees. The earth around many of the perimeter trees was so eroded that the roots were left high and dry. They looked like giant spider legs holding up the trees.

The third platoon set up security just inside the wood line along the northwest side of the clearing, and once everyone was in place, George asked Sanh and me to take out a patrol. We grabbed Binh and Ly and two other Bodes and in a single column moved up a tree-laden hill to the northwest. The foliage near the ground was relatively thin, and we could see thirty to fifty meters in all directions. With Binh leading on point, and high ground to our front and right, we quickly neared the top of the hill.

Whump-whump-whump. A round whistled by my right ear and thumped into a tree trunk. It couldn't have missed by more than an inch. Whack-whack-whack. Binh returned fire and hit the ground. I ran forward to his position and spotted two Vietcong in black firing at us from fifty meters ahead.

I returned a burst and saw one of them fall before I hit the ground next to Binh. Because of the waist-deep grass, I couldn't see anything from my prone position. By the time I got to my knees, both Vietcong had disappeared. I fired the remainder of my magazine into the area where I had last seen them.

"How many you see?" I yelled to Binh as the remainder of the patrol deployed on line.

"Two, Bac-si."

I considered advancing to where the Vietcong had disappeared but decided against it. In relatively open terrain, two men could easily kill the six of us. "Move to the high ground," I said to Binh while pointing to our right front. With Binh leading the way, we ran to the top of the hill.

"I hit one," I said to Sanh as we ran. "We'll flank 'em."

"*Oui,* Bac-si," he panted.

Thirty meters down the reverse slope of the hill, I stopped. The underbrush was much thicker than it had been on the other side. In between the trees the ground was thick with scrub brush and ferns that grew waist high. "Sanh, spread 'em out. Whoever makes contact will lay down a base of fire." He nodded. "I only saw two, but there could be more," I continued. "If we get into deep shit, we'll RV back at the MSS." I motioned for Ly to give me the handset.

"Swamp Fox, this is Fox Three, over," I radioed Gritz.

"Fox Three, this is Swamp Fox, over."

"Swamp Fox, this is Fox Three. Made contact with two VC. One WIA, both withdrew northwest. We're in pursuit, over."

"Roger, Three. Let me know if you need assistance. Swamp Fox, out."

As soon as Sanh had the Bodes briefed, we spread out and began moving in the direction I thought the enemy might be. Our advancing line extended over fifty meters, and with one of the Vietcong wounded, I felt we had a good chance of finding them. Glancing twenty meters to my right I saw Binh creeping forward; thirty meters to my left Sanh advanced with his M-16 at the ready.

Whump. Whack-whack-whack. An exchange of rifle fire to my left front. A rush of adrenaline surged into my system, and I saw Sanh firing from behind a tree. By the sound of the fire I judged the enemy to be a short distance downhill from Sanh. It sounded like only one of the VC soldiers was returning fire.

Binh, Ly, and I continued downhill and stopped after having moved another thirty meters. I dropped to one knee and pointed in the direction of the enemy. Ly was to my left and Binh to my right. We moved toward the sound of the enemy weapon. It was easy to distinguish the sharp "whack" of Sanh's M-16 from the heavy "whump" of the enemy's weapon.

Approaching the top of a fern-covered rise, I detected movement ahead. As I crawled forward among the ferns, my elbows sank into the soft earth. When I reached the top of the rise, I saw a black-uniformed Vietcong firing at Sanh from behind the buttressing roots of a large cypress tree. He was armed with a long rifle, and after firing a round, he worked the bolt to reload. The second Vietcong was nowhere to be seen.

I had a good shot at him but decided to try to get closer. If we could take him prisoner and treated him well, he might be willing to talk about enemy activity in the area. Crawling forward I saw Sanh's rounds knocking chunks out of the gray mottled trunk that protected the enemy soldier. I stopped when I came to a tree; using it as a shield, I rose to a kneeling position. Resting my M-16 against the trunk, I positioned the top of my front site blade under his ear and took up the slack on my trigger.

"*Da sun xuong,*" I yelled for him to drop his weapon. He swung it in my direction.

Whump . . . thump. A round smacked into the trunk and pieces of bark hit my face.

Whack-whack-whack. My first round tore out a section of his upper arm and his weapon flew into the air. The second round blew off part of his right shoulder; a split second later, his head twitched as the third round ripped open the side of his neck. With everything appearing to happen in slow motion, I ran forward and reached him just as he was slumping to the ground.

''Ahhhh,'' he moaned as blood pumped from his neck wound like water from a faucet. He appeared to be about sixteen; he was in shock. I grabbed him under his arms and sat him up against the tree just as Sanh, Ly, and Binh arrived.

I removed a battle dressing from my harness, tore it from its wrapper, and pressed it against his neck wound. Warm blood quickly soaked the dressing and continued to flow over my hand and down the front of his chest. His upper arm was fractured and a bloody section of bone protruded from the oozing flesh. Most of his right shoulder was gone, but I didn't see any serious bleeding coming from the gaping wound.

''Yaaaa!'' he screamed and pushed my hand away. The other two Bodes arrived and set up security around us.

''Sanh, hit him with morphine. Ly, hold him down,'' I said. Ly grabbed his shirt and pressed him against the tree. While Ly restrained him, I removed a hemostat clamp from my pocket and, reaching under the dressing, pushed it deep into his neck wound and clamped as much flesh as I could grasp.

''Uhhhh.'' His body jerked and a bellyful of vomit spewed from his mouth.

''Sanh, where's the morphine?''

I couldn't see the torn artery but knew it was there. The pulsating bleeding slowed but didn't stop. A steady stream was still flowing down his chest. Sanh squatted next to me and I noticed a can of serum albumin taped to his harness. "Give me the albumin," I barked.

"Let him die, Bac-si."

"Gimme the damned can." I removed a syrette of morphine from my pocket. I injected the painkiller into the top of his leg and saw that his right foot had been shot off during the initial exchange of fire. He had been walking on a dirt-covered stump. There was a tourniquet tied just above the wound. His comrade must have applied it before leaving him.

"Yaaaa!" His body jerked again. When I looked at his face, I saw the faraway look of death.

"He die," Sanh said. With his head slumped against the tree and his mouth agape, the soldier's dying scream would remain frozen in time. I unclamped the hemostat from his neck, wiped it on my trousers, and put it back in my pocket.

"Got some water?" I asked Binh. He removed his canteen from his harness and poured some water on my hands. As I rubbed them together, the blood and vomit washed to the ground. "He was a human being," I said to Sanh. "Let's get the hell outta here."

Sanh picked up the dead man's rifle. It was an old Soviet 7.62-mm Mosin Nagent, but it had been well maintained and was free of rust. Its wooden stock had been shattered by one of my rounds. Before heading back to the Drop Zone, I updated Gritz on the contact.

Moving back down the hill we stopped for a few minutes while Sanh buried two M-14 Toe Poppers on our back trail. As we waited, I listened to the drone of the FAC aircraft and thought about the dead Vietcong. His World War I–vintage bolt-action rifle was a good sign that he was a local rather than main-force Vietcong. The fact that he wasn't carrying a rucksack or food was an indication that he was operating out of a nearby base camp. Since he had a recent haircut, appeared well fed, and had a well-maintained weapon, I also had to conclude that he was well trained and had good logistical support.

An educated guess was that he was part of a two-man tracker team that had been moving cross-country on an assigned route. They and other teams were likely crisscrossing the area trying to pick up our trail. That one had gotten away was bad news. He was probably on his way back to his unit to report our location. The good news was that the Vietcong generally had poor communications, and it would take them a while to react to the information.

By the time we neared the bottom of the hill, I heard a Skyraider making its drop. When we reached the Drop Zone we saw the silver napalm containers with their attached camouflaged parachutes lying in the clearing. We found George standing in the wood line distributing the new uniforms, rucksacks, BAR belts, and boots we had ordered.

"Damn, you stink," he told me. My fatigue jacket was wet with blood and vomit, and the hot sun on the Drop Zone only served to intensify the odor. While George finished handing out the gear, I tried to rinse my jacket. As soon as Jarvis finished booby-trapping the empty napalm containers, we departed in two different groups. Gritz had decided that two groups would provide us with the ability to cover more ground and at the same time make it more difficult for enemy trackers to get a fix on us. Group I—the first and third platoons and the headquarters section—would continue moving east-northeast through the swamp. Group II—recon and the second platoon—would follow the main trail to the northeast.

Group I moved out, the third platoon on point. With Danh leading we moved into an area of dead and decaying trees and knee-deep swamp water. The barren trees reminded me of those found in Buffalo, New York, in the dead of winter. Those lying in the stagnant water were soft with decay and crawling with insects. On many of the fallen trunks, black-headed red birds chirped as they pecked at insects. Vines that were once green and filled with water were now dry and crawling with ants. When we pushed them aside, they broke into small pieces and fell into the black swamp water.

An hour into the swamp, we stopped abruptly when we heard a "wooshing" sound approaching from the north. Seconds later, four large black-and-white birds flew over our column. The wooshing was the sound of their wings.

At 1400 we hit dry ground and, an hour later, stopped on the twenty-foot high bank of a fast-moving east-west stream that didn't appear on my map. It measured a good ten meters across, and its swirling, muddy water appeared to be quite deep. A few meters downstream we found a bridge. Three long pieces of bamboo had been lashed together with vines; four feet above them, a hemp rope was tied to trees on both sides of the stream.

"Go," I motioned Danh to move across the bridge.

"Numbah ten, Bac-si." He didn't think it was a good idea.

"I'll go first." Slowly advancing out onto the bamboo, I gripped the rope and watched the fast-moving water twenty feet below. Maybe Danh was right about it not being a good idea. When I reached the center of the bridge, I heard a crack, and suddenly I was falling. When I splashed into the water, I immediately knew it was over my head; the current dragged me downstream like I was a rag doll.

Instinctively, I didn't want to let go of my M-16 or my rucksack. My feet hit bottom for a second time, and I pushed up as hard as I could. With my head above water, I took in a quick breath before going under again. I was struggling in the muddy current and was about to dump my rucksack when my arm hit something. I grabbed what felt like a tree branch and pulled myself toward the surface. When my head broke the surface, my lungs were burning and I gasped for air. I was holding onto a large root that was growing out of the far bank. Looking up and to my rear, I saw George and Danh preparing to jump into the water.

"You okay?" George yelled.

"Yeah." I raised my M-16 and felt good that I hadn't lost it. My lungs continued to burn and I coughed to clear them of water. Looking back again I saw two Bodes talking to George.

"Jimmy," he bellowed, "got a bridge downstream."

"Okay." Looking at Danh, I felt foolish that I hadn't taken his advice. I dug my toes into the soft mud and used the large root to pull myself to the top of the bank. Once there, I sat for a minute catching my breath. Then I walked the short distance downstream to where I found George and the Bodes crossing the stream on a fallen tree trunk. The enormous trunk measured a good four feet in diameter, and its top had been worn flat and smooth by years of foot traffic.

After crossing the stream, we continued north through the swamp and soon reentered ankle-deep black water covered with a crust of green algae. Observing our movement from a fallen tree were creatures with frog-like heads and fish bodies. As we passed, a firefight erupted to the northeast, and the creatures slithered from the rotting trunks and disappeared beneath the murky water.

George closed the distance between us and held the handset so I could hear.

"Fox Two, this is Fox Four, over." It was Cawley trying to make contact with England's platoon.

"Fox Four, this is Fox Two, over," England responded.

"Fox Two, this is Fox Four." It sounded like he was talking on the run. "Made point contact with three locals moving south on the trail. One's down. The other two beat it to the north. We're in pursuit, over."

We continued to splash through the swamp.

"Roger, Four," England said. "We're at the clearing, over."

Whack-whack-whack. Another burst of fire.

"Fox Four, this is Fox Two," England radioed.

Danh flushed two large brown birds, and the sudden flapping of their wings scared the hell out of me.

"Fox Two, this is Four." It was Cawley again. "We lost them. We'll RV at the clearing, over."

"Roger, Fox Four. I'll remain in place. Fox Two, out."

"Fox Two, this is Swamp Fox, over." It was Gritz calling England.

"Swamp Fox, this is Fox Two, over."

"Fox Two, this is Swamp Fox. Do you have a prisoner? Over."

"That's a negative, Swamp Fox. That old boy lost his head during the initial contact. He was Cambodian VC, over."

"Swamp Fox, this is Fox Four," Cawley interrupted.

"This is Swamp Fox. Roger, Two; go ahead, Four."

"Swamp Fox, this is Fox Four. Got a company-size base camp on the north side of the clearing. Doesn't look like anyone's been here for years, over."

"Roger, Fox Four. Swamp Fox, out."

At 1730 we reached dry ground. Thirty minutes later, we stopped near the Phuoc-Long/Long-Kanh Province border to set up our MSS. The bamboo thicket was alive with mosquitoes, frogs, and crickets. Group II set up twenty-eight hundred meters to the northwest.

When I opened my rucksack I was relieved to see that my rubberized nylon bag had kept everything dry. While George fixed us a meal of rice with Tabasco sauce and hot peppers, I detail-stripped and cleaned my M-16. After dinner I removed the five hundred rounds from my magazines and wiped each of them down with a dry rag. By then it was almost dark. George and I sat whispering for a while, then I crawled into my hammock and fell asleep.

Sometime later, a distant explosion woke me. I checked my Seiko; it was 0100. A hand touched my arm.

"Bac-si." It was Sanh squatting next to my hammock. He had the 2400-to-0200 watch.

"Yeah, Sanh." I rolled on my side.

"Bac-si, I sorry I cannot do," he whispered.

"Can't do what?"

"When we go patrol, I cannot give VC morphine."

"Hey, my friend, don't worry about it."

"In America maybe you do not like other man, but in Vietnam it not same," he said. "Our hearts have much anger."

"I understand."

"Bac-si, you cannot understand." He put his hand on my arm. "Let me tell you. Before I come Ho-Ngoc-Tao, I have son who take Saigon bus to Can-Tho. Vietcong stop bus and take my son. He only seventeen." His voice trembled with building emotion.

"Was he a soldier?" I asked.

"*Oui*, Bac-si. But he not have weapon. He go Can-Tho to see his mamma-son."

"What happened?" I hesitated to ask. Sanh started to shake.

"Vietcong cut bamboo one meter from ground and sit my son on bamboo till he die."

"Jesus." His words left me shaken and incensed.

"When they find him, bamboo come out his mouth."

"I'm sorry."

That night I lay in the darkness for hours thinking about what Sanh had told me. He was right. There were things we would never understand.

CHAPTER FIFTEEN

0900, 26 JANUARY 1967

OUR BLACK-AND-GREEN column snaked north along the west bank of a stream called the Da-Bongkua. Howard's first platoon was on point, followed by the headquarters section and the third platoon. High in the trees the morning mist was beginning to burn off, and the dew sparkled as the first rays of sunlight penetrated to the jungle floor. In our world beneath the canopy, a tangle of thorn-covered vines tore at our skin, and our boots sank ankle deep into soft black mud.

Following a short break at 1200, we waded in chest-deep water as we crossed the Da-Bongkua and headed northeast toward the Dong-Nai River. Whack-whack-whack. A stream of fire erupted to the north. George closed the gap between us.

"England's in a company base camp seven hundred meters north-northeast," he whispered. "Three VC beat it out the back door." We struggled northeast through the thorns and mud, and at 1430 we hit dry ground and began moving uphill past clumps of dead bamboo. The once bright-green stalks had turned brown and brittle and were bowed to the ground by the weight of their wilted leaves.

Twenty minutes later, we linked up with recon at the top

of the hill, and for the first time, I could smell the waters of the Dong-Nai. The area was cluttered with hanging vines, shoulder-high ferns, clumps of green bamboo, and four-story cypress trees whose gray-and-white trunks measured eight to ten feet in diameter. In the branches above us, large black monkeys with small heads and long arms cried "hoot, hoot, hoot" as they scurried to the higher branches.

"Third herd, zero to 120 degrees." Kindoll pointed to the eastern side of the perimeter. Once the Bodes were in place, we lowered our rucksacks to the ground a few meters from where Doyle was setting up his PRC-74 radio. As soon as George left to set up a listening post to the east, I added water to a couple of bags of rice and dried shrimp. Some of the more curious monkeys dropped to the lower branches and continued to hoot as they gracefully swung from branch to branch. Others appeared to float in slow motion as they bounded great distances between the trees.

Dah-dit-dah, dit, dit-dah-dah, dah-dit-dah. Doyle was tapping out Morse code. I picked up my meal and walked to where he was sitting on his poncho. He had a Diana Onetime cryptopad open on his leg and was using it to decode a message. "What's the good news?" I asked, seating myself next to him.

"Just received a message from the C-Team," he answered while writing in the pad. "Intel thinks the 9th VC Division's in the area." His words sent a chill up the length of my spine.

"Any details?"

"No, that's about it."

"Hey, it's good to see you haven't killed old Kindoll," I joked.

"No," he grinned, "I had the ass when he pulled me outta Saigon, but I gotta admit it's been a good experience."

"Where you from?" I used a C-ration spoon to eat my rice.

"River Rouge, Michigan."

"This your first tour?"

"No, I was at Hiep-Hoa [Special Forces camp] and Muc-Hoa [Special Forces camp] back in '63 and '64. We were TDY [temporary duty] from the 5th when the group was still at Bragg. From there I went to the 7th for a few months and then volunteered to come back to Nam. On my second tour I was with the A-Team at Trang-Sup [Special Forces camp] and the B-Team in Tay-Ninh [Special Forces compound]."

"So this is your third tour."

"Yup. Got to the B-Team in Song-Be in March of '66. Later in the year I became the commo chief at Duc-Phong."

"A short timer."

"Yeah, two months to go. I put in for Bad-Tolz," he smirked. "Snow, German beer, and schnitzel." As Doyle and I talked, George, Rinh, and Sanh returned from setting up the listening post.

"I'll catch you later," I said before returning to where George was stringing his hammock.

"LP's seventy meters out at ninety degrees." He used his scarf to wipe the sweat from his face. "Everything's quiet."

"What d'ya say we take those stitches out?" I asked.

"Won't argue with that." He sat on the ground and began unlacing his boot.

"You wanna take 'em out?" I asked Rinh.

"Yes, Donahue." He picked up his M-5 kit and placed it at George's feet. Spreading George's toes with my fingers, I looked at his stitches and saw there wasn't any sign of infection.

"I can't believe it," I said. "A week of sweat and mud and it ain't infected."

"Miracles do happen." George grinned.

While Rinh prepared to remove the stitches, Sanh and I left to check the perimeter. Having heard about the 9th

Division, I wanted to make sure everything was squared away. "Change the batteries on the HT-1s," I told Sanh as we walked. "They've been in for eleven days."

"*Oui*, Trung-si."

"And watch for moisture condensing on the inside of the radios," I continued as we reached the perimeter. "Whenever you get a chance, lay 'em out in the sun. If you don't, they'll corrode."

Passing each position, we checked the Claymores and warned the men not to fire during the night unless we were being overrun. We didn't want to compromise our location by firing at night noises or shadows.

By the time we got back to our hammocks it was almost dark. George, Sanh, Rinh, and I sat in a small circle listening to the listless sounds of the night. At 2100 the radio bristled. "Swamp Fox, this is Fox Four, over," Cawley whispered.

"Fox Four, this is Swamp Fox, over," Gritz responded.

"Swamp Fox, this is Fox Four. My LP just reported that seven VC loaded supplies on a sampan and crossed the river west to east, over."

"Roger, Four. Can you take them under fire? Over."

"That's a negative, Swamp Fox. They disappeared into heavy mist, over."

"Roger, Fox Four. Swamp Fox, out."

"Cawley's two or three klicks up the river," I murmured to George. We sat whispering for a good hour or so, then fell into a deep sleep under a moonlit sky. Something woke me abruptly. I raised my head over the side of my hammock and listened. It was the sound of a motor somewhere to the east of the perimeter. "George." I sat up and slipped into my boots.

"I hear it." I moved to where he and Sanh were standing in a shaft of moonlight. "It's a boat."

"Yeah." It reminded me of boats I'd heard moving up the Niagara River. "It's moving north."

Dit-dah, dit-dit-dit-dah, dah-dit-dit. The muffled sounds

of Doyle transmitting Morse code broke the stillness.

"I'll see what's going on." I picked up my M-16 and felt my way to Doyle's position. I lay on the ground next to him and stuck my head under the poncho. The space beneath the poncho was warm, glowed red, and smelled like the inside of a radio. Doyle was sitting cross-legged, with his commo key attached to his leg and his cryptopad lying on the ground between his knees. Kindoll was sitting next to him, illuminating the pad with a red-tipped pen flashlight.

"Trying to get an operational immediate message to the C-Team ALO [air liaison officer] in Bien-Hoa," Kindoll told me. "Gritz wants a Sky Spot on the boat."

"They're not responding," Doyle shook his head. "Can't figure it. My only commo problems have been in the morning when the ionosphere's changing."

"Would a doublet antenna work any better?" I asked.

"No, gotta go with a long wire," Doyle said. "In this terrain it's the only way to go. It's gotta penetrate a good two hundred feet of overhead cover."

As we talked, I heard someone else sending Morse code over the same frequency. "That the C-Team?" I asked.

"No, the B-Team in Song-Be telling Bu-Dop to get off the air. We've got priority."

"I'll catch you guys later," I said before returning to where Sanh and George were sitting next to our PRC-25 radio. At midnight the sound of the engine stopped. A few minutes later the radio crackled again.

"Swamp Fox, this is Fox Four, over," Glossup whispered.

"Fox Four, this is Swamp Fox, over," Gritz responded.

"Swamp Fox, this is Fox Four. A powerboat picked up personnel on the east bank at right 2.0, up 1.0. They picked up a platoon and drifted downstream with three sampans, over."

"Roger, Fox Four. Swamp Fox, out."

"Let's take a look," George said as he spread his map

on the ground and covered it and himself with his poncho. Sanh and I ducked under the poncho and George illuminated his map with his red-tipped flashlight. "Here you go." George pointed to a location on the map. "Glossup's twenty-three hundred meters upstream."

"If those boats are drifting south, they're heading in our direction," I observed.

"Yeah, they gotta know we're in the area," George confirmed.

"VC look for us," Sanh said. George switched off the light and rolled up his poncho.

Dit-dah, dit, dit-dit-dit, dah-dah-dit, dit. It was 0015, 27 January, and Doyle was sending Morse code again. I felt my way back to his position and found him and Captain Gritz under his poncho.

"Finally got two-by [faint contact] with the C-Team," the captain said as Doyle continued to tap out code on his leg key.

"Okay, sir. Gimme the Sky Spot coordinates," Doyle said.

Gritz squinted closely at his map. "I've got four targets," the captain said as Doyle removed a pen from his pocket. "I want the first one at 519 786, the second at 520 783, the third at 519 787, and the fourth at 520 789."

"Yes, sir." Doyle encoded the coordinates.

"Those are pretty close," I suggested.

"Eight hundred meters," Gritz said. "The map shows structures on both sides of the river. Could be where those boats are heading."

"ALO's got plenty of time to put the strikes in before first light," I volunteered.

"Jimmy, tell George I want your platoon to conduct a BDA [bomb damage assessment]."

"Yes, sir."

Doyle continued to tap out code and I returned to where Sanh and George were waiting. I briefed them on the Sky Spots, and Sanh used his HT-1 radio to alert the squad leaders. The three of us then took up positions behind a large tree and waited. I was just beginning to fall asleep at 0145 when George nudged me. "Listen." Ssssshhhhh. A faint whistle filled the air.

Suddenly, the sounds of the jungle stopped. Karoumph, karoumph, karoumph. Bombs flashed to the east. "That was close," George gasped. Forty-five minutes later, I detected the sound of a jet aircraft high above our perimeter. Sssssshhhhh. The whistle of more bombs.

"Get down," I whispered. The three of us lay flat behind the giant cypress. Karoumph, karoumph, karoumph. The ground shook as bombs exploded even closer to our perimeter. Seconds later, pieces of shrapnel cut through the foliage above our heads.

An hour before dawn the monkeys began hooting in the branches above our hammocks. Some of their voices were high pitched, others low. They reminded me of a choir tuning up for a concert. At first light the hill was blanketed with a thick mist that smelled of the river. When we had enough light to see, the third platoon moved downhill with Danh on point. Two hundred meters east of the perimeter we stopped at the edge of a fifty-foot cliff. A hanging garden of vines, ferns, and small banana plants grew over the edge. We used the vines to slowly descend to the ground below.

While waiting for the remainder of the patrol to descend, Danh sank up to his knees in quicksand. I grabbed his hand but couldn't pull him from its surprisingly strong grasp. He tossed his Sten to Sanh, and, with George pulling his other hand, we slowly freed him from its suction. We noticed that the strips of quicksand appeared light brown. Zigzagging around those areas, we continued east past moss-covered bamboo and dead and dying trees. High above the trees, an invisible crow cried "kaw, kaw, kaw" as it circled the area.

An hour later, Danh stopped suddenly at the edge of a grassy area. I moved forward to where he had dropped to one knee; the smell of cordite and burning thatch assaulted my nostrils. "VC cut." He pointed to small stumps that had been cut with a sharp instrument. On the far side of the fifty-meter-wide area, hundreds of bleached punji stakes extended a few inches above the grass.

"What d'ya got?" George and Sanh squatted behind me.

"Looks like a base camp," I replied. "They've cleared fields of fire and put in punji stakes."

"Check it out," George told Danh, who zigzagged in a low crouch before disappearing into the foliage on the far side. "Get 'em on line," George ordered. Sanh extended both arms parallel to the ground. The Bodes quickly deployed on line at five-meter intervals. If we made contact, we'd be in a position to instantly direct all of our firepower against the enemy. If we encountered a large force, we'd use the same firepower to break contact and run like hell.

Ten minutes later Danh returned. "VC camp," he whispered. "VC dead."

"Keep 'em on line," George told Sanh, who stood and gave the signal to move forward. Halfway across the clearing, we encountered row after row of foot-long punji stakes. They had been fire hardened and had needle-sharp tips. While moving through them, I spotted what appeared to be a mound of dirt just inside the line of foliage. Nearing the mound, I saw that it was a bunker with a machine-gun aperture cut across its front. I vaulted into the foliage at the side of the bunker and was joined there by George and Ly. "Need something heavy to knock this sucker out," George whispered while pointing to a dirt-covered roof. Under three feet of dirt were logs that measured a good eighteen inches in diameter.

"Let's check it out," I said. At the rear of the bunker we squeezed through a narrow entrance. Except for the light around the machine-gun aperture, it was dark and smelled of mold. Looking out through the aperture, I saw that the punji stakes had been laid out in a "V" pattern to funnel advancing enemy troops to the front of the bunker—and certain death. To prevent a grenade from being thrown into the bunker, the Vietcong had stretched chicken wire across its front.

"Lucky it wasn't manned," George sighed.

"No shit. They woulda kicked our ass," I shuddered.

George picked up a bamboo mat in the corner and discovered a concealed tunnel. "Have more bunker," Sanh said as he and Danh entered. "One bunker north, two south."

"Got a tunnel here." George used his pen flashlight to peer into it.

"Escape tunnel," Sanh told us.

"Jim, you wanna check it out?" George asked. He handed me his flashlight, and I dropped into the four-foot hole. It was a tight fit, and at its bottom I found a narrow tunnel whose walls were covered with mold and crawling with large black spiders. I didn't much care for tight underground spaces or spiders.

"Tunnel leads northeast," I called out.

"I go you." Danh sat on the edge of the hole and prepared to drop in behind me. Crawling on my belly, I had my selector switch on "automatic" and my finger on the trigger. Danh and I felt claustrophobic as we inched twenty to thirty meters through the damp tunnel before coming to a small, one-man bunker with four narrow firing slits. Looking through one of the slits I could see George, Sanh, and Ly standing a few feet away. If I were a Vietcong, they'd be dead. From what I could see, the camp's defense was classic VC. Bunkers were well camouflaged and set up, in-depth, with interlocking fields of fire. The one-man bunker not only supported the larger first line of bunkers, it could also be used as a fall-back position if the main line of resistance fell.

"George," I hissed.

"Jim?" He peered through the narrow slit. "Anything down there?"

"No. The tunnel goes north."

"Go ahead and follow it. We'll RV down at the river."

After Danh finished burying an M-14 Toe Popper in the tunnel's floor, we crawled another thirty to forty meters. The roof of the tunnel had been weakened by the bombing; parts of it were close to caving in. It was a tight squeeze, and I considered turning back. As I was crawling through loose dirt, my light's beam suddenly flashed across someone's head and shoulders. Whack-whack-whack. I instinctively fired a burst.

Aaaah! The head jerked and there was a groan. My ears were left with a high-pitched ringing. I crawled forward and saw it was a black-clad enemy soldier. His head looked like a watermelon that had been hit by a baseball bat; the ground beneath was wet with blood, cerebral fluid, and chunks of skull and brain. I tried to crawl over the body but found there wasn't enough room to squeeze by.

"Shit." I suddenly felt closed in and worried that the Vietcong might attack while we were stuck in the tunnel. Flashing the light over the top of the body, I saw the end of the tunnel only five meters away. I also noticed that most of the flesh had been blown from one of the dead man's legs—only the bone remained. "Looks like he crawled in here after the Sky Spot," I said to Danh as I handed him my M-16. I put a hand on each of the dead man's shoulders and began pushing him ahead of me. It was slow going, and by the time we reached the end of the tunnel, I was wet with my sweat and his body fluids.

Unbuckling my BAR belt, I found I had just enough room to squeeze over the body. Above the dead man we crawled into another machine-gun bunker. It was a relief to be out of the tunnel. Outside, smoke filled the space beneath the canopy. To our left, the stilts of what had held three elevated huts were silhouetted against the waters of the Dong-Nai. To our front, George and Ly stood between a steaming bomb crater and a charred cypress whose leaves had been stripped by the blast.

Danh and I ran to where George was talking into his

radio handset. "Got a dead VC in the tunnel," I said.

"Yeah, and there's another one over there." George pointed to an arm lying on the ground. I noticed a large mass of red-and-white oozing flesh sticking to the charred trunk of the cypress. It reminded me of a bug splat on a car's windshield. "What the hell's that?" I hesitated to ask.

"Damn, it's a man." George cringed as he looked closer. "Those are human teeth."

We moved toward the river and stopped at the base of the stilts to search through pieces of thatch, torn baskets, and gardening tools. A few meters past the stilts, we came to the water's edge. The river measured a good one hundred meters across; on the far side, a thick mist obscured everything but the tops of a few trees. Upstream and to the northeast, purple-and-green-tinted mountains rose high above the mist.

"I'm gonna wash up," I said to George. He and Ly continued south along the muddy bank. "Come on," I motioned to Danh. We waded waist deep into the river and used our hands to rub the body fluids and dirt from the fronts of our fatigues. A few minutes later, we caught up with George and Ly at a small inlet. On its bank a fallen tree lay across the shattered hull of a red and green sampan. At its center, a dead pig bobbed upon the stilled water. We found Thach just past the inlet, rolling a dead Vietcong into the river.

"Two VC go Saigon," he grinned and pointed to a second body floating south with the current.

"Anything beyond here?" George pointed south.

"Two bunker," Thach said.

"Trung-si," Sanh ran to where we were standing. "VC have eight bunker. Two north, two south, and four west. All bunker very good. Number one soldier live here."

"You're right," George said. "Best bunkers I ever saw."

"*Khleang krob!*" Danh yelled from the center of the camp.

"Ammunition bunker," Sanh said. We followed Danh between two burning elevated huts and around the edge of another bomb crater. The ground was littered with rice, kitchen utensils, broken bottles, and earthenware vats. It looked like a direct hit on the camp's kitchen. A short distance past the crater we arrived at a fenced-in pigsty where we found a couple of Bodes standing next to a hole in the ground.

"VC hide bunker under shit," Danh said. George, Sanh, and I knelt in the pig shit at the edge of the hole and peered inside. At the bottom of the bunker were a dozen wooden boxes partially covered with dirt. The wall closest to the bomb crater had buckled, and most of the roof was caving in. "I go in," Danh volunteered.

"No," I shook my head, "could cave in."

"Booby traps in place?" George asked Sanh.

"*Oui*, Trung-si."

"Okay, clear the camp," George ordered. "Danh, get me a Claymore." Sanh raised his radio to his mouth and said a few words. When Danh returned with the mine, George removed it from its canvas bandoleer. With the blasting cap already in the detonator well, he used the mine's firing wire to lower it into the hole. Once it touched down on the bottom of the bunker, he carefully laid it face down on top of what appeared to be a box of Chinese fragmentation grenades. We then walked backwards and unraveled the mine's one hundred feet of S-rolled firing wire.

"All clear, Trung-si," Thach said to George as we took cover behind a machine-gun bunker. George swung the safety to the armed position and squeezed the handle on the mine's firing device. Whoomph. An earth-rending explosion pounded my eardrums. Looking around the side of the bunker, I saw logs from the bunker's roof falling through thick black smoke.

"Swamp Fox, this is Fox Four, over." It was Chilton calling Gritz.

"Fox Four, this is Swamp Fox, over."

"Swamp Fox, this is Fox Four. We're in a battalion-size base camp at right 2.4, down 0.5. Looks like a city under the trees: twenty large structures, a dispensary, a boat dock, and bunkers on all sides. There was a squad here—probably camp security—but they deedeed [left in a hurry], over."

"Roger, Fox Four. Set up a couple of ambushes in the area. As soon as we get the FAC up in the morning, we'll put some air on it, over."

"Roger, Swamp Fox. Fox Four, out."

"We've got base camps north, east, and west of the MSS," I said to George as thousands of leaves drifted through the still air and settled to the ground around us.

We rendezvoused with the rest of the patrol and, with Danh on point, headed west. Two hundred meters from the camp, we stopped to set up an L-shaped ambush along our back trail. We remained in position until the shadows began to lengthen, then headed west under a crimson sky. Fifteen minutes later, we arrived at the base of the cliff.

As we used thick vines to scale the precipice, the crimson sky was suddenly darkened by thousands of bats. Seconds later, the frenzied flapping of their wings faded to the north. While we waited for everyone to reach the top, George radioed that we were two hundred meters out. Only the shadows remained when Danh's movement was challenged by our perimeter security.

On the morning of 28 January, Gritz called a team meeting, and, as monkeys hooted overhead, he informed us that we would be moving twenty-six hundred meters north-northwest to link up with recon. The rendezvous would take place on a hilltop four hundred meters west of where Glossup had reported the powerboat making the pickup.

At 0730 the jungle was already a steam bath. Howard's first platoon departed on point, and a few minutes later they were followed by England's second platoon and the headquarters section. The third herd was the last to leave, and by the time we were halfway down the hill, I was soaked with sweat. It was going to be another hot one.

At the base of the hill, we entered an area where everything appeared in shades of green. The undergrowth was thick with leaves of every size and shape; the tree trunks were covered with moss and wrapped tight with lime green vines. Even the ground was covered with a crust of green algae. With every step our feet crunched through the crust and sank into a creamy black mud. Laboring under a heavy rucksack, I sweat so much my eyes were soon burning and I could taste salt on my lips. By 0800 the morning mist was beginning to burn off. Soon thereafter, I could hear the hum of the FAC's O-1E approaching from the west.

"Sidewinder, this is Swamp Fox, over," Gritz radioed.

"Good morning, Swamp Fox. It's gonna be another beautiful day, over."

"He must've had a good night," George whispered from behind me.

As we continued through the mud, Gritz requested an air strike on the battalion-size base camp Chilton had reported a day earlier. At 0900 I was swallowing two salt tablets as a flight of jets arrived over our column.

Whoomph . . . pop. The FAC marked the base camp with a white phosphorous rocket round. Minutes later, a jet screeched low over the canopy. Karoumph, karoumph, karoumph. Seven-hundred-fifty-pound bombs exploded a few hundred meters to the east. Their shock waves pounded my eardrums; rivulets of sparkling dew fell from the leaves. As soon as the first jet cleared the air space above the base camp, a second jet streaked in and another load of bombs exploded. With each blast, the fluting wail of shrapnel punctuated the air high above our heads.

"Napalm," George hissed. A third jet knifed through the air at treetop level. Kawhoosh—the sound of the liquid hell spilling down through the trees. Karoumph, karoumph. There were two muffled explosions before the roar of the jets faded to the south. The only sound that remained was that of our boots crunching through the algae, followed by the sucking sound as we pulled them from the mud's suction.

Ten minutes later, Chilton radioed that all bombs were on target. The pungent petroleum odor of burning gas drifted through the ranks. An estimated fifteen structures and four boats had been destroyed. The two secondary explosions were ammunition bunkers. "Any KBA [killed by air]?" I asked George as he continued to monitor the radio.

"Can't tell," he responded. "Everything's on fire." By the time we took a break at 1300, everyone looked spent. "Jim, one of the Bodes from the tail-gunner section's down from the heat," George said.

"Rinh and I'll take care of it," I volunteered. The two of us picked up our rucksacks and retraced our boot prints to the south. Fifty meters down the trail we crossed a shallow stream; one hundred and fifty meters farther south, we found Binh sitting in the mud with his back braced against a tree. His eyes were closed and his mouth hung open, wide. The other members of his four-man team had set up a small defensive perimeter around him.

Rinh and I lowered our rucksacks to the ground and squatted next to Binh. The front of his jacket was covered with vomit, his skin was hot and dry, and his pupils were constricted. "Heat stroke," I diagnosed as I pulled three blood-filled leeches from Binh's face. "Gotta get his temperature down."

"Do you want to put him in the stream?" Rinh asked.

"Yeah. Tell the guys what we're gonna do and make sure they maintain security." I lifted my rucksack and swung it around onto my back. We struggled north under the weight of our rucksacks and Binh's body, our boots sinking deep into the mud with every step. When we arrived at the stream, we dropped our rucksacks on the bank and placed Binh on his back in a couple of inches of water.

Up and down the stream from our position were moss-covered rocks, large ferns, and a few palms reaching high into a blue sky. While I splashed water over the length of

Binh's body, Rinh held a thermometer in his mouth, and the tail-gunner section set up security around us. Just over our heads, small yellow birds chirped and fluttered from branch to branch.

"One hundred six degrees." Rinh wasn't surprised. If we didn't get it down quick, brain damage could result. I checked Binh's pulse. It was fast and weak.

"Gotta get it down to 102," I said. "Let's get an IV going." While Rinh taped a bottle of normal saline to an overhead branch, I placed Binh's arm on the bank and wiped the back of his hand with a piece of alcohol-soaked gauze. When everything was ready, Rinh extended the plastic tubing and needle and handed it to me. I carefully slipped the needle into Binh's vein. "Good," I sighed. Rinh opened the regulator on the tubing, and saltwater began flowing into Binh's body.

I began massaging Binh's arms. "Gotta maintain circulation. We need a fan." Rinh removed a four-foot oval leaf from a nearby plant, folded it in half, and began fanning Binh. I unbuttoned Binh's fatigue jacket, removed a few more leeches from his chest, and started massaging his legs. An exchange of fire erupted somewhere to the north of our position. Rinh looked at me with concern but continued to fan Binh. Over a period of an hour, the stream's cool water brought his temperature down to 104 degrees. By then, both banks were crowded with hundreds of inch-long brown leeches trying to get at us.

"Did you know that Binh was an engineer?" Rinh asked.

"Someone told me he went to school in France."

"Yes, his family owns property in Tay-Ninh Province. When he returned from France his father wanted him to go to school in America. I think it was M-A-T in Boston."

"That's M-I-T." I smiled. "The Massachusetts Institute of Technology. How come he didn't go?"

"He wanted to be a soldier. One day he wants to live in a free Cambodia. His father was very angry."

"His father's a fool," I said. "Old Binh's Special Forces. He may not look like much, but he's one hell of a soldier."

"Yes, Donahue. When he was wounded near Song-Be he did not have to come back."

"Attitude's what makes him special, and attitude's what makes Special Forces special," I nodded. "It's not how big you are, or how strong you are, or how many schools you've been to. It's attitude."

"I agree, Donahue."

"My friend, someday you and Binh and the others will be rewarded for your sacrifice."

"Freedom will be our reward."

"That and more. One day, when you're old and gray, you'll be sipping tea at a sidewalk café in Saigon, and the people will point and say, 'That's Rinh. He fought with the Mobile Guerrilla Force. The finest light infantry there ever was.'"

"Donahue," he whispered, tears welling in his eyes, "the café will be in Phnom-Penh, and you will be there with me."

"Wouldn't it be great to grow old together?"

"Yes," he said, "I would like our children to be friends."

"Someday I'd like to take you to some of my old fishing holes," I grinned.

Another forty-five minutes passed before Binh's temperature was down to 102 degrees, and by then he had regained full consciousness. "Let's sit him up," I said. "If his temperature falls too far, we'll lose him to hypothermia." Rinh positioned himself near Binh's head, and as we helped him to his feet, his body shook and dripped with water from the stream. "Gotta watch him for two or three days," I prescribed.

While Binh held onto a branch, I picked up my rucksack, brushed the leeches from it, and swung it around to my back. Rinh and I then draped Binh's arms over our shoulders and slowly labored north through the heat, mosquitoes, and mud. Sometime later, we came to a bright, open area that was dotted with decaying stumps and fallen trees. We followed boot prints through the shade along the west side of the clearing. On the east side we spotted Gritz, Kindoll, Cawley, Montgomery, and a few Bodes standing in the wood line. Their images appeared to shimmer in the waves of heat rising from the clearing.

Near the top of the hill, we reentered thick vegetation and found the support site. It had been set up in an area of tall cypress trees and clumps of bamboo. To our rear, I could hear the faint wap, wap, wap of a helicopter approaching from the south. After passing through a section of the perimeter defended by Howard's platoon, we came to the headquarters.

"Hey, Jim. How's that boy doing?" Doyle asked as he adjusted a knob on the PRC-74 radio.

"He'll be okay." We sat Binh against a large tree and gave him a canteen.

"What's the chopper for?" I questioned Doyle.

"Captain's bringing in a rubber raft. He, Monty, and Cawley are gonna cross the river tonight. Captain Yedinak's here to take command of the headquarters section." A few feet away, Yedinak sat with his map spread on the ground and his radio handset pressed to his ear.

"Where's George set up?" I asked. Doyle pointed to the west. I found George and Sanh sitting on a fallen tree examining an HT-1 radio.

"One of the Bodes pressed the auto-destruct button." George shook his head. I lowered my rucksack to the ground and laid my M-16 against it. The HT-1 had a classified, state-of-the-art circuitry, and a red auto-destruct button that was to be pressed only if the radio was in imminent danger of falling into enemy hands.

"What?"

"Said he wanted to make sure it worked." George smiled. His words struck me as hysterical, and I started laughing uncontrollably, falling to the ground. "He's gone off the deep end," George laughed.

"Gotta be the heat," I said as I regained my composure and sat up. "Hey, what was that shooting I heard a while back?"

"VC base camp a few hundred meters northeast of here. Twelve hooches. Maybe company size."

"Everyone okay?"

"Yeah, we porked four pigs. One VC dropped a ruck full of food and ran toward the river."

"Old trick," Sanh explained as the chopper made a pass over the nearby clearing. "VC know American stop to look in rucksack. Then they run away." I removed a couple of salt tablets from my pocket and swallowed them with a long drink of water.

"Fox Two, this is Swamp Fox, over." It was Gritz trying to contact Yedinak.

"Swamp Fox, this is Fox Two, over," Yedinak responded.

"Fox Two, this is Swamp Fox. There's no damned air pump with the raft." Gritz sounded pissed. "Look, there's an extra PRC-25 radio antenna attached to Fang's rucksack. One of its sections should fit over the air valve, over."

"Roger, Swamp Fox. It's on the way. Fox Two, out."

"He's gonna blow it up by mouth!" I exclaimed.

After dinner I went to headquarters to check on Binh and later returned to assume the 2200-to-2400 watch.

"Fox Two, this is Fox Five, over." It was Kindoll calling Yedinak. It was 2300; the sky was white with stars.

"Fox Five, this is Fox Two, over," Yedinak responded.

"Fox Two, this is Fox Five. They're in the water, over."

"Roger, Fox Five. Fox Two, out."

"They're on their way," George whispered in darkness. "They're gonna use the moon to move inland. Wake me if you hear anything."

For close to thirty minutes I sat listening to the sounds

of the jungle and watching clouds sweep past the man in the moon.

"Fox Two, this is Fox Four, over." It was Chilton trying to contact Yedinak. The lieutenant was in an ambush position upstream from the crossing point.

"Fox Four, this is Fox Two, over."

"Fox Two, this is Fox Four. We've got a sampan full of Victor Charlie drifting south on the river, over."

"George," I hissed. There was a swish in his hammock, and a second later he was standing next to me.

"Roger, Four. Can you take them under fire? Over," Yedinak asked.

"This is Fox Five," Kindoll broke in. "Do not open fire. I repeat, do not open fire. The VC are between Fox Four and Swamp Fox, over."

"Roger, Fox Five . . ."

"They've spotted our raft," Kindoll interrupted Chilton. "They're rowing ashore."

"Does Gritz have a radio?" I asked George.

"No. No way of warning him."

"Fox Two, this is Fox Five." It was Kindoll calling Yedinak again. "They're on the bank checking out the raft, over."

"Roger, Fox Four. If they move inland, take them under fire," Yedinak ordered. A long couple of minutes of silence followed.

"Fox Two, this is Fox Five," Kindoll radioed Yedinak. "Mister Charles is back in his boat and drifting south, over."

"Whew, that's a relief," sighed George.

"Fox Five, this is Fox Two. What about the raft? Over."

"Fox Two, this is Fox Five. They left it in place. Must think it's one of theirs, over."

"Roger, Fox Five. Fox Two, out."

CHAPTER SIXTEEN

0515, 29 JANUARY 1967

WITH THE FIRST LIGHT of day the stars quickly faded, and beneath the canopy the shadows came alive with yellows, tans, greens, and browns. High in the trees, bright-blue birds sang their morning arias while the faint hint of cinnamon bark filled the air. As George and I sat on a log finishing our breakfast, Captain Yedinak called the team to the headquarters. When we arrived we found Doyle dumping the contents of his rucksack on the ground.

"Termites moved in during the night," he lamented, shaking his head.

"Listen up," Yedinak said as Doyle brushed hundreds of the insects from his gear. "Gritz, Cawley, and Montgomery didn't cross the river until close to midnight, and I don't expect to hear from them until mid-morning."

"Sir. What's their objective?" Jarvis asked.

"Surveillance. Intel suspects that the village of Bu-Khiu may be a center for VC activity."

"Sir. Do we have any additional intel on the 9th Division?" Howard asked.

"No, and I don't expect any," replied the captain. "My one concern is our closeness to the river. If we make heavy contact, we don't have much room to maneuver."

"Don't wanna get pinned up against that river," Howard agreed.

"If we run into trouble and get split up, our emergency resupply will be dropped at," Yedinak paused to look at his map, "459 818. A clearing forty-six hundred meters west-northwest of here."

Everyone marked the location on their maps.

"What about camp security?" George asked.

"I want each platoon to leave your machine-gun section and one squad. Just in case the in-laws drop in." He smiled. "Okay, I've got your patrol assignments and want everyone on the DZ by 1630."

"Drop's scheduled for 1700," Doyle announced.

"Okay, today's first assignment goes to the third herd," the captain said while looking at George. "Take two squads eighteen hundred meters southwest to the RP, then patrol east toward the river. If you run into trouble, the headquarters section will be your reaction force."

Fifteen minutes later, we departed, moving downhill into a mist-filled swamp. There were no prominent terrain features in the area so we had to rely on our navigational ability. The sameness of the terrain made it similar to navigating at sea. While I kept Danh on the correct compass azimuth, George counted the paces and kept track of the distance we had moved. We had become good at the technique and could generally calculate our position to within one hundred meters.

It was an uneventful morning; by 1150 we were moving southwest through bamboo and soft mud. "Hold it up," George whispered while counting the knots on a piece of parachute line he had tied to his belt. "We're there. Eighteen hundred meters, right on the button."

I pointed Danh east-northeast in the direction of the Dong-Nai River, and at 1430 we were moving past fifty-foot palm trees and shoulder-high ferns. We were three hundred meters west of the Dong-Nai, and the hot afternoon air was filled with the smell of the river.

"Swamp Fox, this is Fox Two, over." It was England.

"This is Swamp Fox. Go ahead, Fox Two," Gritz responded.

"They made it back across the river," George whispered from behind me.

"Swamp Fox, this is Fox Two. We've got two hooches and an estimated one thousand kilos of rice at right 1.9, up 1.5. We've dumped the rice in the river, over."

"Roger, Two. Swamp Fox, out."

"They're five hundred meters northeast of the MSS," I reported to George.

While we were moving downhill through thick undergrowth, Danh stopped abruptly. I moved forward and found him crouched at the edge of a north-south trail that measured a meter across and cut a tunnel through the undergrowth. Its surface was covered with six-inch-long grass, much of it flattened by foot traffic.

"Sanh, get security up and down the trail," George commanded, "and pass the word to stay off of it." He was concerned because our jungle boots left a pattern that was well known to the enemy. Also, Americans left prints that were longer and narrower than those left by the Cambodians and Vietnamese.

"You wanna set up a Claymore?" I asked.

"Yeah," nodded George while extending his head out over the trail, "down to the left."

"Security in place," Sanh told us.

"Okay, Jimmy," George said, "you position the mine. Sanh and I'll rig the trip-wire."

Sanh handed me a Claymore mine, and I moved through the brush to the point where the trail turned toward the river. Looking south, I saw thirty meters of straight trail before it disappeared. I removed the olive-drab fiberglass mine from its canvas bandoleer and laid it flat on the ground. Twenty meters down the trail, George and Sanh extended a fine trip-wire across the grassy trail. In the branches above their heads, two bright green parrots sat silently watching.

After spreading the mine's scissors-type folding legs, I held it in front of me. Looking through the peep sight on top of the mine, I aimed it down the center of the trail and slowly pushed its legs into the soft earth.

In the front section of the Claymore were spherical steel fragments embedded in plastic. Behind the fragments, the device was packed with C-4. When detonated, the exploding C-4 would propel a pattern of steel fragments, which—fifty meters out—would measure fifty meters wide and two meters high. When detonated, the mine would kill or wound everyone along the thirty-meter section of trail in front of me.

On the left side of the trail Sanh tied the end of the trip-wire to a sapling. Across the trail, George used pliers to crimp a nonelectric blasting cap to a pull-type firing device. He then taped the firing device to a stalk of bamboo and tied the trip-wire to the device. The wire was stretched tight across the trail and ran shin high through the grass. With the wire in place, Sanh reached out over the trail and adjusted individual blades of grass around the wire so it wouldn't be easily spotted by someone walking down the path. When everything was in place he gave George a thumbs-up. George then tore off another piece of green tape to secure the end of a thirty-foot section of white detonating cord to the nonelectric blasting cap attached to the pull-device.

Sanh left Danh near the trip-wire to make sure no one accidentally set it off, then he crossed the trail to where George was waiting. Once everything was set, George walked backwards in my direction, unraveling the detonating cord. Sanh followed him and covered the milky white cord with leaves.

"Mine ready?" George dropped to his knees next to me.

"Right down the center of the trail," I said.

He removed a small wooden box from his pocket and

pulled a second nonelectric blasting cap from it. While Sanh and I stood guard over him, he used the pliers to crimp the blasting cap onto the end of the detonating cord. With the blasting cap firmly attached, he inserted it into the detonating well on the Claymore.

"She's all set." George covered the mine and detonating cord with leaves. "Sanh, call in security."

We moved to a position fifty meters west of the trail, and I pointed Danh in the direction of the MSS. Minutes later, George signaled me to wait while Sanh rigged a booby trap on the trail we were leaving.

Whoomph. A loud explosion to our rear. "What the hell was that?" George asked. He, Ly, and I ran to the rear of the column. The thought that Sanh might have accidentally triggered his own booby trap gave me a sick feeling. When we reached the end of the column, it was a relief to find him squatting next to a tree.

"Claymore," he told us.

"That was quick," George said. "Let's take a look."

"We be careful," Sanh cautioned. "One day I kill VC on trail and company come behind him." Sanh raised both arms parallel to the ground; we then began moving in the direction of the explosion. At a distance of twenty meters I smelled the exploded C-4 and saw something blue lying on the trail. It was an enemy soldier. We stopped for a few seconds to listen. Except for the sound of an animal screeching in the distance, everything was silent.

"Get security in place," George told Sanh, who then raised his HT-1 radio to his lips and gave instructions to the squad leaders. As soon as security was in place, we moved forward. Ten meters behind the first Vietnamese was a second blue-uniformed soldier lying on the trail.

The soldier closest to the Claymore looked as though he had been torn apart by a shotgun blast at close range. Much of his face was gone, and the front of his uniform was wet with blood. He had been carrying a rucksack full of rice. Its contents and a green pith helmet were blown down the trail behind him. The second soldier had been hit by a single fragment. It left a round hole in the center of his forehead. He had fallen back on top of his rucksack and lay with his mouth and eyes wide open.

"What d'ya wanna do with them?" I asked George as we stood next to the second soldier.

"Leave, 'em," he replied. "Rig a grenade under this guy's ruck."

"Ahhhh." A long breath gurgled from the soldier closest to the mine, and his legs began to quiver. We ran to him and knelt at his side. His eyes, nose, and upper jaw were gone, but somehow his lower jaw and tongue remained in place. I checked his pulse.

"He's dead," I announced.

"Go ahead and rig the ruck," George said. "I'll update Gritz."

Sanh and I walked back to where the second soldier was lying. "VC from 9th Division," Sanh commented as I removed a fragmentation grenade from my harness. "They have good uniform and equipment."

By removing the grenade's time-delay element, we had rigged it for instant detonation: there was no longer a four-second delay. While Sanh pulled the rucksack from the dead man's back, I pulled the safety pin and held the grenade on the trail with its safety lever facing up. Sanh then placed the rucksack on top of my hand. Being careful to maintain pressure on the safety lever, I slid my hand out from under the rucksack. If pressure on the safety lever were relaxed, the striker would rotate and detonate the grenade. It was called "milking the grenade"; it was especially dangerous when rigging a grenade whose time-delay element had been removed. With everything set, we recalled our security teams and headed back to our perimeter.

Ten minutes later, we stopped while Sanh booby-trapped our trail. As we waited, Cawley radioed Captain Gritz that his section had found a well-used east-west trail twenty-seven hundred meters northwest of the support site.

At 1615 we arrived at the clearing on the south side of the perimeter; forty-five minutes later, three Skyraiders dropped sixteen napalm containers of food, ammunition, and supplies. Following the drop, Jarvis supervised the booby-trapping of the Drop Zone and all of the southern approaches to our perimeter. Returning to our positions, we recovered our rucksacks and strung our hammocks.

After dinner, Sanh took out a short patrol while George and I conducted detailed inspections of the platoon's weapons and gear. By the time we finished, the sun was sinking into Cambodia, and the colors of the day were quickly fading. When we returned to our hammocks Rinh had hot tea waiting, and we sat talking softly well into the night. Around 2200 I crawled into my hammock and, under a star-filled sky, nodded off to sleep.

"Jim." George shook my hammock.

"Yeah?" I checked the luminous hands on my Seiko; it was 0310.

"Gritz has a bad feeling. Says we gotta move."

"Okay." I stuffed my hammock into my rucksack and by the time I had it on my back, England's second platoon was moving out on point. A few minutes later, Danh followed England's last man, and the headquarters section fell in behind us. Howard's first platoon brought up the rear. A short distance from the perimeter, we picked up a north-south trail and began following it north. With the help of the moon it was easy going and a pleasant change from humping a rucksack during the heat of the day.

At 0800 we cut off the trail, crossed a knee-deep stream, and stopped in a bamboo thicket while Doyle made radio contact with the C-Team. While we waited, Jarvis, Howard, and Montgomery slipped back across the stream to booby-trap the trail we had traveled. Thirty minutes later, Doyle completed his radio contact and we continued northwest under a double canopy.

Whoomph. An explosion boomed to our rear. It was 0900 hours. "Booby trap," George confirmed as we pushed through a tangle of vines and leaves. Whoomph. A muffled explosion from the same area. I turned and gave George a victory sign.

Whoomph. Another muffled explosion. "Jarvis is good," George smiled.

"Looks like Gritz was right," I told him. "Mister Charles must want our ass."

A few minutes later the radio came to life. "Swamp Fox, this is Fox One, over." It was Howard.

"Fox One, this is Swamp Fox, over," Gritz responded.

"Swamp Fox, this is Fox One. We checked the booby traps and found three heavily armed trackers killed by the Claymore. Two others stepped on Toe Poppers and left blood trails heading south, over."

"Roger, One. Make sure you reseed the trail. Swamp Fox, out."

Another radio transmission came about fifteen minutes later, but I couldn't hear it.

"Glossup's just north of the new MSS," George told me. "Says there are fresh VC tracks all over the place." We continued to follow the stream bank to the north-northwest. Sometime later, the column suddenly stopped.

"Just hit an east-west trail," advised George. "We'll move across as soon as we get security in place." As we waited, Gritz radioed Howard to sanitize and booby-trap the crossing point after everyone was on the other side.

We continued northwest through thick undergrowth and crossed the waist-deep stream for a second time at the point where it abruptly turned to the east. At 1700 we arrived at the hill that would serve as our MSS. It was an area of tall palm trees with bowed trunks. Between the palms grew clumps of bright green bamboo. Yellow-striped black birds chirped high in their leaves.

"Jim," George said as I strung my hammock, "Gritz wants us at headquarters." I picked up my M-16 and we walked the short distance to where Doyle was sitting on the ground sending code.

"Over here." Gritz was sitting on a fallen palm tree and we gathered in front of him. "A few minutes ago we received a message from Blackjack to proceed across the Dong-Nai."

"Hymmm, hymmm," Jarvis hummed and everyone laughed.

"Sir, they gonna airlift us across?" England asked.

"No, we'll move upriver and build a raft."

"Sir, that current will carry a raft a good distance downstream," Montgomery said. He had served with an amphibious reconnaissance unit in the Marine Corps and was recognized as the team's expert on waterborne operations.

"I know," Gritz said. "I want you and Buck to come up with a solution."

"Could get sticky if we get hit during the crossing," Howard said.

"That it could," Gritz answered.

"Sir. Any chance of reinforcements?" Jarvis asked.

"None. If we lock horns with the 9th Division, we're on our own. It's critical that we maintain our aggressive patrolling and booby-trapping." He paused to look at his map. "Okay, tomorrow's assignments." Gritz looked at Howard. "Jim, take your platoon thirty-one hundred meters north-northwest to link up with recon at 485 865. They're on a hill overlooking the crossing site."

"Yes, sir."

"Okay, Yed and Dale. I want you to patrol to the west. Make sure Clyde isn't moving in from that direction."

"Got some hooches a klick out," Yedinak looked at his map. "Could be a base complex."

"Check it out," Gritz looked closely at his map. "George and Jimmy, we got a Sky Spot coming in at 485 855. I want you to conduct the BDA."

"Yes, sir," we answered in unison.

Following the meeting we returned to our hammocks. Under a striped crimson-and-gray sky, we prepared our evening meal. I had the 2200-to-2400 watch; at 2330 I heard the Sssshhhh of bombs falling through the still night air.

"Sky Spot," I hissed. Everyone rolled from their hammocks and thumped to the ground. Karoumph, karoumph, karoumph. Exploding bombs lit the night and shook the ground beneath my chest.

At 0630 we departed with Danh on point and moved downhill to the south-southwest. We were slowed at the bottom of the hill by thick underbrush and thorn-covered vines. Thirty minutes later, we stopped at the edge of a bright clearing lined with shoulder-high elephant grass. Fifty meters into the clearing two sun-bleached thatch roofs extended above the elephant grass. Beyond the roofs a grass hill was pockmarked with blackened bomb craters and the remains of a few huts. At the top of the hill, a thick veil of morning mist drifted high amongst the leaves of tall gray-trunked trees.

"Sanh, have Danh check it out," George said.

While Danh pushed through the elephant grass, we formed a small defensive perimeter and waited. Fifteen minutes later, he returned and whispered a few words to Sanh, who reported, "VC dead." We deployed both squads on line and waded forward through the tall grass. Beyond the grass, we found two large thatch-roofed structures with open sides and bamboo floors. Thach and I checked the one on the right and found a blackboard at one end and a large propaganda banner hanging at the other.

"School," Thach said. We entered the second structure and found George and Sanh standing over a large wooden box.

"Demo and booby-trap supplies," George remarked. "A school for sappers."

I looked inside the box and saw American and Russian firing devices, two American "Bouncing Betty" type antipersonnel mines, a few cast-iron fragmentation grenades, a block of TNT with the number four hundred and Russian letters printed on its side, a box of Chinese blasting caps, a bottle of French potassium chlorate, two satchel charges made of rope and strips of bamboo, and numerous parts to mines and booby traps.

"Sanh," George said, "leave a couple of men here. As soon as we clear the area, have them blow the box."

"*Oui*, Trung-si."

Outside the classrooms, we deployed on line again and moved south through more elephant grass. On the far side of the shoulder-high grass we entered the impact area: a large open space covered with foot-high grass. The black-rimmed bomb craters were still steaming. Just up the hill from them we came to three huts that had been flattened by the blasts.

"Move 'em through and set up security," George barked the order to Sanh.

I found a dead Vietcong in khaki lying on the ground to the left of the huts. One of his arms and part of his chest had been blown away.

Whoomph. The box of explosive materials exploded. Looking back, I saw flames and thick gray smoke. As I examined the dead man's plastic wallet, George and Thach and a few Bodes searched through the remains of the flattened structures.

"Throw everything in the hole and blow it," George said to Thach, who then yelled instructions to the Bodes. Everyone began dropping whatever they were carrying into a foxhole.

"Bac-si," Sanh yelled. He and Danh were squatting on a path leading to the only hut left standing. "Come, I show you." I put the wallet in my pocket and walked to where they were standing. "Mine." Sanh pointed to three metal prongs sticking out of the hard-packed path.

"How in the hell did you spot them?" I asked in amazement.

"Bounce mine," he said. "VC leave warning on trail."

"A Bouncing Betty," I commented. "When I was in

Cuba, a Marine lost both of his legs to one of these suckers."

"I move mine." Sanh removed his knife from its sheath.

"Don't mess with it," I said.

"*Oui,* Bac-si. Come, I show you warning." Sanh left Danh to make sure no one triggered the Bouncing Betty, and we walked a short distance down the path.

"Fire in the hole," George yelled. Sanh and I hit the ground. Whoomph. Black smoke billowed from the hole.

At the beginning of the path, Sanh showed me three rocks: one at the center of the path and one at each side. "Three rock or three string mean danger," he said. "No VC live house. It booby-trap house."

"Guest quarters," I mused as I removed the rocks from the trail and tossed them into the grass.

"Come, I show you."

As we walked up the path to the thatch-and-bamboo hut, I saw it had a bamboo door and an open window to the right of the door. To the left of the hut were a dozen orange trees with dark green leaves; to its right were smaller trees with drooping branches. I think they were lemon trees.

"Do not touch door," Sanh said as we approached.

Sanh climbed in the window and I followed him into the musty room. "See, Bac-si." He pointed above the door.

"Looks like a C-ration can," I said. Looking closer, I saw that the olive-drab can had been tied to the door frame and that inside the can was what appeared to be a gray VC fragmentation grenade. I carefully brushed spiderwebs from around the can and saw that the grenade's safety pin had been removed. One end of the wire was attached to the grenade, while the other was tied to the top of the door.

"If soldier open door, wire pull grenade out of can, and soldier die," he said.

"Let's get outta here," I said. We crawled back out the window and Sanh used his lighter to set the thatch roof ablaze.

"Jim!" George circled his arm over his head. Sanh and

I picked up Danh and ran to where George, Ly, and Thach were waiting. "Let's go," George said.

As our column moved uphill through more elephant grass, George briefed Gritz on our bomb damage assessment. Looking back at the valley, I couldn't see much through the black, gray, and white smoke that billowed from a half-dozen fires. At the top of the hill we entered dense foliage, and as we moved downhill into a dark valley, a distant firefight erupted.

A few minutes later, George closed the gap between us. "Howard made contact with six VC," he told me. "They're in a battalion-size base camp seventeen hundred meters north-northeast of the MSS."

"Any casualties?" I asked as we pushed through an almost impenetrable tangle of leaves and green-and-brown vines.

"No," he said. "Howard said they had a picture of Uncle Ho hanging in the kitchen and that one of the hooches was filled with propaganda leaflets."

At 1245 we arrived at the top of the hill. I was about to tell Danh that it was time to take a break when he unexpectedly froze, then slowly took a few steps to the rear.

"*Pos!*" He pointed to a four-foot gray snake with black and yellow bands.

"Krait." If disturbed, it was one of the deadliest snakes in the jungle. "Go around him," I instructed Danh. He took a few steps to his right and stopped again.

"*Pos!*" He pointed to another krait slithering across the dark jungle floor. If it weren't for its yellow bands, it would have been almost invisible.

"Jimmy," George hissed from behind me. "They're all over the place."

"Must be a nesting area," I said as George cut an eight-foot section of sapling with a vee at its top.

"Snake stick," he said. "Danh, gimme your machete." George slung his M-16 over his shoulder; with the snake stick in one hand and the machete in the other, he parted the vines and moved downhill to the east.

"Big one," he blurted out as he jumped to his right and positioned the stick's vee behind the snake's head. With its head pressed tight against the ground, the viper's jaw flared wide and the remainder of its body whipped violently back and forth.

"Don't let that boy get loose," I pleaded from behind him. George reached forward and, with a swing of the machete, decapitated the snake. For a few seconds the headless viper sprayed the area with blood as it continued to whip from side to side.

At the bottom of the hill, Danh and I slid down a muddy bank into a clear, slow-moving stream. While standing in knee-deep water we submerged our canteens and they bubbled full of cool water. As George and Ly slid down the bank, I added Halazone tablets to my canteens and noticed that the far bank was crawling with red ants.

"Fire ants," I told George as a distant firefight resounded through the jungle. We followed the stream for a short distance. When we were well past the fire ants we climbed atop the muddy bank and continued on our easterly azimuth through a dense entanglement of leaves and vines.

"Cawley made contact with an undetermined number of VC," George reported. "They're three hundred meters south of where Howard's platoon made contact with the six VC." George held the radio handset between us.

"Fox Four, this is Swamp Fox," Gritz radioed Cawley. "Are you in the same base camp as Fox One? Over."

"Negative, Swamp Fox. This is a farming area. We found two thousand kilos of rice and two acres of corn and beans under cultivation. The hooches are well built. All of them have tunnels leading to well-constructed bunkers, over."

"Roger, Four. Set up an overnight ambush. Clyde should be back when he thinks it's safe, over."

"Roger, Swamp Fox. Fox Four, out."

We hacked our way uphill through leaves and thorn-covered vines and paused when Danh arrived at a large fallen tree. I removed my map and laid it on the trunk.

"Better not go any farther east," I cautioned. "Might hit some of the booby traps we left yesterday."

"Yeah," George agreed, "shoot an azimuth back to the MSS." I placed my lensetic compass on my map and rotated it until its north-south grid lines lined up with the compass's north-oriented needle. With the map thus oriented, I used the scale on the side of the compass to measure the distance back to the support site.

"Eighteen hundred meters north-northeast," I told him.

"Let's get on home," he said. I pointed Danh in the right direction, and at 1700 we arrived at the perimeter. While George briefed Gritz, I returned the Bodes to their positions. High above our heads, palms and clumps of coconuts were silhouetted against a deep blue sky. A while later I found George kneeling next to his hammock with his map spread on the ground.

"Everything's a go for the crossing," he said.

"What's the plan?" I removed cans of C-ration bread and peanut butter from my rucksack and sat on the ground opening them.

"A ferry," he smiled. "Kindoll says that Gritz, Cawley, and Montgomery are gonna swim a ferry line across."

"That's a long way to swim a rope."

"Montgomery says it can be done. Once the rope's across, they'll tie it to trees on both sides. Then they'll connect the raft to the ferry line with a short rope and snap links."

"The C-Team sending us another raft?"

"No. Howard and Jarvis are gonna build one. Once the raft's in the water and linked to the ferry line, they'll attach ropes to its bow and stern so we can pull it back and forth across the river."

"The Dong-Nai Ferry," I joked.

CHAPTER SEVENTEEN

THE MID-MORNING SUN was high in the sky, and in our dark, wet world beneath the canopy, Danh dripped with sweat as he used a machete to cut a path through a tangle of leaves and vines. With the third platoon leading on point, we moved north along the east bank of a slow-flowing stream called the Da-ko. Following our boot prints through the soft mud were the headquarters section and Howard's first platoon. Five hundred meters to the west, England's second platoon was moving parallel to our route of march. Sixteen hundred meters to the north, recon patrolled the area of our planned river crossing.

Karoumph, karoumph, karoumph. A string of five-hundred-pound bombs exploded to our rear. Seconds later, an F-100 screeched overhead. Its target: the battalion-size base camp that the first platoon had located a day earlier. Captain Gritz had requested the follow-up air strike because he was convinced the enemy would return to the camp once they were sure we were out of the area.

An hour later we were moving in and out of the shadows of the great trees. Packed between their trunks were lush green ferns that grew to a height of ten feet.

Chunk-chunk-chunk. Danh fired a quick burst from his

silencer-equipped Sten. George and I ran forward to where he had dropped to one knee.

"Two VC," he told us as I looked for movement. "I see two face." He snapped his fingers. "Maybe one second." Twenty meters ahead the roofs of two thatch huts glowed in the bright sunlight of a small clearing. George turned to Sanh.

"Get 'em on line." Sanh raised his HT-radio to his mouth. He whispered instructions to the squad leaders, then raised both arms parallel to the ground. As the Bodes ran forward and deployed to Sanh's left and right, George used his PRC-25 radio to brief Gritz.

"Move 'em through and set up security on the north side of the clearing," George instructed Sanh. "Headquarters will conduct the search. First platoon's got rear security."

With the platoon on line, George raised his hand above his head and lowered it forward. We advanced at a fast walk and quickly moved through the camp. Both huts were open sided, and between them a fire pit smoldered under a blistering sun. We moved twenty meters back into the jungle on the far side of the clearing and set up security as George made contact with Gritz.

"Captain says it's a way station," George advised. "He wants you to take a look at some medicine they found." ·

I moved back to the clearing and found Gritz standing just inside the wood line talking to the FAC over his radio. Kindoll and Fang were kneeling on the ground next to the fire pit. Spread out on the ground in front of them were three Russian bayonets, a few black uniforms, some cooking utensils, and a small cardboard box.

"Bac-si," Fang smiled as I approached.

"What d'ya got?" I asked.

"ID card with 'C-123' printed on it." Kindoll put the card in his pocket. "Probably the 123rd VC Company."

"Could be a C-123 pilot," I kidded.

"They local VC," Fang assured me.

"Yeah," Kindoll agreed, "guides for main-force VC and NVA moving through the area."

"George said you found some medical supplies," I said.

"Not much." Kindoll pointed to the box. I squatted next to it and found that it contained a package of French band-aids, a bottle of American APCs (aspirin, phenacetin, and caffeine), and bottles labeled Casphosuljonate, Norodiena-dine, and Nicethamide.

"Nothing I'd want," I said to Kindoll.

"We'll booby-trap it," Kindoll said as I stood to leave.

"Roger, Sidewinder," I heard Gritz say to the FAC as he looked at his map. "We've got a way station at left 1.2, up 0.2, over."

"Swamp Fox, this is Sidewinder. Are you requesting fast movers? Over."

"Negative, Sidewinder. We've got a half-dozen Victor Charlie living this location. We'll put a Sky Spot on it tonight. Might just catch 'em at home, over."

"Roger, Swamp Fox. I'll relay a Sky Spot request to the ALO for sometime after 2400. Sidewinder, out."

We continued northeast through thick undergrowth; at 1640 we began moving uphill around clumps of bamboo. We reached the top of the hill fifteen minutes later and set up a defensive perimeter in an area of green bamboo and three-story-high trees. We were four hundred meters west of the Dong-Nai River. While George and I cleaned our weapons, Sanh took out a patrol to the north.

Whack-whack-whack. Whump-whump-whump. The stutter of automatic rifle fire to the west of our perimeter. George picked up the radio handset. A few tense minutes later, England's voice broke the silence.

"Swamp Fox, this is Fox Two. Made point contact with some locals who withdrew west. We counted six, but don't know how many were bringing up the rear. One of 'em dropped a lighter with '504' engraved on it, over."

"Roger, Two. What's your location? Over."

"Swamp Fox, this is Fox Two. We're at left 1.5, up 0.7,

over." Looking at my map, I saw they were eight hundred meters west of our perimeter.

"Roger, Two. Set up an overnight ambush. In the morning, continue to patrol until I give you the word to close this location, over."

"Roger, Swamp Fox," England said as I wiped down the outside of my M-16 with a silicon cloth.

Dit-dit, dah-dah-dit, dah-dit, dah-dit-dah. It was 1900, and Doyle was sending Morse code from a position a few meters to our rear.

"He's trying to get confirmation on tomorrow's drop," George informed Sanh when he returned from his patrol.

"When and where?" I asked.

"On the far bank at 1000. Three hundred meters north-northeast of the crossing point," George replied as Kindoll arrived.

"We're moving," Kindoll told us. "Gritz wants to get closer to the river."

I disassembled my cleaning rod, and a few minutes later we were moving downhill toward the river. After covering about two hundred meters, we stopped in an area of dead and dying bamboo to set up another perimeter. The soft, moist earth was crawling with leeches; in the branches overhead, light brown monkeys cried, "ka, ka, ka" as they fled. While stringing my hammock between two saplings, I noticed that even the branches were thick with leeches. In anticipation of a bad night, I stood in the shadows applying a fresh coat of mosquito repellent. With everything set, I lay in my hammock eating rice with Tabasco sauce and hot peppers. To the north, the occasional trumpeting of an elephant could be heard over the chirping and croaking.

"Gritz and Kindoll went down to the river to recon the crossing point," George whispered in the darkness.

Sanh was on watch near the foot of my hammock and used his HT-1 radio to alert the squad leaders. We didn't want anyone accidentally firing on the captain and Kindoll. Thirty minutes later the radio crackled, and Kindoll radioed

Howard that it was too dark to see anything. He and the captain would remain at the crossing point until the moon came up.

When I finished my rice, I lay in my hammock watching fireflies drift in the still black air.

"Fox One, this is Fox Five," Kindoll murmured over the radio. "We've got three sampans coming up the river from the south. Do not, I repeat, do not respond to this transmission. If you're receiving me, break squelch [key your radio handset] twice, over."

Psssss, psssss came the rushing sound of Howard keying his radio handset. I slipped into my boots and felt my way to where George was squatting next to our radio.

"Fox One, this is Fox Five," Kindoll whispered again. "All three boats are coming ashore."

"Shit. Bring everyone to full alert," George told Sanh. "No noise." Sanh whispered instructions to the squad leaders as fireflies flashed around him.

"Too much bamboo for us to move," I cautioned George. "They'd hear us all the way to the river."

"Fox One, this is Swamp Fox." It was Gritz. "They may be here to RV with the unit Fox Two made contact with earlier. We're in bamboo and can't move or get a clear shot at 'em. Have to wait this one out, over."

Psssss, psssss. Howard responded on his radio handset as the faint odor of Vietnamese cigarette smoke suddenly filled the air. We sat for hours, occasionally removing slimy, wet leeches from our skin. When the moon finally came up, everything appeared in shades of gray.

Karoumph, karoumph, karoumph. A string of bombs flashed to the south. "The way station?" whispered George.

"Fox One, this is Swamp Fox," Gritz whispered to Howard. It was 0300. "Two sampans are drifting south. One to go, over."

Psssss, psssss was the reply.

At a few minutes past 0400, the monkeys began to

screech in the branches above our heads. Whack-whack-whack. Whump-whump-whump. Two bursts of automatic rifle erupted to the east.

"Kindoll's M-16 and Gritz's Swedish K," I cheered under my breath as my heart shifted into second gear. "I didn't hear any AKs."

"Fox One, this is Swamp Fox, over," Gritz's Oklahoman twang broke the silence.

"Swamp Fox, this is Fox One, over," Howard responded.

"Fox One, this is Swamp Fox. We took 'em under fire as the last sampan was pulling out. Splashed one VC, over."

"Sanh," George whispered, "pass the word that they'll be reentering the perimeter from the east."

When the jungle began to glow with the first light of day, George and I found our bodies covered with hundreds of leeches. Most of the slimy brown creatures were bloated with our blood, like balloons full of air. We stripped and, standing nude in the morning mist, removed them one at a time. One had even attached itself inside George's ear; we had to fill his ear canal with mosquito repellent before it would release its hold. By the time we finished doing each other's back sides, our hands were sticky with blood and slime.

With yellow-eyed brown monkeys watching, we deployed on line and moved downhill toward the crossing point. Nearing the river, the higher elevations of the great trees disappeared into the thick morning mist. Between their trunks grew clumps of green, tan, and brown bamboo. At the water's edge, a muddy bank dropped three feet into the murky waters of the Dong-Nai. Fifty meters from the bank, everything disappeared into the mist.

We quickly formed a half perimeter at the water's edge, with our backs to the river. The third platoon defended the northern part of the half circle, Howard's first platoon the southern. Chilton's recon platoon was two hundred meters to the north and was returning from an overnight ambush.

England's second platoon was five hundred meters to the west and would continue to patrol until it was time for them to make the crossing. Soon after our perimeter was in place, the recon platoon moved inside the perimeter and began preparing their gear for the crossing.

Gritz's plan was to have recon cross first. Once on the far bank, they would move to secure the Drop Zone. They would be followed by England's second platoon, Howard's first platoon, and the headquarters section. The third herd would be the last to cross. George, Sanh, Ly, and I set up just inside the perimeter; ten meters to our rear, the Bodes were busy clearing a path for Doyle's radio antenna. Kindoll had tied two 120-foot sections of half-inch nylon rappelling rope together and stood on the bank coiling it.

To Kindoll's right, Gritz, Cawley, and Montgomery sat on the bank removing their boots. Twenty meters upstream from the crossing point, Jarvis and Howard and a few Bodes were busy cutting bamboo for the raft. The noise worried me.

Dit-dit-dit-dah, dit, dit-dah-dit, dit-dit-dit-dah. The morning mist was beginning to burn off, and Doyle sat on the ground sending an Operational Immediate request that our resupply drop be delayed until 1400. There was no way we were going to get everyone across by 1000.

"Current looks strong," Kindoll said to Gritz as he finished coiling the rope. "This half-inch rope may be too heavy to swim across."

"Let's give it a shot." Gritz stood on the bank tying his trousers tight around his waist. His body was covered with scrapes and sores. "You know," he smiled as he examined his belly button. "When I started this operation I had an inner. Now I've got an outer."

"The sign of a true guerrilla," I laughed. "If the White Mice [South Vietnamese police] checked belly buttons instead of ID cards, they'd round up every VC in Saigon."

"What type of knot you got there?" Gritz asked Kindoll.

"Square knot with half hitches on both sides," he said.

"It won't slip. In fact, the strain will pull it even tighter."

"Let's do it before the mist burns off." Montgomery had his trousers tied tight around his waist. Attached to a piece of parachute line, a .45-caliber pistol hung loosely around his neck.

"I'm ready." Cawley was the only one still wearing his trousers. Gritz sat on the bank, grabbed a few roots, and lowered himself into the water. On the far bank, the shadows of a few large trees could be seen through the fading mist.

"We'll use one of those trees as our anchor point," Gritz pointed as the lieutenant and Montgomery slipped into the water next to him. "As soon as we're tied in, you take up the slack on this side," he told Kindoll.

"Yes, sir." Kindoll had taught mountaineering in Germany and knew everything there was to know about knots and ropes. "Be sure you use a bowline as your anchor knot."

"Right," Gritz said as he pushed off into the murky waters with the rope tied around his waist. Cawley grabbed the rope a few meters behind Gritz, and Montgomery a few meters behind the lieutenant. As the three of them faded into the mist, I walked north along the bank and found Howard and Jarvis standing chest deep in water. They were using parachute line to lash the last few sections of bamboo to the raft.

"Noah's ark," Jarvis joked.

"That thing gonna hold the weight?" I asked.

"Hey," Howard smiled and pointed at Jarvis, "the world's foremost raft designer."

"Yeah," Jarvis chuckled, "I'm glad recon's going first."

Returning to the crossing point, I found Gritz sitting on the bank coughing. He appeared to have come close to drowning. To his left, Kindoll and Doyle pulled the rope from the water and re-coiled it on the bank. Cawley and

Montgomery had made it to the far side and were standing on the bank.

"Kindoll was right," the captain conceded. "Once the current got hold of that half-inch rope, it dragged me under like an anchor. Cawley had to dump his trousers. He damn near drowned."

"Sir, d'ya wanna go with the 550 cord?" Kindoll asked.

"Yeah." He took a deep breath. Kindoll removed a roll of olive-drab, 550 parachute line from his rucksack; the captain slid back down into the water.

"Here you go, sir." Gritz grabbed the end of the line and tied it around his waist.

"See you on the DZ." The captain swam the breast stroke off into the current for a second time.

"Just like fishing," Kindoll smiled while holding the unraveling roll of 550 cord.

A few minutes after Gritz reached the far bank, Montgomery held his hand above his head. They were ready to pull the heavier rope across. With the 550 cord stretched across the river, Doyle tied it to the end of the heavier rappeling rope.

"You use a double sheep bend?" Kindoll asked.

"Yup." Doyle stepped on the rope and pulled the knot tight.

"We're ready." Kindoll raised his hand above his head, and a few seconds later the 550 parachute line pulled the first of the rappeling rope into the river. When it was finally across, Gritz, Cawley, and Montgomery tied it to the base of a tree. Kindoll then ran our end of the rope around the base of a large cypress. With the assistance of a half-dozen Bodes, we pulled it until it stretched just above the water. While we held it in place, Kindoll tied it off with a bowline.

"We're in business," Kindoll grinned as Doyle used a snap link to attach a twelve-foot section of rappeling rope to the ferry line. With the ferry line ready, Jarvis and Howard floated the raft downstream. When it arrived at the crossing point, Doyle crawled on board and tied the other end of the twelve-foot section of rope to the raft. A few meters to our rear, Chilton and his recon section were waiting to make the crossing.

While Howard and Jarvis tied tow ropes to the bow and stern of the raft, I returned to the perimeter. I found George kneeling next to his rucksack taping a time-delay explosive device to a three-foot section of white detonating cord.

"Ferry's ready," I announced as what sounded like a hand grenade exploded to the south of our perimeter.

"Hope it doesn't take too long," he fretted. "I got a feeling Mister Charles is closing in."

I helped George attach trip-wires to a half-dozen fragmentation hand grenades and then returned to the crossing point. Kindoll and Doyle were standing on the bank; Chilton and his recon section were halfway across. The ferry line was stretched tight by the raft and was pulled into a vee just above the surface of the water.

"She gonna hold?" I asked Kindoll.

"Sure is," he boasted. "Nylon's got a breaking point of thirty-six hundred pounds."

"It'll stretch a good 30 percent before it breaks," Doyle confirmed.

As soon as Chilton's group off-loaded on the far bank, Glossup and his recon section began pulling the raft back to our side of the river. I returned to the perimeter and reached George just as the second platoon was returning from its patrol.

"Lotta activity out there," Yedinak said as he passed.

With the second platoon inside the perimeter, George and I moved down the line to make sure everyone was alert and that our Claymore mines were properly positioned. After checking the troops, we moved to the crossing point and saw the last of England's platoon off-loading on the far bank. Howard's first platoon was next to cross. When they left their positions on the perimeter, George and I pulled in the third platoon to form an even smaller perimeter. While waiting for the first platoon to make the crossing, George and Sanh moved outside the perimeter to rig a few more Claymore mines and fragmentation grenade booby traps.

By 1130, George, Sanh, Ly, our machine-gun section, and I were the only ones remaining on the west bank of the Dong-Nai. We had set up a small perimeter at the water's edge and were waiting for the raft to off-load on the far bank.

Whoomph. Whump-whump-whump. An explosion followed by a burst of automatic rifle fire. It couldn't have been more than two hundred meters west of our position. "Claymore and AK-47," George surmised while wrapping a section of white detonating cord around the ferry line. "Probably one of England's booby traps."

"Yeah," I agreed, "VC probably thought it was an ambush and opened up."

"VC very close," Sanh said with a strained expression.

Someone on the far bank signaled: the raft was ready. Ly, two members of the machine-gun section, and I strained to pull it back to our side of the river. Our machine-gunner remained in position with his finger on the trigger.

"Gimme some green tape," George said. Sanh removed a roll from his rucksack, and while George held the detonating cord against the ferry line, he taped them together. George had a thirty-minute time-delay fuse attached to the end of the detonating cord. A half hour after the pin was pulled, it would explode and cut the line.

My arms ached as we pulled the raft to within twenty meters of the bank. To our rear, George rigged a trip-wire attached to a fragmentation grenade. The grenade had a two-hour time-delay device attached to it. If the enemy didn't trip it within two hours, it would explode. By the time George finished rigging the grenade, we had the raft piled high with our gear. Sanh, Ly, and two members of the machine-gun section were in the water holding onto the sides of the raft. The machine-gunner and I lay on the bank with our weapons at the ready.

"All set." George covered the grenade with a handful

of leaves and someone tripped one of our booby traps less than a hundred meters to the west.

"Let's move it," I urged George, who ran to the ferry line and pulled the pin on the time-delay device. When he arrived at the bank, he signaled the far side that we were ready to cross. Ta-tow-tow-tow-tow. Our machine-gunner opened up with a long burst; my heart shifted into high gear. With my finger on the trigger, I searched for movement. I didn't see any. The three of us slid down the bank into the cool water, placed our weapons on top of our rucksacks and web gear, and grabbed the side of the raft.

George gripped the raft to my right. "We're on our way," he said with a sense of relief. I didn't say anything, but I suddenly felt very exposed and vulnerable. I worried that the Vietcong might appear on the bank and blow us out of the water. Once we got beyond the branches which grew out over the water, I saw a straight section of river on our downstream side. Upstream, the river turned sharply to the north and disappeared into the purple and green of the mountains. To the south, a layer of black smoke drifted above the canopy and mixed with what was left of the morning mist.

"Way station's still burning," I pointed.

"Can't believe we made it," George shook his head.

"River come from mountain in II Corps and go Saigon," Sanh told us.

"Let's cut the rope," I kidded, "and we'll drift down to Bien-Hoa."

"*Oui*, Bac-si," Sanh grinned, "I take you to La Plage. It is my favorite French restaurant."

Hanging on with one hand, I submerged my head in the cool water and rubbed my face. My boots had filled with water and it felt good to move my toes up and down. Halfway across the river we found Montgomery waiting at the knot in the ferry line. The current had him pressed tight against the rope.

"Last load," George said. "You look like a drowned

rat.'' Whoomph. Another explosion on the west bank. I watched for movement but didn't see any.

"Grab the rope," Montgomery said. George and I grabbed the ferry line with one hand and held the raft with the other. With his belly pressed against the rope, Montgomery disconnected the snap link and reattached it on the other side of the knot. When the raft started moving again, he grabbed hold between George and me. A few meters from the bank my knees hit soft mud.

"Made it," I sighed, relieved that we now stood knee deep in the muddy water. We picked up our gear and, struggling through ankle-deep mud, moved to dry ground.

Whoomph. An explosion on the west bank. "The charge on the ferry line," George asserted.

"A short fuse," I said. "Danh, gimme your machete." With one quick swipe I cut the ferry line, and like a languid snake, it slipped into the river and disappeared. It was noon.

I stood a moment on the bank and noticed, for the first time, that Montgomery wasn't wearing trousers.

"This the uniform of the day?" I asked, pointing at his bare legs.

"That damned Cawley pulled rank on me," he laughed.

"What?"

"Cawley almost drowned and had to dump his in the middle of the river."

"So what happened to yours?" George asked.

"Hell, he pulled rank and took mine. Said it wasn't proper for an officer to be walking around without trousers."

"What d'ya expect from a second lieutenant."

"You better hope we don't run into thorns," George smirked.

"We got two-dozen pair coming in with the drop," replied Montgomery.

We followed a winding trail north through scrub brush and bamboo until we came to a large open area surrounded by tall trees. After George talked to Kindoll we moved to the wood line on the north side of the clearing and waited while Sanh positioned the Bodes. At 1330 the FAC appeared overhead; thirty minutes later, three camouflaged Skyraiders arrived and dropped our supplies. For some reason, nine of the sixteen napalm containers weren't attached to parachutes. They tumbled lazily through the air until landing with a "thud" near the center of the clearing.

One of the containers was packed tight with tiger-striped fatigues and cold cans of Budweiser—one for every man in the company. Standing in the hot sun we chugged the beer. After weeks in the jungle, I felt drunk from just that one can. While waiting for Jarvis to finish booby-trapping the Drop Zone, Yedinak suggested we leave the empty beer cans in full view. He was convinced that the sight of them would have a dramatic impact on enemy morale.

We departed the clearing—my head spinning from an alcoholic buzz—and headed northeast under a blazing late afternoon sun. Recon led on point, followed by the second platoon, then the first, the headquarters section, and the third. Fifteen minutes after leaving the Drop Zone, what sounded like a Claymore mine exploded to our rear.

"The DZ," George whispered from behind me.

"Had to be watching us during the drop." I used my scarf to wipe the sweat from my eyes. It was quickly becoming apparent that this side of the river was also crawling with enemy troops. At 1900 we arrived at a bamboo thicket located atop a small hill and stopped to set up our MSS. Except for a Sky Spot at 0215, and what sounded like one of our booby traps at 0340, it was a quiet night.

The next morning—3 February—at 0700, the recon platoon departed. Their mission: to conduct a reconnaissance of a possible support site located twenty-six hundred meters to the northeast. An hour and a half later, the main force departed and followed a ridge line northeast into the mountains.

At 1030 Gritz stopped the unit to inform us that we would be splitting into three groups. The third platoon and the headquarters section would continue northeast along the ridge. England's second platoon would move downhill to the northwest to survey a stream area at the base of the mountain. Howard's first platoon would move downhill to the east and follow a stream called the Da-Din-Bo. The captain reasoned that three groups would be able to cover more ground and make it more difficult for enemy trackers to follow us.

Soon after the first and second platoons departed, we moved out with Danh on point. Whump. What sounded like a .30-caliber round was fired a few hundred meters to our rear. "Warning shot," I turned and whispered to George.

The air became cool and fresh as we moved higher into the mountains; I suddenly found myself full of energy. Far below and to our rear, the Dong-Nai River appeared as a twisting brown ribbon on a green felt table. By late afternoon we reached the top of the mountain and set up a small defensive perimeter. It was an area of trees, one and two stories high, topped with thick clumps of leaves. Little vegetation grew under them.

Once the Bodes were in position, I took out a short patrol and set up a listening post one hundred meters to the north. By the time I got back, the sky above the Dong-Nai had turned a fiery red.

"First platoon's a thousand meters to the south," reported George, using a piece of C-4 to heat a cup of water. "Second's twelve hundred meters west."

A soft breeze blew along the side of the mountain as I strung my hammock between a couple of saplings. The light of day was quickly fading; our mountain soon turned inky black. It was a beautiful night, and I fell asleep listening to the wind and the rustling of leaves.

"Jim!" a voice called. I opened my eyes and found myself lying on a cold, hard slab, a glaring white light above my head. I couldn't move. To my right, a gray, headless man lay on another table. Beyond him, a charred body lay stiff on another slab. His blackened legs, arms, and fingers were twisted, bent, and stiff. Although he lay in silence, I could feel the pain that was forever etched on his face. It was a morgue. I was dead.

"Jim!" It was George tugging on my hammock. I had been dreaming. I pulled the parachute nylon from my head and saw his outline standing in the shadows.

"Yeah?"

"Got flashlights coming up the mountain." His words scared the hell out of me.

"Okay." I slipped into my boots and, under a moonlit sky, quickly stuffed my hammock into my rucksack. Moving through the shadows, I felt my way to where Gritz, Doyle, Kindoll, and George were standing. Downhill, and to the west, I saw what appeared to be a line of flashlights moving up the hill.

"Strange," Kindoll commented while using a lensetic compass to take an azimuth on one of the lights. "They haven't moved in ten minutes."

"Maybe they're not flashlights," George volunteered.

"Think you're right," Gritz said.

"The wind's moving the trees," Doyle said. "Could make it look like they're flickering. Like someone walking with a flashlight."

"Might be fires," I suggested.

"There's a village down on the Dong-Nai called Bu-N'Dreng," Kindoll said. "It's due west of here."

"How far?" Gritz asked.

"About three klicks."

"I don't think they're that far," the captain said. "Check your map." Kindoll removed a poncho from his rucksack and pulled it over himself and the map. I lay on the ground next to him and ducked my head under it as he turned on his red-tipped pen flashlight.

"Here you go, Jim." Kindoll pointed to a village located on the east bank of the Dong-Nai. "Thirty-two hundred meters."

"What about this ridge?" I pointed to a lower ridge line located between us and the river.

"Yeah, they're on the next ridge," he said, "not the river." Kindoll snapped off the flashlight and removed the poncho.

"They're on a ridge line eighteen hundred meters west-southwest," Kindoll reported to Gritz.

"Al, get an Operational Immediate request for a Sky Spot to the ALO," Gritz ordered. "Give 'em the coordinates and elevation of the target and the speed and direction of the wind. With Yed and England that close to the target, it's gotta be right down their smoke stack."

"Yes, sir." Doyle felt his way to his PRC-74 radio and Gritz picked up the handset to his radio.

"Fox Two, this is Swamp Fox, over," he whispered.

"Swamp Fox, this is Fox Two, over," England responded in his familiar West Virginian drawl.

"Fox Two, this is Swamp Fox. I'm requesting a Sky Spot on a string of fires seven hundred meters southwest of your location, over."

"Roger, Swamp Fox. They're not visible from down here on the stream. Everything's quiet, over."

"Roger, Two. Anticipate the strike sometime after 2400 and plan to conduct a BDA at first light, over."

"Roger, Swamp Fox. Fox Two, out."

George and I returned to the perimeter and waited. As I lay in my hammock, I realized that my nightmare was probably the result of one of my visits to Saigon. A year earlier, I had gone to the 3rd Field Hospital to trade a few Montagnard crossbows and spears for medical supplies and equipment. While walking around the hospital, I took a wrong turn and ended up at the morgue. At the time, I was somewhat naive, and the sight of a room full of torn and deformed bodies was one of the more sobering experiences of my life—one I wouldn't forget.

Before I had a chance to leave, a mortician asked if I would help him lift a corpse from a stretcher to a slab. I agreed. As I walked out the door, he smiled and gibed, "Don't worry about a thing, Sarge. If things don't work out, we'll take good care of you." I didn't fear death, but for some reason the thought of them processing my body bothered me. There was something unnatural about it. If I were killed, and had a choice, I would prefer to be buried where I fell. With my friends.

Dit-dah, dah-dit-dah, dit-dit-dit-dah, dit. A few meters to our rear Doyle tapped out the Sky Spot request. George and I lay in our hammocks chatting quietly for a while. A few minutes past midnight, a series of flashes lit the sky to the west. In an instant, the fires disappeared.

Karoumph, karoumph, karoumph. The sound of the exploding bombs reached our eardrums. "Right on target," George whispered in the shadows. I quickly fell back to sleep and, hours later, awoke to the predawn sound of birds chirping. A star-filled, black sky slowly turned blue, and for the first time in days our perimeter wasn't shrouded in mist. Far below and to the west, mist-filled valleys and mountains, mottled green and purple, continued for as far as I could see.

I led a patrol to the north and, before returning, moved our outpost fifty meters farther north. During the day, I didn't like leaving an outpost in the same location for more than a few hours. By the time I got back to the perimeter, a bright orange sun hung low in the clear morning sky and the branches were alive with yellow-striped black birds. I was sitting in my hammock sipping tea when the sun's first rays touched my face.

"Swamp Fox, this is Fox Two, over." It was Yedinak.

"Fox Two, this is Swamp Fox, over," Gritz responded.

"Swamp Fox, this is Fox Two. BDA completed. All bombs on target. We've got twelve Victor Charlie KBA and, judging from the number of blood trails, I'd say they've dragged a few more out of the impact area, over."

"Roger, Two. Booby-trap the area and RV this location, over."

"Roger, Swamp Fox. Fox Two, out."

Gritz was concerned about enemy activity and kept the third platoon in place to provide perimeter security. The welcomed break provided George and me with the opportunity to conduct a detailed inspection of everyone's weapons, ammunition, and equipment.

At 1300 Howard's platoon closed from the southeast, and fifteen minutes later England's entered the perimeter from the west. Gritz called the American platoon commanders to a meeting; when George returned, he informed me that we had received orders to continue the mission past Tet. The Bodes were visibly shaken by the news because we had assured them that they would be back in Bien-Hoa for the Tet holidays. Within minutes of the announcement, the Bodes began digging foxholes along the perimeter—something they had never done before.

"Let Gritz know what's going on," George said. "I gotta find Sanh."

I ran the short distance to headquarters and found Gritz talking to Howard, Kindoll, and Fang. "Sir," I interrupted, "there's something strange going on. The Bodes are digging in."

"I know," he said. "Fang, get the platoon sergeants."

A few minutes later, David—a tall, good-looking interpreter—arrived with a delegation of seven Bodes. Sanh and Thach were among them.

"Okay, what's the problem?" Gritz asked Fang.

"Captain Gri," David began, "Cambodian soldier ask me to speak."

"I have no problem with that."

"Captain Gri," David said, "before we come this operation, you say we go home for Tet."

"David, that's exactly what I was told, and I do understand your disappointment," the captain replied with concern in his voice. "But this morning we received orders to press on, beyond Tet. As soldiers, we may not always agree with orders, but, as soldiers, we obey them."

David interpreted the captain's words for the delegation. "Captain Gri," David continued, "we must go our family. If Colonel Blackjack want us kill VC, we kill many VC, then we go Bien-Hoa." He smiled.

"What are you talking about?" Gritz asked.

"All soldier dig hole," David said. "Soon many VC come here and we kill them. Then we go Bien-Hoa." The Bodes smiled and nodded.

"Look, I appreciate your concern, but this isn't a democracy. In exactly twenty minutes we move out and press on to the north."

David finished his translation and Thach stepped forward, snapped to attention, and saluted. "Captain Gri," he said, "if American soldier in jungle long time, money go his wife. If Cambodian soldier not go home, his family not have money for food." His scar-covered leather face filled with emotion. "Captain Gri, we have no one take care our family." He grabbed the arm of a Bode from the second platoon. "Luc not want his wife fuck soldier in Saigon so she buy food for three baby." His eyes welled with tears. "Captain Gri, you know I jump Dien-Bien-Phu with 5th Parachute. I not afraid VC. When we give money our family, we go jungle for you."

I felt sorry for the Bodes and found myself being overcome by emotion. I sensed that the captain was moved, but he showed no sign of emotion. "David," he said, "you have three options. First, everyone moves out in twenty minutes, and we continue the mission until we are ordered to terminate it." David relayed his words and the Bodes shook their heads that it was not an agreeable option.

"Second, you turn in your equipment, including weapons and ammunition. If you then decide to leave, no harm will come to you from any member of the Mobile Guerrilla Force." The Bodes again shook their heads. The captain's cold blue eyes peered at David, and I sensed that the young Bode felt uncomfortable serving as a go-between.

"Third, if you elect to remain separate, and do not turn in your weapons and equipment, you will be considered enemies of the Mobile Guerrilla Force and will be treated as Vietcong."

"Oh, shit," George whispered from behind me.

To the west a flight of F-100s arrived over the area bombed by the Sky Spot during the night. Gritz reached down and picked up his radio handset.

"Sidewinder, this is Swamp Fox, over." Gritz called the FAC.

"Swamp Fox, this is Sidewinder, over."

"Sidewinder, this is Swamp Fox. Direct one of your fast movers to buzz this location, over."

"Say again, Swamp Fox. I didn't copy, over."

"Sidewinder, I say again, direct one of your F-100s to buzz this location, over."

"Roger, Swamp Fox. You got it."

Seconds later, a jet screeched over our perimeter at tree-top level. "Are there any questions on the options?" Gritz asked as thousands of leaves drifted to the ground around us and the air filled with the odor of burnt aviation fuel. The Bodes huddled and talked in muted whispers.

"Sidewinder, this is Swamp Fox, over."

"Swamp Fox, this is Sidewinder, over."

"Sidewinder, this is Swamp Fox," Gritz said. "If I don't make radio contact with you in five minutes—repeat, five minutes—I want you to drop heavy ordnance—repeat, heavy ordnance—this location, over."

"It's crunch time," George mumbled. My heart pounded in my chest as I thought of what might take place during the next few minutes.

"Roger, Swamp Fox. I read you five by five [loud and clear]. Sidewinder, out."

The Bodes finished their discussion and David stepped forward. "Captain Gri," he said, "we are soldier. We go north."

"Whew," I sighed.

"We move out in ten minutes," Gritz said. "One, two, headquarters, and three." We moved out as the captain had ordered and at 1900 arrived at our MSS.

CHAPTER EIGHTEEN

0750, 5 FEBRUARY 1967

WITH LOW GROUND TO our left and right—and little growth beneath the canopy—we were making good time moving north-northeast along the spine of the ridge. It was another cool morning, and at 0900 we stopped so Doyle could make radio contact with Bien-Hoa. At a team meeting that morning Captain Gritz informed us that we would be breaking down into two groups. Group I—recon and the second platoon—would go north twenty-five hundred meters to conduct a reconnaissance of a suspected enemy base area. Group II—the headquarters section and the first and third platoons—would go five thousand meters to the northeast to a stream called the Da-Dimbo. Both groups would rendezvous for a scheduled resupply drop at 1000 on 7 February.

At 0950 Group II moved out. Our order of march: the third platoon, the headquarters section, and the first platoon. With Danh leading on point, we moved downhill into a dark, triple-canopied valley and slowly worked our way up to another ridge line. The ridge was relatively flat, but our movement was slowed by thick undergrowth.

"Jimmy," George whispered from behind me. I turned

and saw him walking with the radio handset pressed to his ear.

"Yeah?" I waited for him to close the gap.

"Montgomery and Jarvis ran into four Montagnards armed with crossbows."

"What happened?"

"They shot two arrows at 'em and ran like hell. Must've been a hunting party."

"Probably scared the hell outta the poor Yards."

We continued northeast; at 1205 Danh stopped at the edge of a well-used east-west trail. Tall trees and brush grew up to both edges of the trail, making it look like a tunnel winding through the jungle. Looking closer, I saw that bicycle and rubber-sandal tracks had been cast in the hard, dry surface.

"Gritz says to follow it east," George said. At one time, an order such as that would have scared me to death. During our time in War Zone D, however, I had learned that not all trails were to be avoided. In contested areas, of course, or those areas controlled by American or South Vietnamese forces, moving on a trail could be a deadly mistake. In those areas controlled by the Vietcong, though, the enemy rarely booby-trapped the trails. If one was mined, it would be marked with a warning.

Fifty meters down this hard-packed trail, I passed a small piece of blue plastic lying at its center. I didn't pay much attention to it, but after passing a second and a third piece, I realized that they were roughly one hundred paces apart—a pattern. I stopped and called Sanh forward.

"VC mark trail," he confirmed for George and me. "When soldier come from North Vietnam, VC guide say follow this, so they not get lost."

"We may be on to something big," George murmured. He relayed the information to Gritz, and, as we continued southeast, we passed numerous pieces of sharpened wire. Each had been bent to remain upright and was intended to keep barefoot Montagnards off the trail—another indication that we were on to something.

At 1450 Danh stopped at a fork in the trail. The main trail continued to the southeast and another led downhill and to our right. The way to our right was blocked with a few branches. Danh pulled a leaf from one of them and crumpled it between his fingers. "One or two day, Bac-si."

George approached with the handset pressed to his ear. "Gritz says to stay on the main trail." I signaled Danh to move out; fifty meters down the trail, we passed another piece of blue plastic. Sanh was right about the plastic being used to guide enemy troops through the area. The branches blocking the fork also served to keep them moving in the right direction and provided additional evidence that out-siders—main-force VC or NVA units—were in the area. My guess was that they were elements of the 9th Vietcong Division.

Whack-whack-whack. Whump . . . poing . . . whump. A firefight erupted less than a hundred meters to our rear. George and Sanh ran forward to where I was, crouched down on one knee at the side of the trail. "VC at the fork," George confirmed as the shooting continued. "Gritz wants us to get down the trail behind 'em." He grabbed Sanh's arm. "Stay here with the first and second squads. Third squad," he pointed to Thach, "let's go."

We dropped our rucksacks, and, with George leading on point, we pushed southwest through thick undergrowth. At the bottom of the hill, we found the other trail. "Get 'em on line," George ordered in soft but clipped tones as the firefight continued and a few friendly rounds cut through the foliage around us. Thach raised his arms parallel to the ground; half of the squad quickly deployed to the other side of the trail. Suddenly, we heard the singsong chatter of Vietnamese voices coming down the trail. I hit the ground to the right and switched my M-16 to automatic. George took up a position on the other side of the trail and quickly crawled forward a few meters to position a Claymore mine on the far side of a large tree. Hopefully, its trunk would absorb the back blast when the mine was detonated.

A couple of seconds after George crawled back to his position, I caught a glimpse of blue moving in our direction. My hands were slippery with sweat, and I could hear my heart pounding in my ears. I settled into a good prone position and took up the slack on the trigger. "Here we go," I said to myself. I glanced to my left. George held his M-16 with the barrel resting on an elevated root. In his left hand he cupped the Claymore's electrical firing device and used his thumb to push the safety bail to the firing position.

Turning back to my front, I saw two blue-uniformed enemy soldiers running in my direction. Both wore pith helmets and carried AK-47 rifles and rucksacks. "*Nhanh-lēn,*" the first man yelled as he looked to his rear. When he turned back around, his mouth dropped open and a look of terror distorted his face. "*Dich!*" he screamed. Whoomph. Whack-whack-whack. George detonated the Claymore and I fired a long burst. In what appeared to be slow motion, the top half of the first man's body flipped through smoke and dust and landed face first on the trail. For a split second everything was quiet.

"*Tov muk peat!*" Thach yelled. Everyone jumped to his feet and ran forward through the dust and smoke as hundreds of leaves drifted to the ground. Thach stopped the advance ten meters past the second enemy soldier. When we were convinced no more enemy soldiers were coming down the trail, we formed a hasty perimeter around the bodies. While George used the radio to update the captain, I checked the bodies. The first had been cut in half, just below the rib cage, and lay on the trail in a pool of body fluids. We found his lower half lying in the brush alongside the trail. The second man had multiple gunshot and steel-fragment wounds from the Claymore—everything above his mouth was missing.

"Look, Bac-si," Thach said as he examined the first

man's rucksack. It was filled with cookies and rice cakes. Thach removed what appeared to be a receipt and handed it to me. "Caravelle Hotel, 23 Lam-Son Square, Saigon," I read aloud. "These guys go first class."

"Roger, Swamp Fox. Fox Three, out," George said into the handset. "They got three more at the intersection," he turned and reported. "Let's get up there." George and I picked up the blood-stained rucksacks and left Thach with a three-man security detail to booby-trap the trail. When we arrived at the intersection, we found Kindoll, Doyle, and Howard removing bags of candy, cookies, and rice cakes from three additional enemy rucksacks. Gritz was on the radio talking to Chilton.

"Well, well, well," Kindoll clucked as he pulled two bottles of whiskey from one of the rucksacks.

"Getting ready to celebrate Tet," Doyle said.

"Dump the whiskey and pass the food out to the Bodes," Gritz said.

"Sir," Howard said, "Jarvis can booby-trap the whiskey."

"Just make sure they stay full," Gritz smiled. George and I swung two of the enemy rucksacks over our shoulders and headed back down the main trail toward the third platoon. While Sanh passed out the captured goodies, George and I enjoyed a few sugar cookies. Shortly after Thach and the third squad returned, we continued along the trail.

Whack-whack-whack. Poing . . . whumph. An exchange of fire to the west. "Group I," George called quietly as we walked.

"Cease fire, cease fire," someone yelled over the radio. It sounded like Chilton. The firing stopped.

"Fox Four, this is Fox Two, over." England broke in. "You're in contact with friendly forces. I repeat, friendly forces, over."

"Fox Two, this is Swamp Fox," Gritz broke in. "What the hell happened?"

"Swamp Fox, this is Fox Two," England responded.

"We were moving west on the trail and made point contact with recon. Negative casualties, over."

"Swamp Fox, this is Fox Four," Chilton broke in. "Fox Four Alpha and two Bodes were hit by M-79 frags, over."

"Oh, no," I moaned, "that's Glossup."

"Roger, Four," Gritz said. "How serious?"

"Swamp Fox, this is Fox Four. Fox Four Alpha's got a piece in his leg. One of the Bodes was hit in the arm and another in the forehead. Got a lotta blood, but nothing life threatening, over."

"Roger, Four. Are you in need of assistance? Over."

"Negative, Swamp Fox. We've got a cross-trained medic and an M-5 kit, over."

"Cawley's cross-trained," I assured George as we continued down the trail. Forty-five minutes later, we cut off the path and crunched through dead bamboo to the top of a small, steep hill. Under the spreading branches of tall cypress trees we set up a small defensive perimeter with Howard's first platoon defending the eastern half. Once the third platoon was positioned along the western half, George, Sanh, Danh, Ly, and I set up just inside the perimeter. I took a patrol two hundred meters to the west, and on my way back I dropped off a three-man listening post seventy-five meters west of the perimeter. When I returned I found George sitting in his hammock. It was almost dark.

"Sanh's down on the trail with a four-man Claymore ambush," he advised me.

"Good." I was worried about us setting up so close to a high-speed trail. "Any word from Group I?"

"Yeah, they're thirty-eight hundred meters northwest of here," he said. "Cawley took care of Glossup and the two Bodes."

"Cawley's a good medic."

"Two Bodes from the first platoon came down with malaria," he said. "Rinh's with 'em."

"Latent malaria hasn't been the problem I thought it would be," I said.

"Phuc-yoo, phuc-yoo." A three-inch green lizard balanced on a nearby branch. "Hey, George . . ." A small brown monkey-like creature pounced on the lizard and grabbed it with suction-cup tipped fingers. The furry animal had small round ears, bulging brown eyes, and a ratlike tail.

"What on earth is that?" George asked. Gripping the squirming lizard with its long fingers, the creature bit a chunk out of the reptile's midsection. With what appeared to be a smile on its face, it sat on the branch munching its meal. Once it had eaten everything between the head and tail, it dropped the remains to the ground and leaped into the shadows.

At 2130 George and I were sitting on the ground enjoying a cup of hot tea. "Fox Three, this is Swamp Fox, over." It was the captain.

"Swamp Fox, this is Fox Three," I whispered.

"Fox Three, this is Swamp Fox. One of our LPs just reported a large enemy force—repeat, large enemy force— two hundred meters east of here. Bring everyone to full alert, over."

"Roger, Swamp Fox. Fox Three, out." Fumbling in the shadows, I quickly stuffed my gear back into my rucksack, slipped into my ammunition harness, and picked up my M-16.

"Jimmy," George said softly, "I'm gonna check the perimeter. See if you can get some more info."

"Okay." Moving through the shadows, I felt my way the short distance to the headquarters section. There I found what appeared to be two people huddled under a poncho. Kindoll was standing next to them with his M-16 at the ready. "What's going on?" I whispered.

"Gritz and Howard are figuring the coordinates for a Sky Spot," he replied.

"Any update on the size of the unit?"

"Just what the LP told us."

"What's that?"

"They radioed that beaucoup VC were setting up on the next hill. Then we lost contact with 'em.''

I lay on the ground and slipped my head and shoulders under the poncho. Gritz had a map spread on the ground and Howard held a red-tipped flashlight a few inches above it. "We're at 565 929." Gritz used a grease pencil to mark the spot. "Clyde's on the next hill." He pointed 250 meters east of our location.

"Sir, we may have a problem," Howard said with concern.

"What's that?"

"Sir, we've got three hills here." He used a pen to point to the locations on the map. "You're saying that Clyde's on the middle hill and that we're on the one on the left. I think we're on the middle hill, and that Clyde's on the one on the right. If you're wrong, the Sky Spot's gonna hit us, not them."

"Well, there's only one way to find out," Gritz responded. "Jimmy, tell Al I've got a Sky Spot request for him."

"Yes, sir." I slipped out from under the poncho and saw Doyle standing a few feet away. Doyle ducked his head under the poncho and Kindoll and I squatted to listen.

"Al, I want you to send an Operational Immediate request to the ALO in Bien-Hoa," Gritz ordered.

"Got the coordinates?" Doyle asked.

"Yeah, here you go." Gritz paused. "565 929."

"Sir," Doyle said following a moment of silence, "that's only 250 meters from here. They won't approve a Sky Spot any closer than six hundred meters to friendly forces."

"By God, you're right," Gritz exclaimed.

"Sir," Howard said, "we could report that we're five hundred meters west of where we actually are."

"That would give us 750 meters," Gritz said.

"Innovative map reading," Doyle mused.

"It's a gamble, but a necessary one. Let's do it."

"It's called 'You bet your ass,' " Kindoll said.

When I returned to the platoon, I found George and Thach sitting next to the radio and updated them on the situation. "No use scaring the hell outta the Bodes," George said. "If the captain's wrong, it won't make any difference."

"You're right," I agreed. "If he's wrong, we won't live to see the sun come up." The thought that I might be killed by friendly fire bothered me. If I had to die, I wanted it by an enemy bullet, not an American bomb.

"Thach," George whispered, "pass the word that we've got a Sky Spot coming in to the east. Get down on the west side of the trees. And do it quietly."

Dah, dit-dah-dah, dah-dah, dit-dit-dit. We could hear the muffled sound of Doyle sending the Sky Spot request. George, Thach, and I moved our rucksacks to a position behind a large cypress. "What d'ya think?" George asked.

"No easy solution," I said. "The sides of the hill are covered with dead bamboo. If we try to bug out, we're gonna sound like a herd of elephants."

"Yeah. If we don't call in the strike, and wait for first light to move, one of their LPs is gonna pick up our movement. They'd be on us like stink on shit."

"Wouldn't be a problem if we had reinforcements standing by. With air support, we could hold the hill until they got here."

Two hours later we sat waiting for the unknown, and every now and then the smell of wood smoke and Vietnamese cooking filled the still night air. High above our perimeter, whispering death fell through the still night air. "Here we go," I whispered. George put his arm over my shoulder, and I could hear my heart pounding in my ears. Suddenly, the animals became silent and a flash lit our world beneath the canopy.

Karoumph-karoumph-karoumph. Bombs flashed, the earth shook, and concussions pounded our eardrums. "On target!'' I slapped George's shoulder and had to restrain a strong urge to stand up and cheer.

"Thank you, God," George prayed, as debris rained down on us.

At first light on the morning of 6 February 1967, a thin veil of smoke drifted among the leaves and the smell of cordite and wood smoke filled the air. We kept everyone absolutely still until we had enough light to see and then slowly moved out with Howard's first platoon on point. They were followed by the headquarters section and the third platoon. Moving downhill through dead bamboo was slow going because each step had to be measured: one "crunch" would give us away. When the third platoon reached the trail we had been following the day before, we picked up Sanh and the members of his ambush and waited while George buried a few Toe Poppers along the trail.

Fifty meters farther down the trail we stopped again. While we waited, George moved into the undergrowth along the left side of the trail and rigged a trip-wire attached to a Claymore mine. Sanh did the same on the right side. We figured that if the enemy tripped one of the Toe Poppers, the remaining members of the unit would move to either side of the trail and begin skirting it. When we caught up with the headquarters section's last man, Howard picked up the pace.

At 0901 the lead platoon cut off the trail and moved a hundred meters into the undergrowth. While Doyle cleared a lane for his radio antenna, we set up a hasty perimeter around him. Once everyone was in place, George sent Sanh and three Bodes on a short patrol to the north. While we waited we sat leaning against our rucksacks. "Have you talked to Sanh about the Tet problem?" I asked George.

"Yeah, they're still upset, and I can't say I blame 'em."

"You know, if the Bodes were extracted, we could press on with the mission," I said.

"Just the Americans?"

"Why not?"

Dit-dit, dah-dit-dit, dit, dah-dah, dit-dah. A short distance to our rear Doyle was sitting on the ground with his commo key attached to the thigh of his outstretched leg. A mischievous smile appeared on George's face. "You're right. Thirteen men could do it. We could go north to the II Corps border. All we'd need is an extra FAC to give us continuous daylight coverage."

"Yeah, and maybe two emergency extraction choppers standing by at Duc-Phong," I whispered. "Just in case we got into deep shit." There was a commotion and the sound of Cambodian voices. Something was wrong. The Bodes were always excellent at maintaining noise discipline.

"Jim, check it out," George directed, as Sanh returned. Nearing the headquarters section, I saw two Bodes lying on the ground kicking their feet. Others were jumping up and down.

"They gone crazy?" I asked Kindoll.

"Just got a message from Blackjack," he grinned. "We're being extracted at 0800 tomorrow morning."

I ran back and relayed the news to George and Sanh, who grabbed my hand and squeezed it. With tears of joy brimming in his bloodshot eyes, Sanh proclaimed, "Good, Bac-si. I very happy." Within a few minutes the Bodes were dancing and singing.

"Sanh, calm 'em down," George said. "We ain't outta here yet." I had mixed feelings about the news. I felt happy for the Bodes, but for some unexplained reason I also felt a sense of disappointment.

Fifteen minutes later we departed and again followed the first platoon and the headquarters section northwest on the trail. For forty-five minutes we were moving down the trail at a fast pace. Suddenly, the column stopped. Ten meters ahead, a sparkling stream flowed over moss-covered rocks. I wiped the sweat from my face and bounced a couple of times to adjust the weight of my rucksack.

"Swamp Fox, this is Fox One, over," Howard called in a hushed voice.

"Fox One, this . . ." Whack-whack-whack. Whump-whump-whump. An exchange of heavy fire interrupted Gritz's transmission. We moved into the brush at the side of the trail and watched for movement.

"Swamp Fox, this is Fox One, over." Howard sounded winded.

"Fox One, this is Swamp Fox, over."

"Swamp Fox, this is Fox One. Made contact with an estimated squad at the edge of the biggest base camp I've ever seen. It's a good 150 meters across and goes north for as far as I can see. Negative casualties. VC broke contact, over."

"Roger, One. Assault immediately. Don't give them a chance to set up, over."

"Roger, Swamp Fox. Fox One, out."

"Fox Three, this is Swamp Fox, over."

"Swamp Fox, this is Fox Three, over," George responded.

"Fox Three, this is Swamp Fox. Move two hundred meters north and assault on Fox One's right flank. I'll be with Fox One, over."

"Roger, Swamp Fox. Fox Three, out."

"Two hundred meters." I pointed Danh north, and we pushed through a tangle of leaves and vines.

"Make sure they know we're gonna have friendlies on our left flank," George said to Sanh as we used our hands to push the undergrowth aside.

"*Oui*, Trung-si." Minutes later Danh stopped and raised two fingers. We had reached the two-hundred-meter point. The smell of wood smoke and Vietnamese cooking suddenly filled the air; a cacophony of firing continued to the south. Sanh raised his HT-1 radio to his lips and gave last-minute instructions to the three squad leaders.

"Okay." Sanh flashed George a thumbs-up. Everyone was on line and ready. George raised his hand over his head and, by lowering it forward, gave the signal to move out. A short distance ahead I slipped through the last of the leaves and vines and entered a large area where all of the lower levels of foliage had been cut and cleared. Only the great trees remained, and they supported an umbrella of leaves that screened out much of the light and effectively hid the camp from aerial view. A three-foot blanket of wood smoke hung close to the ground, and the few rays of sunlight that penetrated the canopy appeared as bright, white shafts.

I made a quick visual sweep of the area, but, other than seeing a few long-legged white birds stabbing at insects, I didn't spot any movement. Glancing to my left and right, I saw the remainder of the platoon emerging from the wall of green. A short distance into the clearing we waded across the slippery, moss-covered rocks of the ankle-deep stream. On its far bank, a half-dozen black uniforms and a dingy white bra hung drying on branches. In the dark shadows beyond the uniforms, I counted ten to fifteen bamboo-and-thatch structures.

Whump-whump-whump. Fifty meters into the camp two black-clad Vietcong jumped from a trench. Whack-whack-whack. Poing . . . whump. We returned fire, and a second later they disappeared behind what appeared to be a mess hall. Sanh barked orders to keep on line as we continued forward at a fast walk; the firing continued on our left flank. Whack-whack-whack-whack-whack-whack. Two bursts of M-16 fire on our right flank. The first thatch-and-bamboo structure I came to measured thirty meters long and ten meters across. Its roof, which extended far out over its sides, was covered with green mold. Glancing inside the structure, I saw a dozen bamboo mats lying on the floor.

Whump. A round slammed into the dirt between my feet. "Sniper," I yelled as I ran for cover. Whack-whack-whack. The Bodes returned fire as George and I dove behind a large tree. The shot appeared to have come from a grassy hill on the far side of the camp. "Get some seventy-nine fire on him," I shouted to Sanh. "It came from the clearing." Our M-79 grenade launchers served as our artillery and were very effective in suppressing sniper fire.

Whump. Another round came from the clearing on the hill. Sanh barked out instructions to our grenadiers. Poing . . . whump. Poing . . . whump. Forty-millimeter M-79 rounds began exploding on the side of the hill.

"Sanh," George yelled, "lay down a base of fire with the first and second squads. Jim and I'll take the third on an envelopment."

"*Oui,* Trung-si." George and I ran past the mess hall and a number of other structures. Seventy-five meters to the north we found Thach and his squad waiting in a trench.

"Sniper," George reported. "Let's go." With George leading on point, we ran to the edge of the camp and moved uphill through thick undergrowth. A confused roar of rifle fire and explosions continued to the south. Carrying heavy rucksacks on our backs, we were soon panting and soaked with sweat. At the top of the hill we turned south. Whoomph. A loud explosion at the base of the hill. When we saw the clearing ahead, Thach radioed Sanh to stop firing. We came out of the jungle at the top of the clearing and squinted as we looked down over a field of grass.

"Check the wood line," George told Thach as he used his sleeve to wipe his face. Thach's men swept the wood line and then deployed along the top of the hill. With everyone on line, George gave the signal to move downhill. Halfway down the hill Thach stopped and pointed to the ground in front of him.

"What d'ya got?" I whispered as shooting and explosions continued to the south.

"*Khlang,* Bac-si." He pointed to a square section of faded yellow grass surrounded by green.

"George," I hissed. He ran to where we were standing and squatted next to the faded grass. "Trapdoor."

"Thach, make sure there isn't another exit," George ordered.

"Want me to lift it?" I asked as we lowered our rucksacks to the ground.

"Yeah." We squatted in the glaring sun, and George removed a fragmentation hand grenade from his harness. "Go ahead."

"On three," I said. George pulled the safety pin from the hand grenade and I grabbed handfuls of the faded grass. "One, two, three." I lifted the trapdoor a foot in the air. George tossed in the grenade and I dropped the lid back into place. We grabbed our M-16s and ran a short distance before hitting the ground. For all we knew, it could have been an ammunition bunker, and we didn't want to be killed by the explosion.

Whoomph. A muffled underground explosion. We jumped to our feet and ran back to the trapdoor. I lifted it again and cool, moldy air and thick gray smoke poured from the hole. George fired four bursts into the hole while I dropped the trapdoor to the ground next to the hole. It had beveled edges and four inches of dirt on top of a wooden bottom.

"*Dira*," Thach yelled into the hole, but no one answered. "I go in," he volunteered.

"It's my turn," George said as Thach peered into the smoke-filled hole. "See anything?"

"Bunker, Trung-si." With a flashlight in one hand and his rifle in the other, George lowered himself into the hole. It was a tight squeeze, and he immediately began coughing from the smoke. "Got a tunnel leading uphill," George hollered.

"Thach," I pointed uphill, "check it again for an exit." Whump. A shot fired in the bunker startled me. I leaned down into the hole and saw George squatting in the smokey shadows.

"You okay?"

"Yeah." He fired a burst down the tunnel. I slid into the reeking chamber and found George next to the tunnel, his back up against the wall. "He's gotta be a good ten meters down the tunnel," he said as I took up a position next to him. "Gimme a frag." I removed a fragmentation hand grenade from my harness and handed it to him. He pulled the pin, let the safety lever fly free, and counted, "One, one thousand, two, one thousand," before tossing it down the tunnel.

Whoomph. An earth-splitting concussion filled the bunker with red dust and left my ears ringing. "That should do it." His sweaty face was red with dirt.

Whump. A round slammed into the mud wall across from us. "Shit," George mumbled.

"*Cho-de!*" someone yelled from down the tunnel.

"He swore at you," I told George.

"Trung-si," Thach yelled into the bunker, "Captain Gri on radio. He say we go."

"Okay," George agreed.

"No telling where the tunnel goes," I remarked. "Could go left, right, or down. Some of these things have two or three levels."

"Let's booby-trap the entrance and get outta here," George said. I handed him a CS gas grenade and crawled out. Looking back into the bunker, I saw him toss it down the tunnel.

"Want me to rig it?" I asked as I pulled him out.

"Okay." George picked up the radio handset; I replaced the trapdoor. My eyes were burning from the smoke and my ears were still ringing. "Swamp Fox, this is Fox Three, over."

"Fox Three, this is Swamp Fox, over," Gritz responded. "What d'ya got on your end? Over."

"Swamp Fox, this is Fox Three. A hundred-man mess hall and twenty to twenty-five structures. We had an estimated squad here, but they bugged out. We've got one trapped in a tunnel, over."

"Roger, Three. When was it last occupied? Over." As George and Gritz conversed, I used my knife to dig a four-inch hole on the uphill side of the trapdoor.

"Swamp Fox, this is Fox Three. I saw some fresh meat wrappings outside the mess hall. I'd say they cooked for a

large unit sometime during the last twenty-four hours.
Mighta been the unit we called the Sky Spot in on last
night, over.''

"Roger, Three. RV my location ASAP, over.''

"Roger, Swamp Fox. Fox Three, out.''

When the hole was just right, I placed the grenade in it.
It was a tight fit. Looking downhill I saw bright flames and
thick smoke billowing from a half-dozen structures.
Whoomph. A loud explosion shook the ground. Someone
must have blown an ammo bunker. I removed the grenade
from the hole, pulled the safety pin, and carefully pushed
it back into the hole with the safety level pressed against
the side of the trapdoor. If the door were lifted, the grenade
would instantly explode. With everything set, I pulled out
a handful of grass and used it to camouflage the top of the
grenade. By the time I finished, George was at the base of
the hill standing next to one of the burning structures.

"Jimmy," he called, "let's get a picture together. Might
be our last chance.'' I ran down the hill and Thach snapped
a photo of us standing in front of the burning hooch.

We deployed on line and swept south through the camp.
Every structure was ablaze and, with thick smoke trapped
beneath the canopy, it was difficult to see for more than a
short distance. A hundred meters south, we ran into Montgomery, Jarvis, and Thai-Hien-Son—the first platoon's machine-gunner. They had killed two large pigs and were
dumping them down a well. "Let's move it,'' Montgomery
quipped. "I ain't got all day.''

"Hey," I kidded, "I heard four Montagnards kicked
your ass.''

"Don't laugh,'' Jarvis smirked. "One of those arrows
damned near got me.'' He guided us around some of their
booby traps and pointed us in the direction of the headquarters section. Twenty-five meters farther south we found
Gritz, Howard, Doyle, and Kindoll throwing food, uniforms, web gear, pith helmets, engineer tools, and communications equipment into a bunker. When they finished,

Doyle poured a five-gallon can of kerosene over the pile. Howard then placed a Claymore mine—face down—on top of the pile and walked to the rear as he unraveled the mine's firing wire. "Fire in the hole," he yelled from behind a tree.

Whoomph. Thick black smoke billowed from the bunker. "Got a distance to the MSS?" Gritz asked Howard.

"Yes, sir. Sixteen hundred meters."

"Okay, let's get outta Dodge," Gritz ordered. "First platoon, headquarters, third platoon." Howard's first platoon departed on point, and Montgomery and Jarvis returned just as the third platoon was getting ready to move out.

"Gritz wants us to booby-trap everything between here and the LZ," Jarvis explained to George. "We'll follow you out."

"You got any demmo you don't wanna take back to Bien-Hoa?" Montgomery asked.

While Danh and I waited on point, George and Sanh collected our demolition bags, extra hand grenades, and surplus Claymore mines. Ten minutes later we caught up with the tail end of the headquarters section and continued west-northwest through thick undergrowth. At 1600 we linked up with Group I on a ridge line 250 meters east of the Landing Zone. Gritz didn't think the location could be defended against an enemy ground attack and made the decision to move to another location. Fifteen minutes later we moved out.

Whoomph. An explosion came from the area of the base camp. Half an hour afterward, we arrived at the base of a hill and moved up past massive cypress trees. Between the great trees grew smaller ones and saplings. While the three main-force platoons and the headquarters section set up a defensive perimeter, the recon platoon continued eight hundred meters to the south-southwest. Their mission: to set up an ambush along a major trail.

I took a patrol four hundred meters downhill to the southeast; by the time I got back to the perimeter, the sky had turned crimson and gray and the crickets were chirping. It was almost dark when I found George squatting next to his hammock.

"Everything's quiet," I announced as I leaned my M-16 against a tree.

"Dinner's ready." He handed me a cup of hot tea.

"*Monsieur,* may I ask what you are serving?" I asked with a French accent.

"Ah, tonight we have zee house spe-cee-al-ee-tay," he responded in a similar accent. "We have Chef George's gourmet rice, sauteed with his ex-quee-zeet instant soup." George and I sat enjoying each other's company and, at last light, were joined by Sanh, Thach, and Rinh.

"Listen up," George whispered in the shadows, "this is our last night in War Zone D, and I'd like to make a toast."

"What toes?" Thach asked. Rinh whispered something in Cambodian. "Ahhh," Thach nodded.

"Here's to Colonel Francis Blackjack Kelly," George toasted. "The best group commander there ever was."

"To Colonel Kelly," I echoed, and sipped from my cup. "For a month we fought the war our way: the Special Forces way."

"Hear, hear," George cheered.

"Colonel Kelly knows more than the generals," Rinh said.

"When I was Viet-Minh we do not fear Saigon soldier because they are like elephant," Sanh said. "Mobile Guerrilla Force is like tiger."

"You're right," George agreed. "It makes no sense to combat guerrillas with conventional forces."

"When I was with the 6th, we jumped into the desert near White Sands, New Mexico," I recalled. "We were the guerrillas, and some troops from Fort Bliss were the counterinsurgency forces. Even in the open desert we kicked their ass."

"Donahue," Rinh continued, "when we return to Bien-Hoa, will you go to America?"

"Just for thirty days. I'll be back."

"Buffalo in February," George mused. "You'll freeze your butt."

"It'll be great," I countered. "Can you imagine walking down the street without worrying about ambushes, booby traps, or snipers?"

"People back in the States don't appreciate the little things," George reflected as fireflies flickered around him. "After Vietnam, I'm gonna get a lot more outta life."

"I know what you mean. Like reading the Sunday paper with a good cup of coffee."

"Or going for a walk with your kids," George said.

"Someday, I would like to visit America," Rinh sighed. "I have read Thomas Jefferson and would like to visit his memorial."

"Do you have kids?" George asked Rinh.

"Oh, no. Son-Thi-Chua and I were only married in 1965. But someday we hope to have many."

"When we go Bien-Hoa, I not come back Mobile Guerrilla Force," Sanh announced.

"What?" I was shocked.

"Khmer-Serei ask me go Cambodia."

"We'll miss you," George said.

"I very sad," Sanh continued, "but, if I die, I want to die in Cambodia. It is my country."

"My friend," I said, "if it wasn't for you, a lot of us would be dead. You've taught us a lot about soldiering."

"Thank you, Bac-si."

"This may be our last chance to talk like this, and I've gotta say something," George choked back his emotion. "For as long as I live, I'll remember our time together as something special, and I want you to know that I've grown to love you guys, like members of my own family, like brothers."

"Trung-si," Thach sniffled. He too was filled with emotion and couldn't say anything. I put my hand on his back and could feel him trembling.

"My heart feel very good," Sanh said.

"I have toes." Thach took in a deep breath. "To Mobile Guerrilla Force."

"To the Mobile Guerrilla Force," everyone toasted.

"The finest light infantry there ever was," I added.

No one wanted to sleep that night, so we sat whispering under a star-filled sky until the dawn of a new day broke. As soon as there was enough light to see by, I led the first squad back down the hill to the southeast. When I returned, everyone was ready to move to the Landing Zone.

"Gritz wants to minimize our time on the LZ," George said to me. "Recon and the second platoon will be picked up on the south side; headquarters and first and third platoons on the east side. We'll have two choppers at a time landing at each of the pick-up points."

Ten minutes later, we moved out. A hundred meters to the west we came to a large valley. Our side had been cleared for slash-and-burn agriculture and was covered with the remains of thousands of rotting tree stumps. The valley below was filled with mist. To the west, the slope was crowded with large trees and a couple of collapsed huts. Except for the kaw, kaw, kaw of a few crows flying from tree to tree, everything was silent.

We formed a defensive line just inside the wood line. When everyone was in position, Rinh, Danh, and I moved back to the edge of the clearing and lowered our rucksacks to the ground. Gritz, Kindoll, and Fang were standing a few meters into the clearing. The captain had his radio handset pressed to his ear.

"Jimmy," Gritz called. I ran to where he was standing. "Sir."

"Break out the colors."

"Yes, sir!" I smiled. "Sir, would it be okay if Danh carried them? He's been on point for the whole operation."

"Hell, yes."

I ran back to where Rinh and Danh were standing. Near the bottom of my rucksack I found the plastic bag that contained the American and Khmer-Serei flags. Both were wrinkled, but clean. "Rinh," I said. "Cut a pole for the flags." A mischievous smile appeared on his face.

"Donahue, the LLDB will be very unhappy." He pulled a machete from Danh's rucksack.

"And Rinh," I added, "tell Danh the captain wants him to carry the flags into Duc-Phong and Bien-Hoa." Rinh said something in Cambodian, and Danh responded with something I didn't understand.

"He said it is a great honor and that no one will take the flags from him," Rinh said.

"I don't doubt that." A few minutes later Rinh returned with an eight-foot section of green bamboo; while he held the pole, I tied the flags to it. "Okay." I handed the pole to Danh. Keep the pole straight and pressed against your shoulder."

With his rucksack on his back and his Sten gun slung over his left shoulder, Danh carried the flags to where the captain was standing. Wap, wap, wap. To the west a line of choppers appeared black against the clear blue sky. Kindoll popped a purple-smoke canister, and a hundred meters to the south someone popped one with yellow smoke. George and Sanh walked out from the wood line.

"Get 'em ready," George said to Sanh. "One, two, three. Thach's squad and the machine-gun section will be the last to go."

"*Oui*, Trung-si." Sanh used his HT-1 radio to issue instructions to the squad leaders. When the lead chopper reached the far side of the valley, the Huey's nose rose slightly and its forward speed slowed to about fifty miles an hour. With its rotor blades slapping the still morning air, the aircraft descended to our side of the valley. The pilot made a few last-minute adjustments, and at the last possible second, he lowered the nose and set the skids down on the side of the hill. It made me feel good to see the Stars and Stripes blowing in the rotor wash.

Seconds later, another chopper touched down fifty meters

south of the first. Two more landed in front of the recon and second platoons. With four Hueys on the ground, the air quickly filled with blowing dust and JP-4 fumes. High above the Landing Zone the FAC drifted in lazy circles and, to the west, a dozen more choppers circled as they waited their turn to land.

"Jim," George grabbed my arm, "we've got movement to the east." We ran ten meters into the jungle and found Sanh and Thach standing next to the machine gun.

"OP [outpost] see two VC," Thach told me. "Maybe two hundred meter."

"Claymore's out?" I asked.

"Yes, Bac-si."

"Every VC in the area's gonna be moving to the sound of the choppers."

"Sanh," George called, "when the last two choppers are on their final approach, I'll give three blasts on my whistle."

"*Oui,* Trung-si." George returned to the Landing Zone; I stayed with Sanh and Thach. Within minutes only the third squad and the machine-gun section remained. Wap, wap, wap. The pulsating sound of approaching choppers and three shrill blasts from George's whistle filled the air.

"Let's go," I yelled. "Last flight to Duc-Phong." With their weapons at the ready, everyone remained on line and walked backwards. At the edge of the clearing we found Gritz and George waiting. Two choppers were about to touch down.

"Thach, put your squad on the second chopper," George pointed. "Sanh, you and the machine-gun section come with us." When the first Huey touched down we covered our eyes with our arms and followed the captain down the hill to the side of the chopper. Sanh and the machine-gun section moved to the Huey's far door. We found an anxious door-gunner sitting in the jump seat, his finger on the trigger of his M-60 machine gun. In his pressed uniform and shined boots, he appeared almost unreal—like someone in a dream.

"Hurry it up!" he hollered over the noise of the engine and rotors. Gritz grabbed Ly by the arm and helped him into the cabin while Sanh and the machine-gun section scrambled in the other door. The Huey's nylon mesh seats had been removed so George, the captain, and I sat on its honeycombed aluminum floor with our feet dangling out over the skids. "Who the hell are you guys?" The door gunner shouted.

"Mobile Guerrilla Force Detachment A-303," Gritz yelled back.

With the main rotors slapping the morning air at over three hundred RPMs, the pilot pulled back on his collective and the chopper shook as it lifted to a few feet above the ground.

"Yahoo!" I let out a loud yell.

"By God, we did it!" The captain put his arms around George and me.

Ta-tow-tow-tow. The door gunner opened up with his M-60. Whack-whack-whack. A surge of adrenalin shot into my system as the three of us emptied our magazines into the wood line.

"You see anything?" Gritz called out as we picked up speed and headed down the valley.

"No, sir." George and I shook our heads.

"Saw movement," the door gunner hollered above the noise. Cool, fresh air rushed through the cabin as we climbed high above the broccoli-topped trees and mist-filled valley of War Zone D. Within minutes we were high above the light brown waters of the Dong-Nai River. Everything looked so peaceful. It was good to be alive.

EPILOGUE

On 9 February 1967, Mobile Guerrilla Force Detachment A-303 was debriefed by Col. Francis Kelly, commanding officer, 5th Special Forces Group (Airborne) at the C-Team headquarters in Bien-Hoa. Colonel Kelly informed us that the recovery of the electronic countermeasure system 13A black box had averted a serious blow to the national security of the United States. The colonel also told us that Operation Blackjack-31 clearly demonstrated that American-led indigenous troops could conduct guerrilla operations against enemy forces. During Blackjack-31 the Mobile Guerrilla Force had entered an area previously unpenetrated by conventional military forces, fought fifty-one engagements, called in tactical air strikes against twenty-seven targets, and raided fifteen company- and battalion-size base camps. Following the debriefing, Colonel Kelly decorated each member of the team.

On 12 February 1967, the team was debriefed by Gen. William C. Westmoreland, commander, U.S. Military Assistance Command, Vietnam, at II Field Force headquarters in Long-Binh. Following that debriefing, the general personally congratulated each member of Detachment A-303 and lauded their unequaled performance.

On 20 February 1967, the Mobile Guerrilla Force moved from Bien-Hoa to the Special Forces camp at Trang-Sup in

Tay-Ninh Province. On 1 August 1967, Major Gritz organized Detachment B-36 (provisional); under B-36, Detachments A-303 and A-304 were redesignated Detachments A-361 and A-362. We were also augmented with twenty American Long-Range Reconnaissance Patrol [LRRPs] personnel.

In September 1967 Detachment B-36 moved from Trang-Sup to a villa on the beach at Long-Hai—Cape Saint Jacques. When Projects Omega (Detachment B-50) and Sigma (Detachment B-56) were transferred to the Military Assistance Command, Vietnam, Studies and Observations Group (MACV-SOG), in November 1967 Detachment B-36 assumed the added responsibility of developing tactical and strategic reconnaissance in the III Corps tactical zone of South Vietnam. On 23 May 1968, the Mobile Guerrilla Force was redesignated the 3rd Mobile Strike Force and grew to a force of more than two thousand men. The unit included three light infantry battalions, a reconnaissance company, and a headquarters company.

THE CAMBODIANS AND VIETNAMESE

Rinh—Chief Cambodian Medic

In the spring of 1967, Rinh was wounded on Liberty Blackjack, a raid on a prisoner-of-war camp near Chi-Linh Special Forces camp. He was wounded again in 1968 but remained with the Mobile Guerrilla Force and later the 3rd Mobile Strike Force until 1970.

With the American-sponsored overthrow of Cambodia's Prince Noradum Sihanouk in the spring of 1970, Rinh and the Cambodians of Detachment B-36 were flown to Phnom-Penh, Cambodia. Once the government of Lon-Nol was in power, Rinh was selected to attend the Cambodian Military Academy in Phnom-Penh. He graduated in 1973, was assigned to the 101st Evacuation Hospital in Phnom-Penh, and quickly rose to the rank of captain.

By 1975 the Khmer-Rouge (Cambodian Communists) had taken over in Cambodia and were systematically tracking down and murdering everyone who had served with the Americans or the Lon-Nol government. Rinh avoided capture and, in April, headed back to Vietnam on foot. Twenty-nine days later he arrived at his former village in Vinh-Binh Province. By then the Communists had also taken over in Vietnam, but, with the help of friends, Rinh managed to conceal his past from the Communist authorities.

Rinh's luck ran out in July 1982, when an informer told the police that he had worked with Special Forces. Rinh once again averted capture and headed back to Cambodia, where he hid and lived as a woodcutter near Kompong-Steu. Vietnamese security forces soon tracked him down, but he evaded them and headed northwest to the city of Battambang.

When he arrived there, security forces from the Cambodian National Front arrested and jailed him. After four days of intense interrogation, Rinh convinced his captors that he had never worked with the Americans or the government of Lon-Nol. He also convinced them that he was on his way to a job in Paris and that if they didn't execute him, he would send them money from France. They believed his story, and a few days later Rinh made it to the Thai border and the Site #2 refugee camp. While at Site #2 he applied for permission to emigrate to the United States; in January 1987 he made it to Seattle, Washington, where he found part-time work as a medical interpreter.

Sanh—Platoon Sergeant, Third Platoon
Sanh achieved his dream of returning to Cambodia. He was killed fighting the Khmer-Rouge in 1973.

Thach—Squad Leader, Third Platoon
Thach died in my arms on mission Blackjack-34. He was fatally wounded in a 17 July 1967 battle with an enemy regiment north of Quan-Loi.

Dung—Rifleman, Third Platoon
Dung was medevacked from the black-box mission to Cong-Hoa Hospital in Saigon. After his arm was amputated, he returned to the Mobile Guerrilla Force and joined the camp security force at Trang-Sup.

Danh—Silent Weapon Specialist, Third Platoon
Danh suffered hand and shoulder wounds when the third platoon ambushed a large enemy force south of Dong-Xoai Special Forces camp in May 1967. He returned to the Mobile Guerrilla Force following medical treatment in Bien-Hoa.

Binh—Rifleman, Third Platoon
Binh suffered a chest wound on Operation Picnic, an August 1967 raid on a Vietcong base complex north of Ben-Soi Special Forces camp. When we loaded him on the med-evac chopper he appeared close to death.

Luc—Medic, Third Platoon
Luc was killed in a battle with a large enemy force near Chi-Linh Special Forces camp on 3 May 1967.

Ly—Radio Operator, Third Platoon
Ly was shot through the heart near Phuoc-Vinh in May 1967.

Hoa—Rifleman, Third Platoon
Hoa recovered from the chest wound he suffered on the black-box mission. He was last seen in Bangkok, Thailand, in 1972. At the time he was a lieutenant in the Cambodian army.

David—Headquarter Section Interpreter
David was last seen at a classified site in Thailand in 1972. At the time he was a major in the Cambodian army.

Luc—Section Leader, Recon Platoon

Following Blackjack-31 Luc became the third herd's platoon sergeant. In May 1967 he was shot in the stomach during a battle with a large enemy force near Phuoc-Vinh. I last saw him when I was wounded and medevacked to the 24th Evacuation Hospital in Long-Binh on 18 July 1967. He was skin and bones but still alive.

Kimh—Medic at Duc-Phong Special Forces camp

Kimh became an ARVN infantry officer and was killed in 1969.

Kimh Ly—Platoon Sergeant, Second Platoon

Dale England ran into Kimh-Ly at Ban-Me-Thuot in early 1970. At the time, Kimh was a company commander with MACV-SOG's Command and Control South. In the spring of 1970, Kimh returned to the 3rd Mobile Strike Force at Long-Hai to take part in the overthrow of Cambodia's Prince Noradum Sihanouk. Following the installation of Lon-Nol, he became a captain in the Cambodian army. When the Communists overthrew Lon-Nol in 1975, Kimh was captured by the Khmer-Rouge. He escaped execution by concealing his identity but was sent to a Communist "re-education" camp.

In 1976 Kimh escaped and made it back to Soc-Trang, Vietnam, where he was captured and imprisoned by the Vietnamese Communists. He escaped from the prison camp in 1979, and after making it back to Cambodia on foot, he joined a Cambodian guerrilla group that was fighting the Khmer-Rouge along the Thai-Cambodian border. In August 1982, Kimh was wounded for a ninth time and was treated by the Thai Red Cross at a refugee camp in Thailand. Kimh immigrated to the United States in May 1984; he currently lives in Lowell, Massachusetts.

Thai Hien Son—Machine Gunner, Second Platoon

In 1973 Thai lost a leg while fighting the Khmer-Rouge in

Cambodia. In 1975 he walked back to Vietnam on one leg, and when he arrived in Tay-Ninh Province, he was jailed by the Vietnamese authorities. In 1981 he was released by the Vietnamese; two years later he walked to Thailand. In 1984 Thai immigrated to the United States and is currently living in Philadelphia.

Lieutenant Thoi—LLDB commander at Duc-Phong Special Forces camp

The lieutenant was last seen southeast of Saigon in late 1967. It has been reported that he later lost both his legs to a Vietcong booby trap.

Tranh—Vietcong prisoner captured during the black-box mission

Tranh was medevacked to Cong-Hoa Hospital in Saigon. He convinced the hospital staff that he was a member of the Mobile Guerrilla Force and was subsequently treated and released.

THE AMERICANS

Dale England—Commander, Second Platoon

On 3 May 1967 we made contact near Chi-Linh Special Forces camp with the Vietcong's 271st and 273rd main-force regiments. During the battle the Mobile Guerrilla Force suffered heavy casualties. Dale was wounded early in the afternoon of the day-long battle, and that evening was medevacked to a 1st Infantry Division medical clearing station. From there he was sent to the 93rd Evacuation Hospital in Long-Binh, a hospital in Japan, and finally to Walter Reed Army Hospital.

Following four months of medical treatment he received orders to the 46th Special Forces Company (Airborne) in Thailand. England returned to Vietnam a year later and was assigned to MACV-SOG's Command and Control South at Ban-Me-Thuot. While with CCS he ran cross-border reconnaissance teams into Cambodia. Early in 1970 he was transferred to Project Delta and later in the year returned to B-36 at Long-Hai. At that time, B-36 was training Cambodians and organizing them into infantry battalions. Once trained, they were turned over to the Lon-Nol government in Cambodia.

In September 1970 England returned to Thailand to serve an additional three years with the 46th Special Forces Company (Airborne). In September 1973 he returned to Fort Bragg, North Carolina, to serve with Special Forces Training Group (Airborne) and later the 5th Special Forces Group (Airborne). While assigned to the 5th, England's Mobile Training Team deployed to Liberia, Africa, where they trained the Liberian army cadre that included a master sergeant by the name of Samuel K. Doe. On 12 April 1980, Sergeant Doe and a handful of enlisted men from the Peoples' Redemption Council overthrew the government of President William R. Tolbert.

England also served with the 5th in the Middle East during Desert Storm, after which he returned to Fort Campbell, Kentucky, and retired as a sergeant major. England lives in Clarksville, Tennessee, with his wife and two daughters.

Frank Kelly—Commanding Officer, 5th Special Forces Group (Airborne)

Blackjack returned to Fort Bragg in July 1967 to assume command of the Institute of Strategic and Special Operations. In June 1970 he transferred to Denver, where he served as the senior military advisor to the State of Colorado.

Blackjack retired in August 1972 to become a professor of economics and political science at Loretto Heights College in Denver. The colonel was widowed in 1974. He has four grown children.

Steve Yedinak—Deputy Commander, Mobile Guerrilla Force; Deputy Platoon Commander, Second Platoon

Steve returned to Vietnam in September 1970 to serve with the Regional Advisory Command's Team #50 at Cao-Lamh—southwest of Saigon in Kien-Phong Province. While assigned to Team #50, he coordinated Vietnamese operations in the 44th Special Tactical Zone.

In September 1971 Steve returned to the States and the 101st Airborne Division at Fort Campbell, Kentucky. In 1976 he received orders to attend the Command and General Staff College at Fort Leavenworth, Kansas; a year later he was assigned to the Training and Doctrine Command (TRADOC) at Fort Monroe, Virginia. In 1981 he became the senior Army advisor to the Puerto Rican National Guard. Steve returned to Fort Monroe and TRADOC in 1983; in 1985 he was selected to be the Army's representative at the Center for Low Intensity Conflict at Langley Air Force Base, Virginia.

Steve retired as a lieutenant colonel in November 1985 and lives in Newport News, Virginia, where he owns and operates Home Products, Inc. He has three grown children.

Pat Wagner—Senior Radio Operator, Mobile Guerrilla Force

From Blackjack-31 Pat was medevacked to the 93rd Evacuation Hospital in Long-Binh, where he was diagnosed as having falciparum malaria. After thirty-two days in the hospital he returned to the C-Team compound in Bien-Hoa, where Sgt. Maj. Richard Finn sent him back to the field to replace a radio operator who had been wounded on Blackjack-32, a Mobile Guerrilla Force operation in the Seven Mountains region of Vietnam.

Wagner returned to Fort Bragg in April 1967 to serve as a communications instructor with Special Forces Training Group (Airborne). Following that tour he served in a number of other communications assignments and retired as a master sergeant in December 1976.

Wagner works as a range control supervisor at Fort Bragg and lives in Fayetteville, North Carolina, with his wife and three daughters.

Dick Jarvis—Deputy Platoon Commander, First Platoon

Jarvis retired as a sergeant major and was last reported to be living on a boat in Honolulu, Hawaii.

Jim Howard—Platoon Commander, First Platoon

Howard returned to Vietnam and Detachment B-36 in October 1969 and was assigned to the 3rd Mobile Strike Force's 3rd Battalion. On 5 February 1970 his unit was on an operation in War Zone D when they discovered a Vietcong base camp near Rang-Rang. Early in the battle Howard was hit in the right shoulder. After refusing to be medevacked he suffered multiple gunshot wounds while leading an assault on an enemy bunker complex. Howard lost a rib and parts of his liver, right calf muscle, left femur bone, and right tricep muscle.

He was medevacked to the 93rd Evacuation Hospital in Long-Binh, later to Japan, and finally to Womack Army Hospital at Fort Bragg. He spent fourteen months undergoing medical treatment; in November 1972 he was medically retired as a sergeant major.

Following retirement Howard moved to Colorado Springs, Colorado, where he set up Jim Howard Investigations with his wife, his son, and his daughter.

Lowell Glossup—Section Leader, Reconnaissance Platoon

Glossup was killed south of Saigon in 1969.

Buck Kindoll—Intelligence Specialist, Mobile Guerrilla Force

Kindoll returned to Vietnam in September 1969 and was assigned to MACV-SOG's Detachment B-53 at Long-

Thanh, east of Saigon in Bien-Hoa Province. While at Long-Thanh he trained indigenous personnel in cross-border operations. He later served with the Combined Studies Division's Province Reconnaissance Unit in Bien-Hoa, advising indigenous personnel who were involved in the destruction of the Vietcong infrastructure in Bien-Hoa Province.

In 1970 Kindoll returned to MACV-SOG and was assigned to its Ground Studies Group—OP-35—in Saigon. While with OP-35 he targeted and supported cross-border operations.

Kindoll retired as a master sergeant in February 1978 and moved to Corbin, Kentucky, where he and his wife own and operate the Kindoll Real Estate Company. He has a son and a daughter.

Charlie Chilton—Commander, Reconnaissance Platoon
Chilton survived the war and is believed to be living in Chula Vista, California.

Al Doyle—Senior Radio Operator, Mobile Guerrilla Force
Following Blackjack-31, Doyle was assigned to the 10th Special Forces Group (Airborne) in Bad Tolz, Germany. He returned to Vietnam in September 1970 and served with 2nd Mobile Strike Force units at Ban-Me-Thuot and Pleiku. Following his fourth tour in Vietnam, he was assigned to the 1st Special Forces Group (Airborne) on Okinawa.

In March 1971 Doyle returned to Vietnam for a fifth tour and was assigned to the Special Missions Advisory Group (SMAG) at Nha-Trang. While there he trained former Vietnamese Special Forces and Rangers in cross-border operations. Later in the year he was transferred to the SMAG detachment in Pleiku.

Doyle retired as a master sergeant in May 1977. He and his wife and two daughters live in Tampa, Florida, where he works for the post office.

Joe Cawley—Section Leader, Reconnaissance Platoon
Cawley retired as a major and is believed to be living in the Fayetteville, North Carolina, area.

Dennis Montgomery—Deputy Platoon Commander, First Platoon
Montgomery returned to Fort Bragg in May 1967 to serve as a medical instructor with Special Forces Training Group (Airborne). He returned to Vietnam in March 1968 and was assigned as a mobile advisory team leader at Cao-Lamh.

Montgomery was sent to Fort Sam Houston, Texas, in April 1969, and in September of that year he received orders to attend Spanish language training in Washington, D.C. In January 1970 he completed the course and was assigned to the 8th Special Forces Group (Airborne) in Panama. Following his Latin American tour he served with the 10th Special Forces Group (Airborne) at Fort Devens, Massachusetts.

Having retired as a first sergeant in March 1977, he lives in Manito, Illinois, with his wife and three daughters. He is currently working on a master's degree in history.

Jim Gritz—Commanding Officer, Mobile Guerrilla Force
Gritz left Vietnam in 1968 to attend the Army's Chinese Language School in Monterey, California. When he completed language training in 1970, he attended the Command and General Staff College at Fort Leavenworth, Kansas. After graduating in 1972, he moved to Washington, D.C., to become an aide to Gen. William C. Westmoreland, who was then chief of staff of the Army. Later that year, Gen. Creighton W. Abrams replaced Westmoreland, and Gritz received orders to enroll in a full-time graduate program at the American University in Washington.

Upon completion of his graduate studies in 1974, he became the commander of the 3rd Battalion, 7th Special Forces Group (Airborne) in Panama. In 1976 he returned to the Pentagon to become the chief of congressional relations for the Office of the Secretary of Defense. In 1979 Gritz retired as a lieutenant colonel.

I linked up with him at the 1979 Special Forces Association Convention in Washington, D.C. That night over dinner he told me that in October 1978 he had been asked by Lt. Gen. Harold Aaron, deputy director of the Defense Intelligence Agency, to retire from the military to organize and command a civilian POW rescue operation. He explained that General Aaron and others within the military and intelligence establishments knew that American POWs were being held in Southeast Asia.

Since his retirement Gritz has organized four major POW rescue missions: Velvet Hammer in early 1981; Grand Eagle in late 1981; Lazarus in late 1982; and Lazarus Omega in early 1983.

Gritz and his wife live in Sandy Valley, Nevada, and have four grown children.

George Ovsak—Commander, Third Platoon

George was killed at Trang-Sup on 22 February 1967 and is buried at Fort Snelling National Cemetery in Saint Paul, Minnesota. Shortly after my first book, *No Greater Love,* was published (Daring Books, 1988), I received the following letter from his daughter:

> Dear Mr. Donahue,
>   My name is Dena Ovsak Fullbright. You knew my father, George, in Vietnam. When I found out about your book, and [saw that] my father was on the cover of it, it was a dream come true for me. For years I've prayed that someone who knew my father would surface. God has answered my prayers and I am very grateful to you for being who you are.
>   Contacting you is giving me such mixed emotions. I'm full of joy and yet, I'm afraid. I wonder about the conversations you and my father had. How I would love to have had a conversation with my dad

as an adult. I was only six years old when he died. I was the sick child. I now consider it a blessing because I got special attention from Dad. He was my first love, and I remember being very certain that I was going to marry him when I grew up. Holding his hand as we walked down the green grass from the hospital was the greatest joy of my childhood years.

I still remember [the] sad day [when I learned of his death]. Mom and my sisters and brother, George Junior, were napping. I heard over the radio that "George had died in Vietnam," and I thought to myself that it couldn't be my dad. There were hundreds of men named George in Vietnam. Only a few minutes later there was a knock at the door, and two men in suits were standing there. Mother broke down. I didn't realize how the events of the day would change my life so.

I still take out old black-and-white pictures of Dad and stare at them for what seems like hours. What a handsome and dashing man Dad was. I treasure the magic he possessed that just lit up my whole world. I'm sure had Dad lived, things wouldn't be as perfect as they are in my mind now. But he didn't live, and this is the way my six-year-old's heart remembers him.

The pain never goes away—just like the need for your father never goes away. I'll never get that hug I so desperately need while I'm on this earth.

I hope I'm not depressing you, Jim. I realize that this is probably very hard for you too. I can't imagine what you must be feeling as you read this letter, though I feel somewhat a veteran myself. . . . I wonder if Dad stared at the stars at night and dreamed wonderful dreams. Were you close to my father? I wonder how much of his heart and his thoughts he shared with you.

I'd better close this letter before I bombard you

with questions. I'm finding it harder and harder to resist the temptation.

It's an odd feeling sharing my emotions with a stranger, yet I'm willing to take the risk.

If you can find the time, please write to me. I'll be hanging on to your every word.

With love and prayers,
Dena Ovsak Fullbright

P.S. I hear that you're writing a book on Blackjack-31. I know Dad would've liked that. My husband, David, and I had our first child (a little girl) on January 22, 1988. We took her home on January 26—[what would have been] Dad's 53rd birthday.

APPENDIX

MOBILE GUERRILLA FORCE DETACHMENT A-303

Headquarters Section

Capt. James Gritz	MGF Commander
Sgt. 1st Class Patrick Wagner	Communications
Sgt. 1st Class Aloysius Doyle	Communications
Sgt. 1st Class William Kindoll	Intelligence

Reconnaissance Platoon

1st Lt. Charles Chilton	Platoon Commander
Sgt. 1st Class Lowell Glossup	Section Leader
	Engineer\Demolitions
	Weapons
Staff Sgt. Joseph Cawley	Section Leader
	Medic
	Communications

First Platoon

Master Sgt. James Howard	Platoon Commander
Staff Sgt. Dennis Montgomery	Deputy Platoon Commander
	Medic
Staff Sgt. Richard Jarvis	Deputy Platoon Commander
	Engineer/Demolitions

Second Platoon

Staff Sgt. Dale England	Platoon Commander
Capt. Steven Yedinak	Deputy Platoon Commander
	Deputy MGF Commander

Third Platoon

Sgt. 1st Class George Ovsak	Platoon Commander
Sgt. James Donahue	Deputy Platoon Commander
	Medic

INDEX

ABOUT THE AUTHOR

James C. Donahue joined the Marine Corps when he was seventeen years old and subsequently served with the Marine Barracks in Sanford, Florida; the 2nd Marine Division at Camp Lejeune, North Carolina; and in Guantánamo Bay, Cuba, during the 1962 Cuban Missile Crisis.

Once discharged from the Marines, he enlisted in the Army and volunteered for Special Forces. As a Green Beret, he served with the 6th and 7th Special Forces Groups (Airborne) at Fort Bragg, North Carolina, and with the 5th Special Forces Group (Airborne) in Vietnam. While assigned to the 5th Mr. Donahue fought with Detachment A-343 at Duc-Phong and Mobile Guerrilla Force Detachments A-303, A-304, A-361, and B-36 at Bien-Hoa, Ho-Ngoc-Tao, and Trang-Sup. His major military awards and decorations include the Silver Star, three Bronze Stars, the Purple Heart, two Air Medals, the Cross of Gallantry, the Conspicuous Service Cross, the Cross of the Netherlands, the German Performance Badge, the Combat Medical Badge, and American and Vietnamese Parachute Wings.

In 1967 he enrolled at the State University of New York at Buffalo. After earning a bachelor's degree in anthropology and a master's degree in social sciences there, he went to work for the U.S. Department of Labor's Veterans' Employment and Training Service.

Mr. Donahue's first book, *No Greater Love* (Daring Books, 1988), was awarded the Freedom Foundation's George Washington Honor Medal.

He now lives in Glenwood, New York, with his wife, Sandi. His daughter, Sarah, is a student at the State University College at Buffalo, and his son, Michael, is an air traffic controller stationed at Key West Naval Air Station.